PHILIP'S

SLO...

MAIDENHEAD

CW00386411

www.philips-maps.co.uk

First published 2008 by

Philip's, a division of
Octopus Publishing Group Ltd
www.octopusbooks.co.uk
2–4 Heron Quays
London E14 4JP
An Hachette Livre UK Company
www.hachettelivre.co.uk

First edition 2008
First impression 2008

ISBN 978-0-540-09400-4

© Philip's 2008

This product includes mapping data licensed
from Ordnance Survey®, with the permission
of the Controller of Her Majesty's Stationery
Office.

© Crown copyright 2008. All rights reserved.
Licence number 100011710

Printed and bound in China by Toppan

Contents

II **Key to map symbols**

III **Key to map pages**

IV **Route planning**

2 **Street maps** at 4½ inches to 1 mile

54 **Index**

68 **List of numbered locations**

Key to map symbols

Roads

Symbol	Description
(12)	Motorway with junction number
A42	Primary route – dual, single carriageway
A42	A road – dual, single carriageway
B1289	B road – dual, single carriageway
	Through-route – dual, single carriageway
	Minor road – dual, single carriageway
	Rural track, private road or narrow road in urban area
	Path, bridleway, byway open to all traffic, restricted byway
	Road under construction
	Pedestrianised area
	Gate or obstruction to traffic restrictions may not apply at all times or to all vehicles
P P&R	Parking, Park and Ride
(30) (30)	Speed cameras – single, multiple

Railways

Symbol	Description
	Railway
	Miniature railway
	Metro station, private railway station

Emergency services

Symbol	Description
◆ ◆	Ambulance station, coastguard station
◆ ◆	Fire station, police station
H +	Hospital, Accident and Emergency entrance to hospital

General features

Symbol	Description
+ PO	Place of worship, Post Office
i	Information centre (open all year)
	Bus or coach station, shopping centre
	Important buildings, schools, colleges, universities and hospitals
	Woods, built-up area
Tumulus FORT	Non-Roman antiquity, Roman antiquity

Leisure facilities

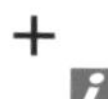

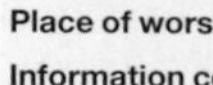

Symbol	Description
⚑ 🚐	Camping site, caravan site
► ✕	Golf course, picnic site

Boundaries

Symbol	Description
••••••••	Postcode boundaries
—— · ——	County and unitary authority boundaries

Water features

Symbol	Description
River Ouse	Tidal water, water name
	Non-tidal water – lake, river, canal or stream
‹		Lock, weir

Scales

Blue pages: 4½ inches to 1 mile 1:14 080

| 0 | 220 yds | ¼ mile | 660 yds | ½ mile |

| 0 | 125m | 250m | 375m | ½ km |

| 44 | Adjoining page indicators The mapping continues on the page indicated by the arrow |

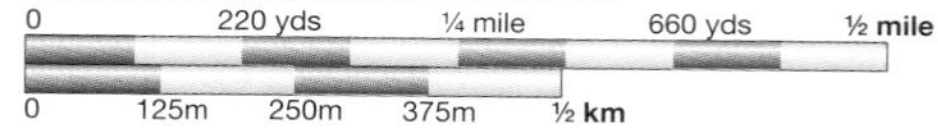

Abbreviations

Acad	Academy	Mkt	Market
Allot Gdns	Allotments	Meml	Memorial
Cemy	Cemetery	Mon	Monument
C Ctr	Civic Centre	Mus	Museum
CH	Club House	Obsy	Observatory
Coll	College	Pal	Royal Palace
Crem	Crematorium	PH	Public House
Ent	Enterprise	Recn Gd	Recreation Ground
Ex H	Exhibition Hall	Resr	Reservoir
Ind Est	Industrial Estate	Ret Pk	Retail Park
IRB Sta	Inshore Rescue Boat Station	Sch	School
		Sh Ctr	Shopping Centre
Inst	Institute	TH	Town Hall/House
Ct	Law Court	Trad Est	Trading Estate
L Ctr	Leisure Centre	Univ	University
LC	Level Crossing	Wks	Works
Liby	Library	YH	Youth Hostel

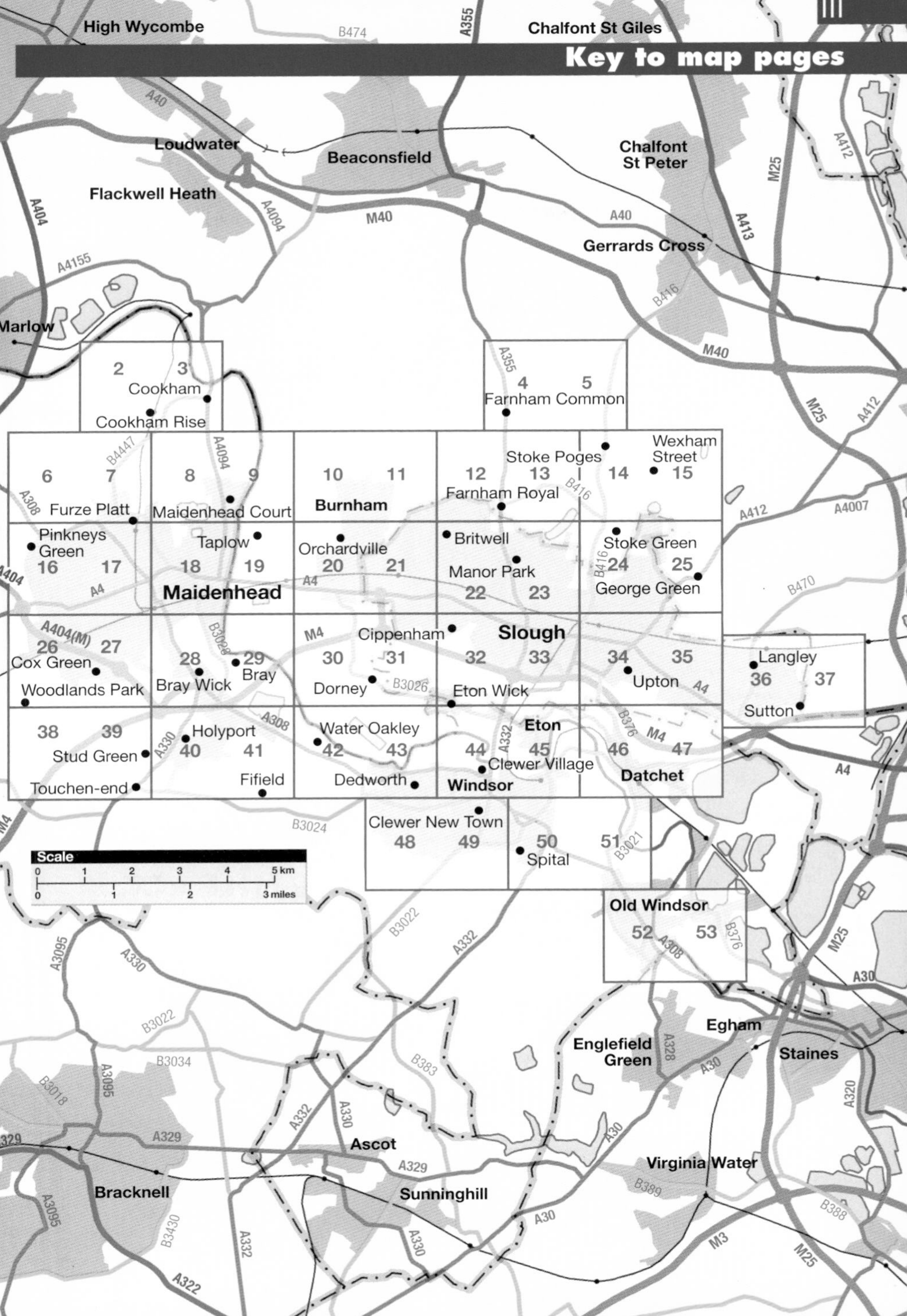

High Wycombe
B474
A355
Chalfont St Giles

A40

Loudwater
Beaconsfield
Chalfont St Peter

Flackwell Heath
A4094
M40
A40
M25

Gerrards Cross

A404
M40
A413
A416

A4155

Marlow
M40

2 3
Cookham
A355
4 5
Farnham Common
M25
A412

Cookham Rise

6 7
8 9
10 11
12 13 14 15
Stoke Poges
Wexham Street

Furze Platt
Maidenhead Court
Burnham
Farnham Royal
A412
A4007

Pinkneys Green
Taplow
Orchardville
Britwell
Stoke Green
16 17
18 19
20 21
22 23
24 25
George Green
B470

Maidenhead
Manor Park

26 27
28 29
30 31
32 33
34 35
Langley
Cox Green
Cippenham
Slough
36 37

Woodlands Park
Bray Wick
Bray
Dorney
Eton Wick
Upton
Sutton

38 39
40 41
42 43
44 45
46 47
Stud Green
Holyport
Water Oakley
Eton
Datchet

Touchen-end
Fifield
Dedworth
Clewer Village
Windsor

48 49
50
Clewer New Town
Spital
51
52 53
Old Windsor

Scale
0 1 2 3 4 5 km
0 1 2 3 miles

Englefield Green
Egham

Staines

Ascot
Virginia Water

Bracknell
Sunninghill

Sheepridge
Sedgmoor
Juniper Hill
Burroughs Grove
Marlow Bottom
Well End
Wooburn Green
Hall Barn
Over's Fm.
Hillmott's Fm.
Seymour Ct.
Munday Dean
SEYMOUR CT. RD.
A4155
MARLOW RD.
Little Marlow
Cores End
Wooburn
Berghers Hill
Dipple Wood
Wooburn Common
Jennings Fm.
Pennlan Fm.
Marefield
A404
Westhorpe Ho.
Spade Oak
BOURNE END
Bourne End
Hawks Hill
Hedsor
Hales Corner
Collum Green
Marlow
MARLOW
Lock
Cock Marsh
THAMES PATH
Hedsor Ct.
The Priory
Abbey Park Fm.
Littleworth Common
A4155
HENLEY RD.
Court Gdn.
Winter Hill
Dial Close
The Grange
Dropmore
Brook End Fm.
Cookham
STANLEY SPENCER GALLERY
COOKHAM
CLIVEDEN (N.T.)
BURNHAM BEECHES
BISHAM ABBEY
Quarry Wood
Cookham Dean
Cookham Rise
White Pl.
Dorney Wood
DORNEYWOOD (N.T.)
East Burnham
Temple Lock
Bigfrith
Temple
Cookhamdean Common
The Mount
A4094
THE THAMES PATH
Rosehill
Priory (remains)
Hurley Bottom
Temple Park
Park Wood
A308
Heron's Ct.
B4447
Hunt's Wood
Cant's Hill
Lee Fm.
Burnham
Park Corner
Ditton Ho.
Furze Platt
FURZE PLATT
Hitcham Park
Speen Hill
Pinkneys Green
North Town
Boulter's Lock
Taplow
Lent
The Priory
FARNHAM RD.
Burchett's Green
Berry Hill
TAPLOW
Lent Rise
Slough Trading Estate
A404
MAIDENHEAD
A4
BURNHAM
SLOU
Robin Hood's Arbour
Maidenhead Thicket
Highway
MAIDENHEAD
West Town
Burnham Abbey
A4 BATH RD.
Holloway
Tittle Row
A4
A308
B3028
Woolley Green
Fishery Estate
Cippenham
Littlewick Green
Altmore
A404(M)
M4
Lake End
Chalvey
Bray Wick
Bray
Cox Green
Dorney Reach
Cold Harbour
A308(M)
Monkey Island
Dorney
B3026
WHITE WALTHAM
Woodlands Park
Lowbrook Fm.
A308
WINDSOR RD.
Eton Wick
Shottesbrooke Fm.
Thrift Woods
Queen's Eyot
Boveney
Down Pl.
Oakley Ct.
RIVER THAMES
WINDSOR
White Waltham
Waltham Pl.
M4
Stud Green
ASCOT RD.
Holyport
Moneyrow Green
ROAD
Clewer Village
Eton
A332
WINDSOR
BROADMOOR ROAD
Foxley's Fm.
B3383
Dedworth
Windsor
Littlefield Green
Paley Street
Touchen-end
B3024
Fifield
Oakley Green
AND
Clewer New Town
Smewins Fm.
Great Wood
B3024
Ledger Fm.
B3024
MAIDENHEAD
MILITARY MUS.
A330
Beenham's Heath
Braywoodside
Haweshill
Clewer Green
Spital
P&R
B3022
New Lo.
St. Leonard's
St. Leonard's Dale
Redstone Fm.
LEGOLAND
Shurlock Row
Buck Fm. Ho.
Foliejon Park
WINKFIELD ROAD
Flemish Fm.
Forest Park
Westleymill
Cruchfield Ho.
Winkfield Pl.
Winkfield Plain
Felix Fm.
A3095
Hawthorn Hill
A330
Chawridge Manor Fm.
Old Dairy Fm.
Cranbourne
WINDSOR
B3018
Jealott's Hill
Binfield Lo.
Winkfield Street
NORTH STREET
B3022
Cranbourne Chase
FOREST
Forest Gate
The Village
Qn. Anne's Ride
Winkfield
A330
Cranbourne
B383
Mount Pleasant
A332
Billingbear Ho.
Woodside
B3034
Binfield
Cabbage Hill
Newell Green
Winkfield Row
Ascot Pl.
Lovelhill
Duke's Lane
FOREST ROAD
B3022
Manor Ho.
West End
B3034
B3017
SUNNINGHILL ROAD
Emmets Nest
Park Fm.
B3018
A3095
Mushroom Castle
B3034
Winkfield Manor
A330
Home Fm.
Warfield Park
Burleigh
Stokes Fm.
Popeswood
Priestwood
Wick Hill
BRACKNELL
Ascot Heath
Cheapside
B3408
Priory
WINDSOR RD.
Bullbrook
Harewood
Temple Cott.
Route planning
Scale
0
1
2
3
4 km

V
Gerrards Cross
Bulstrode Park
Mumford's Fm.
OXFORD
Isle of Wight Fm.
DENHAM
Denham Green
Higher Denham
DENHAM GOLF CO.
Baker's Wood
Tatling End
Denham Mount
Denham
South Harefield
Bayhurst Wood Country Park
Highway Fm.
Newyears Green
Brackenbury Fm.
Ruislip Common
RUISLIP
West Ruislip
Ruislip Manor
Ruislip Gardens
Eastcote Village
LIDO
Ickenham
ICKENHAM
The Manor
NORTHOLT
WESTERN AVENUE
North Hillingdon
Hedgerley Green
Hedgerley Park
Tara
Fulmer Chase
Hall
Fulmer
Oldhouse Fm.
Stoke Common
Langley Corner
Willowbank
Ivy Ho. Fm.
New Denham
Uxbridge Common
Coll.
Holybush Hill
Pinewood Film Studios
BLACK PARK
Black Park
Mansfield Fm.
UXBRIDGE
RAF Station
Stoke Poges
Wexham Street
Grange Fm.
Iver Heath
Warren Ho.
Rowley Fm.
UXBRIDGE RD.
SLOUGH
Hillingdon
Brunel University
Stoke Green
Stoke Pl.
Langley Park
LANGLEY PARK
COLNE VALLEY REGIONAL PARK
Heath Lo.
Love Green
Cowley
Pield Heath
Cowley Peachey
Hillingdon Heath
Colham Green
Hayes End
Wood End Green
Wood End
Yeading Brook
George Green
Love Hill
Shreding Green
Iver
Middle Green
SLOUGH
Trenches Fm.
Parsonage Fm.
GRAND UNION CANAL
Colne Brook
Yiewsley
HAYES
West Drayton
W. DRAYTON
IVER
LANGLEY
Langley
Richings Park
Thorney
THORNEY
HAYES & HARLINGTON
Upton
LONDON ROAD
Ditton Park
Sutton
Old Slade Nature Reserve
COLNBROOK BY-PASS
Sipson
Harmondsworth
HEATHROW VISITOR CENTRE
Harlington
Cranford Park
Cranford
Brands Hill
Datchet
Reservoir
Datchet Common
Colnbrook
THE HOME PARK
WINDSOR CASTLE
Longford
BATH ROAD
Poyle
Horton
Terminal 5
Terminal 3
Terminal 1
Terminal 2
LONDON (HEATHROW)
Heathrow Airport
Royal Gdns.
SUNNYMEADS
R. Colne
Hatton
Old Windsor
Reservoir
WELLEY RD.
WRAYSBURY
Wraysbury
Stanwell Moor
Stanwell Pl.
Terminal 4
Stanwell
East Bedfont
West Bedfont
GREAT SOUTH WEST ROAD
Feltham
Hythe End
Staines Moor
Kg. George VI Reservoir
STANWELL MOOR ROAD
Staines Reservoirs
LONDON ROAD
Cooper Hill
RUNNYMEDE
WINDSOR ROAD
Bishops Gate
Englefield Green
Runnymede Park
STAINES
ASHFORD
Chatern Hill
Lower Feltham
Felthamhill
Egham
Hythe
Knowle Green
Ashford
Sunbury Common
Egham Wick
Thorpe Lea
KINGSTON ROAD
Ashford Common
Queen Mary Reservoir
Gt. Fosters
Callow
VALLEY GDNS.
Charlton
SUNBURY
UPR. HALLIFORD
M25
M4
M3
A40
A413
A412
A4020
A4007
A408
A437
A4180
A4
A312
A30
A3113
A3044
A308
A315
A328
A320
A244
B416
B467
B466
B470
B3021
B376
B378
B3376
B388
B377
B3377
B465
B3026
B483

Thames Path
Noah's House
Patches
Coney Copse
Stonehouse La
Gibraltar La
Winter Hill
Winter Hill
Bradcutts La
Terry's La
Harvest Moon
Greythatch
Hillgrove Farm
Winter Hill
Job's La
Startins La
Victoria Cotts
Dean La
Alleyns La
Herries Sch
Kings La
Cookham Dean Bottom
Lower Ventnor Cotts
Upper Ventnor Cotts
Warners Hill
Hillgrove Wood
Bradcutts La
Wessons Hill
Popes La
Hills La
King's Coppice Farm
Royal Cotts
1 Apsley Cot
2 Hamfield
Cookham Dean
Albion Cotts
Hardings Farm
SL6
Lower Rd
Hatch Pl
Lautree Gdns
Halldore Hill
South View
New Rd
Rosebank Cl
Fair View
High Rd
Cookham Dean CE Prim Sch
School La
Kennel La
PO
Bigfrith Common
Spencers La
Briar Glen
Graham Rd
Worster Rd
Sandpipers Pl
Payton Hos
Gorse Rd
Broom Hill
Whyteladyes La
Bigfrith La
Bedwins La
Woodlands Farm
Church Rd
Hollybush La
Pudseys Cl
Lyndhurst Ave
Penling Cl
Windmill Rd
Hillcrest Ave
Lesters Rd
Dean View
The Shaw
Spring La
Mount Hill
Southwood Rd
A
B
C
1
2
3
4
85
86
87
88
7
The Mount
Lower Mount Farm
Cannondown Rd
Southwood Gdns
Long La

3
Cock Marsh
Bourne End
Ind Est
A4094 Bourne End, A40
30
WALNUT WAY
WALNUT TREE CL
ABNEY COURT DR
JEFFRIES CT
HEDSOR RD
Hollands Farm
HAYWARD PL
HEAVENS LEA
1 SPRINGDALE COTTS
2 COSTERS COTTS
3 BEACONSFIELD COTTS
River Thames
ANDREWS REACH
RIVERSDALE CT
ORCHARD MILL
SL8
Thames Path
Mill House
RIVERSDALE COTTS
RIVERSDALE
Merlins Mead
A4094
HEDSOR RD
Hedsor Wharf
Sewage Works
FERRY LA
Lock Cut
Cookham Bridge
GRANGE LA
TERRY'S LA
GLENORE
BERRIES RD
VICARAGE CL
FERRY LA
ODNEY LA
POUNDFIELD LA
HIGH ST B4447
Stanley Spencer Art Gall
POCKETTS YD
ST GEORGES LODGE
SCHOOL LA
Cookham
BURNT OAK
HEDSOR VIEW COTTS
ANCHOR CT
THE POUND
THE POUND
Moor Hall
Holy Trinity CE Prim Sch
Lulle Brook
STATION RD
ROMAN LEA
Cookham
STATION HILL
LC
ELIZABETH CL
B4447
BLACK BUTT COTTS
ORCHARD GDNS
WOODMOOR END
MILL LA
STATION PAR
CEDAR DR
SUTTON CL
TRINITY HO
SL6
Garden Cottage
WESTWOOD GN
PEACE LA
DANES GDNS
BAYBROOK
SUTTON RD
MAIDENHEAD RD
VIVIEN CL
Sutton Farm House
White Place Farm
GAINSBOROUGH
LIGHTLANDS LA
STRANDE VIEW WLK
Strand Water
Lodge
Widbrook House
BARNFIELD CL
STRANDE LA
A
B
C
89
90
8
86
85
4
3
2
1
A4094

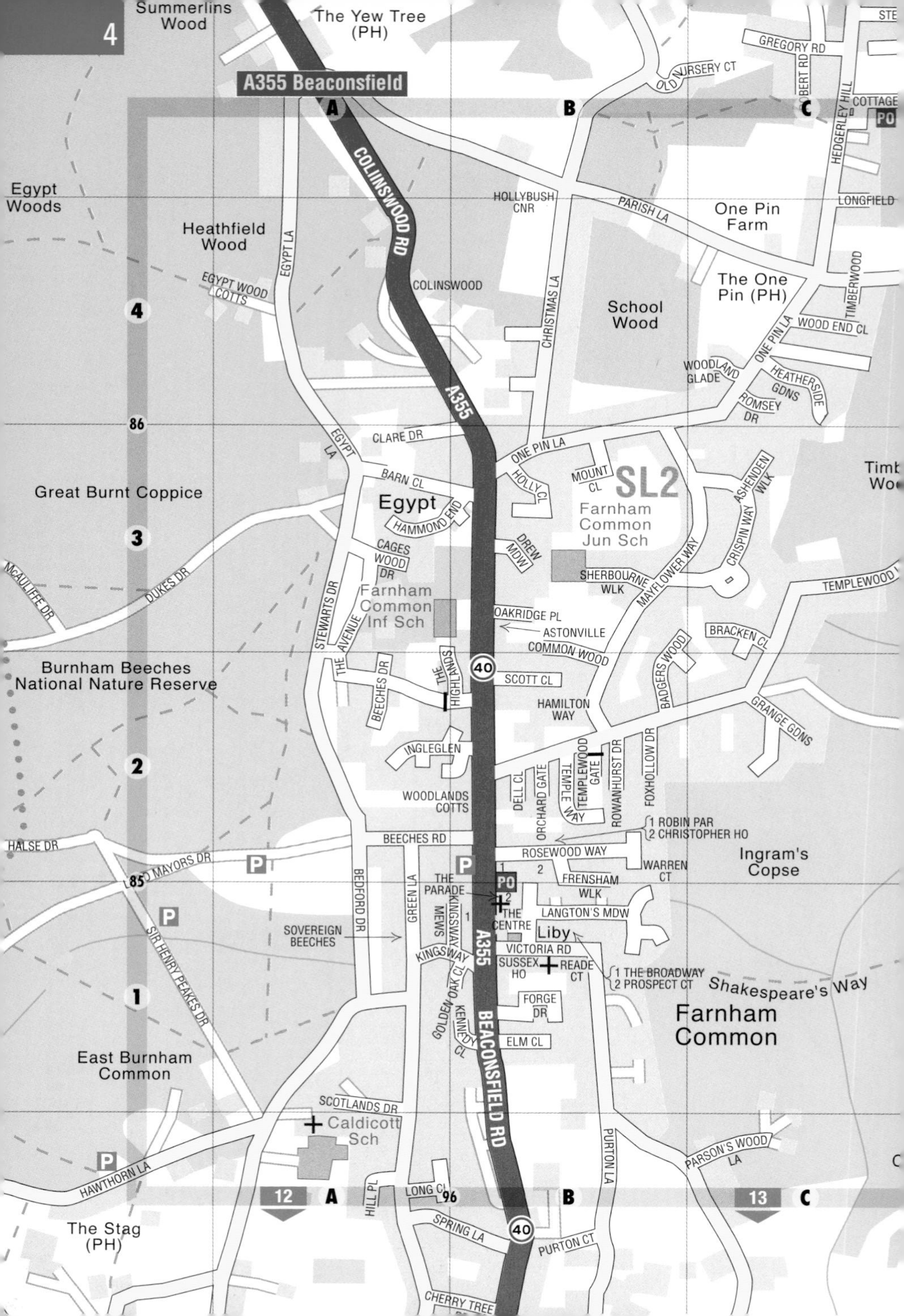
A355 Beaconsfield
Summerlins Wood
The Yew Tree (PH)
Egypt Woods
Heathfield Wood
Great Burnt Coppice
Burnham Beeches National Nature Reserve
East Burnham Common
The Stag (PH)
Egypt
SL2
Farnham Common Jun Sch
Farnham Common Inf Sch
School Wood
One Pin Farm
The One Pin (PH)
Ingram's Copse
Farnham Common
Shakespeare's Way
Caldicott Sch
Liby
COLINSWOOD RD
COLINSWOOD
A355
BEACONSFIELD RD
EGYPT LA
EGYPT WOOD COTTS
HOLLYBUSH CNR
CHRISTMAS LA
PARISH LA
GREGORY RD
OLD NURSERY CT
HEDGERLEY HILL
LONGFIELD
TIMBERWOOD
ONE PIN LA
WOOD END CL
WOODLAND GLADE
HEATHERSIDE GDNS
ROMSEY DR
CLARE DR
BARN CL
HAMMOND END
HOLLY CL
MOUNT CL
ASHENDEN WLK
CRISPIN WAY
MAYFLOWER WAY
SHERBOURNE WLK
DREW MDW
CAGES WOOD DR
STEWARTS DR
THE AVENUE
DUKES DR
McAULIFFE DR
OAKRIDGE PL
ASTONVILLE
COMMON WOOD
TEMPLEWOOD
BRACKEN CL
BADGERS WOOD
GRANGE GDNS
SCOTT CL
HAMILTON WAY
THE HIGHLANDS
BEECHES DR
INGLEGLEN
WOODLANDS COTTS
DELL CL
ORCHARD GATE
TEMPLE WAY
TEMPLEWOOD GATE
ROWANHURST DR
FOXHOLLOW DR
1 ROBIN PAR
2 CHRISTOPHER HO
HALSE DR
LORD MAYORS DR
BEECHES RD
ROSEWOOD WAY
WARREN CT
FRENSHAM WLK
THE PARADE
THE CENTRE
LANGTON'S MDW
BEDFORD DR
GREEN LA
KINGSWAY MEWS
KINGSWAY
SOVEREIGN BEECHES
VICTORIA RD
SUSSEX HO
READE CT
1 THE BROADWAY
2 PROSPECT CT
SIR HENRY PEAKES DR
GOLDEN OAK CL
KENNEDY CL
FORGE DR
ELM CL
SCOTLANDS DR
HAWTHORN LA
PURTON LA
PARSON'S WOOD LA
HILL PL
LONG CL
SPRING LA
PURTON CT
CHERRY TREE
12
13
86
85
96
40

Hanging Wood
Hedgerley Hill
NS RD
Hedgerley Park
Mount Hill Farm
Mounthill Wood
Park House
A
B
C
B416
DUKES VALLEY
SL9
Pickeridge Wood
Cemy
Hedgerley Park Farm
COLLUM GREEN RD
COLLEY HILL LA
4
STOKE WOOD
86
The Pickeridge
GYPSY LA
Stoke Wood
STOKE WOOD
COLLUM GREEN RD
WINDSOR RD
Fox & Pheasant (PH)
3
STOKE COMMON RD
JARDINE COTTS
TEMPLEWOOD LA
SL3
Stoke Common
Shakespeare's Way
SL2
LARCHMOOR PK
2
Duffield Farm
GERARDS CROSS RD
Brockhurst Wood
85
Frame Wood
VINE RD
VINE CT
VINE RD
VINE RD
FIRCROFT CL
FIRCROFT CT
1
DUFFIELD LA
Hornbeam Cottage
NEVILLE CL
CLEVEHURST CL
RICKMAN'S LA
ELDERFIELD RD
WAKEFIELD CRES
HAZELL WAY
FREEMANS CL
FREEMANS CL
Stoke Poges
Hollybush Hill
Brockhurst Park
PENNYLETS GN
30
POST OFFICE COTTS
BROOM HILL
CHERRY ORCH
hard
od
BUNBY RD
98
BELLS HILL GN
P
PO
13
14
ASH GR
Stoke Court
B416
SEFTON PADDOCK
HOLLYBUSH HILL
BOLD'S CT
ROGERS LA
The StokePoges Sch
SCHOOL LA
CHAPEL LA

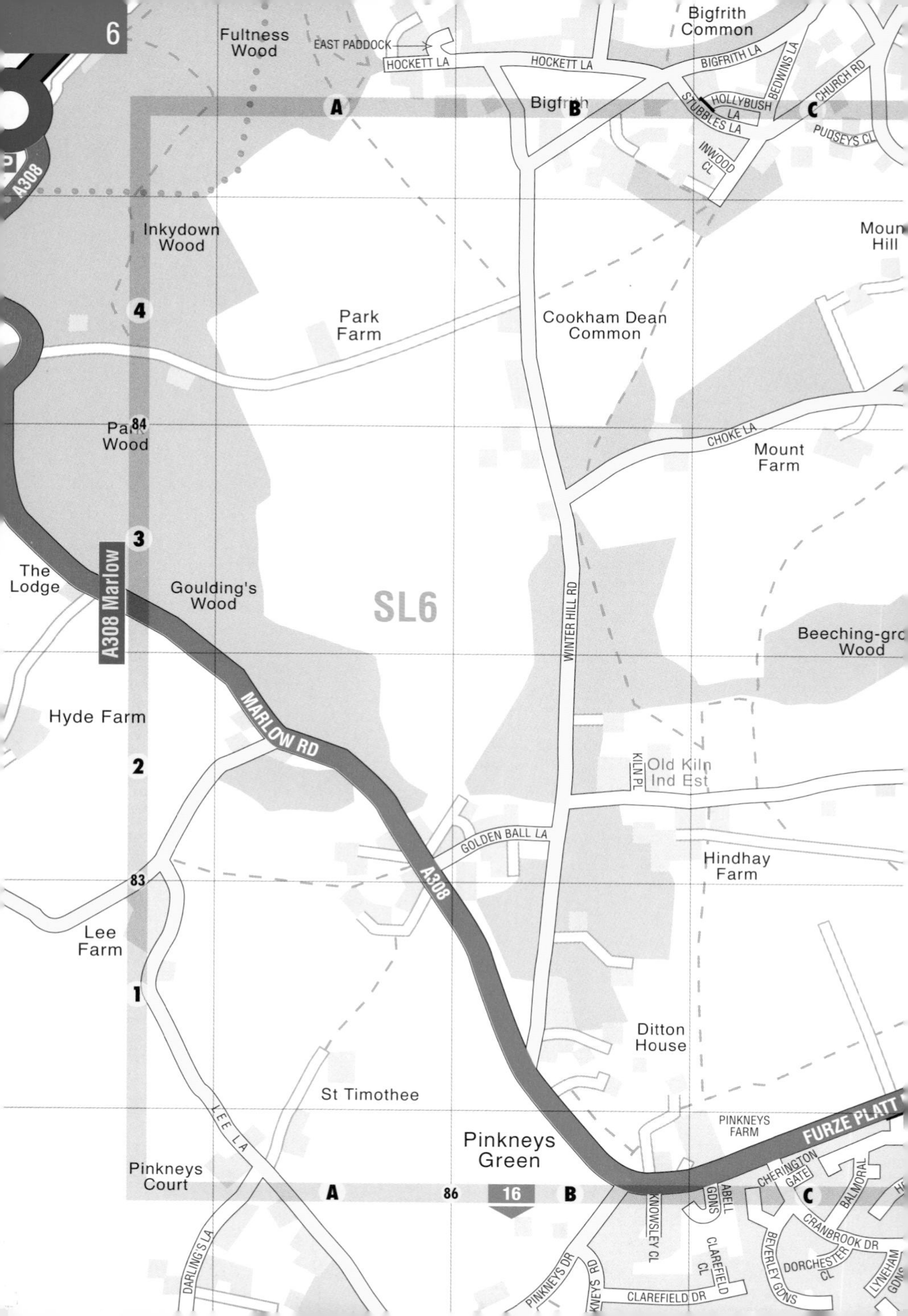
Fultness Wood
EAST PADDOCK
HOCKETT LA
HOCKETT LA
Bigfrith Common
BIGFRITH LA
BEDWINS LA
CHURCH RD
HOLLYBUSH LA
STUBBLES LA
Bigfrith
PUDSEYS CL
INWOOD CL
A308
Inkydown Wood
Mount Hill
Park Farm
Cookham Dean Common
Park Wood
84
CHOKE LA
Mount Farm
The Lodge
A308 Marlow
Goulding's Wood
SL6
WINTER HILL RD
Beeching-gro Wood
Hyde Farm
MARLOW RD
KILN PL
Old Kiln Ind Est
GOLDEN BALL LA
Hindhay Farm
83
A308
Lee Farm
Ditton House
St Timothee
LEE LA
PINKNEYS FARM
FURZE PLATT
Pinkneys Green
Pinkneys Court
CHERINGTON GATE
BALMORAL
ABELL GDNS
KNOWSLEY CL
CRANBROOK DR
CLAREFIELD CL
BEVERLEY GDNS
DORCHESTER CL
LYNEHAM
DARLING'S LA
PINKNEYS DR
KNEYS RD
CLAREFIELD DR
A
B
C
4
3
2
1
A
86
B
C

16

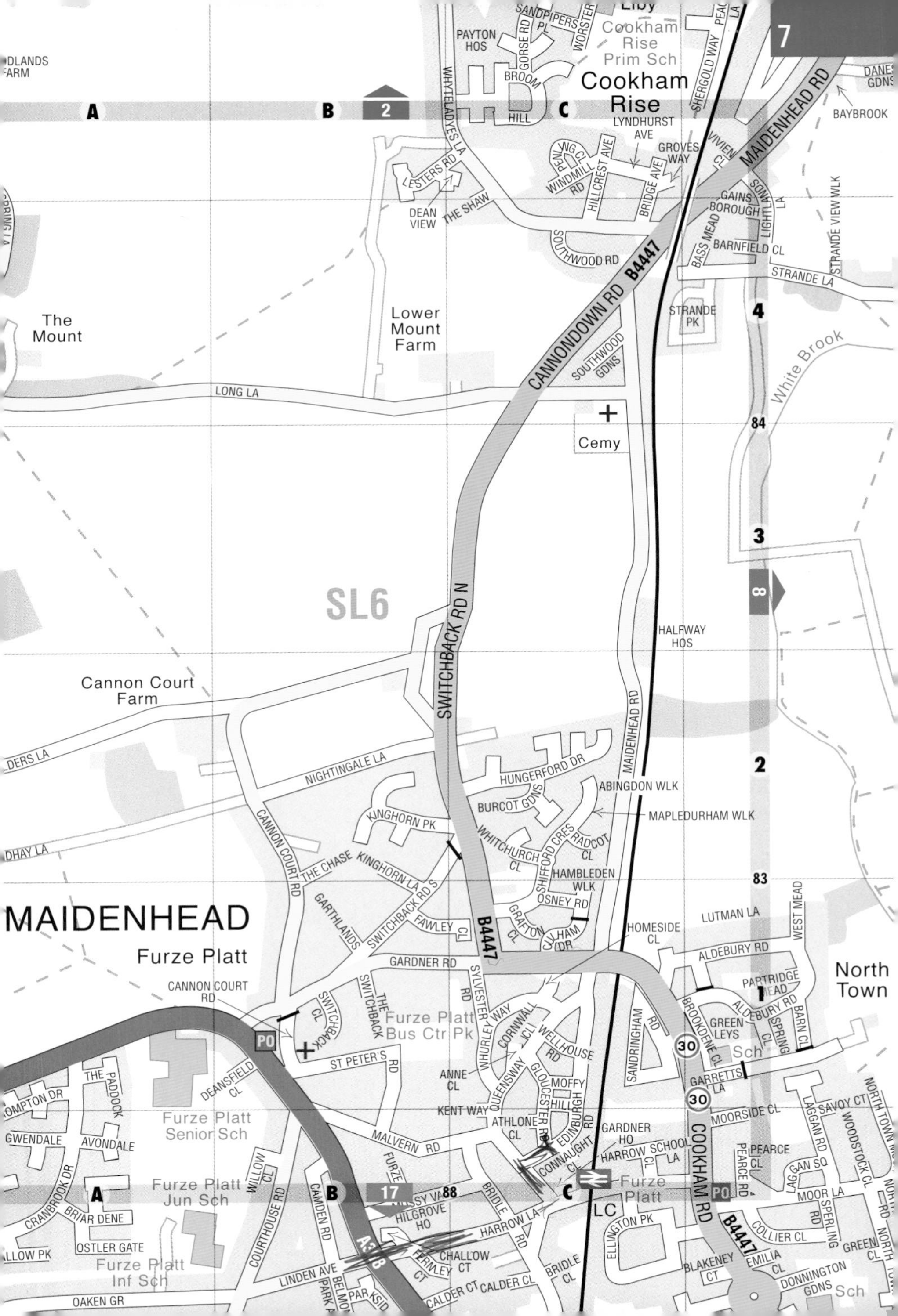
Cookham Rise
Cookham Rise Prim Sch
The Mount
Lower Mount Farm
Cemy
SL6
Cannon Court Farm
MAIDENHEAD
Furze Platt
North Town
Furze Platt Bus Ctr Pk
Furze Platt Senior Sch
Furze Platt Jun Sch
Furze Platt Inf Sch
HALFWAY HOS
White Brook
CANNONDOWN RD
SWITCHBACK RD N
MAIDENHEAD RD
COOKHAM RD
LONG LA
NIGHTINGALE LA
GARDNER RD
MALVERN RD
HARROW LA
B4447
A308
STRANDE LA
STRANDE PK
SOUTHWOOD RD
SOUTHWOOD GDNS
BAYBROOK
HUNGERFORD DR
ABINGDON WLK
MAPLEDURHAM WLK
KINGHORN PK
KINGHORN LA
THE CHASE
CANNON COURT RD
GARTHLANDS
SWITCHBACK RD S
FAWLEY CL
WHITCHURCH CL
SHIFFORD CRES
RADCOT CL
HAMBLEDEN WLK
OSNEY RD
GRAFTON CL
CULHAM DR
HOMESIDE CL
LUTMAN LA
WEST MEAD
ALDEBURY RD
PARTRIDGE MEAD
SANDRINGHAM RD
BROOKDENE CL
GREEN LEYS
SPRING CL
BARN CL
GARRETTS LA
MOORSIDE CL
PEARCE CL
PEARCE RD
LAGGAN RD
LAGGAN SQ
SAVOY CT
WOODSTOCK CL
MOOR LA
SPERLING RD
COLLIER CL
GREEN CL
EMILIA CL
BLAKENEY CT
DONNINGTON GDNS
ELLINGTON PK
BRIDLE CL
BRIDLE RD
CALDER CL
CALDER CT
FERNLEY CT
CHALLOW CT
HILGROVE HO
LINDEN AVE
OAKEN GR
COURTHOUSE RD
CAMDEN RD
WILLOW CL
DEANSFIELD CL
ST PETER'S RD
SWITCHBACK CL
THE SWITCHBACK
SYLVESTER RD
WHURLEY WAY
CORNWALL CL
WELLHOUSE RD
ANNE CL
QUEENSWAY
KENT WAY
ATHLONE CL
GLOUCESTER RD
MOFFY HILL
EDINBURGH RD
CONNAUGHT CL
GARDNER HO
HARROW SCHOOL LA
AVONDALE
GWENDALE
THE PADDOCK
CRANBROOK DR
BRIAR DENE
OSTLER GATE
BURCOT GDNS
WHYTELADYES LA
LESTERS RD
DEAN VIEW
THE SHAW
PAYTON HOS
GORSE RD
SANDPIPERS PL
BROOM HILL
LYNDHURST AVE
GROVES WAY
PENLING CL
WINDMILL RD
HILLCREST AVE
BRIDGE AVE
VIVIEN CL
SHERGOLD WAY
GAINSBOROUGH
BASS MEAD
BARNFIELD CL
LIGHTLANDS LA
STRANDE VIEW WLK
DANES GDNS
LONG LA
LC
Sch
PO

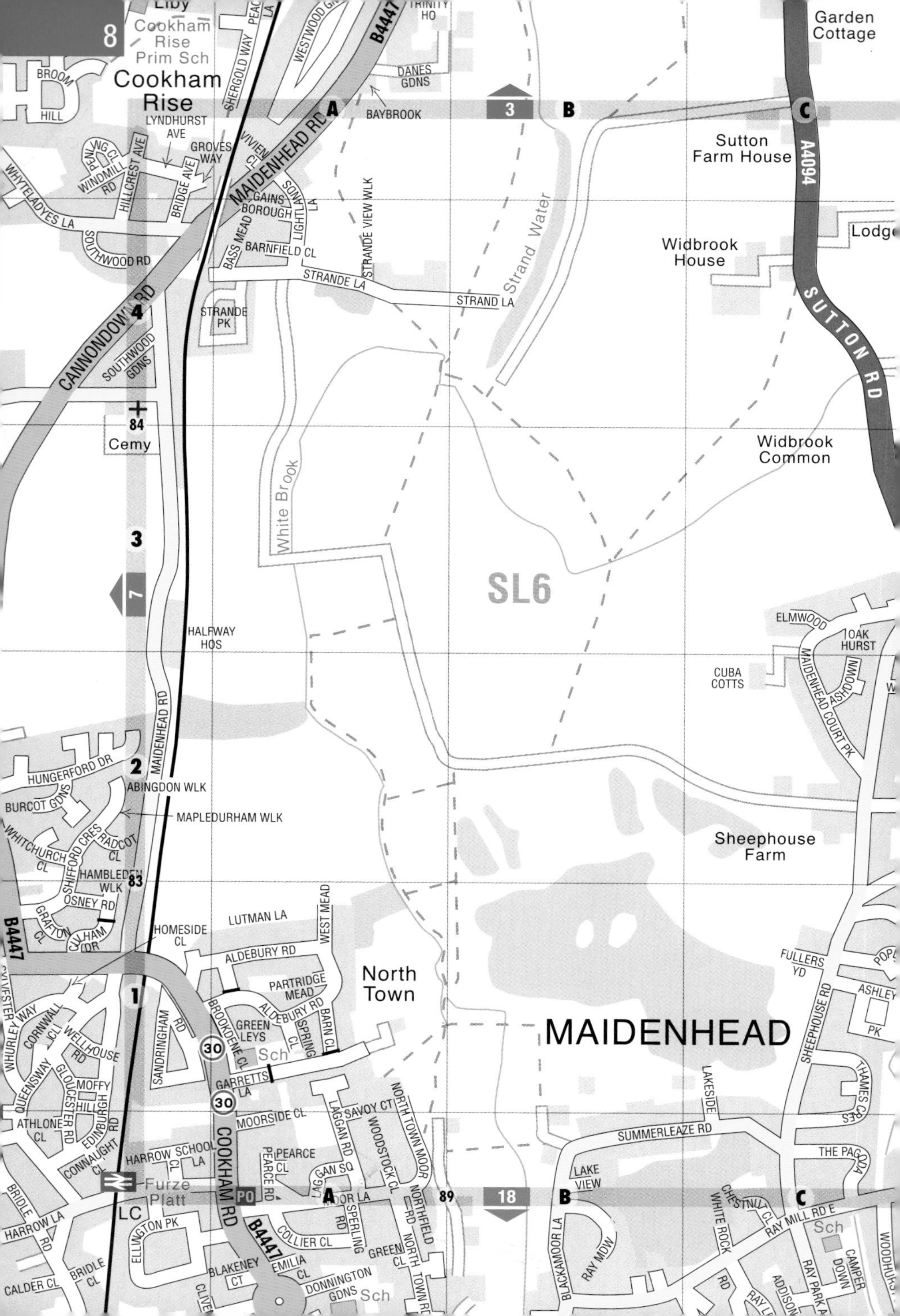
Cookham Rise Prim Sch
Cookham Rise
Garden Cottage
TRINITY HO
DANES GDNS
BAYBROOK
WESTWOOD GN
SHERGOLD WAY
BROOM HILL
LYNDHURST AVE
GROVES WAY
PENLING CL
WINDMILL RD
HILLCREST AVE
BRIDGE AVE
VIVIEN CL
MAIDENHEAD RD
B4447
WHYTELADYES LA
SOUTHWOOD RD
GAINSBOROUGH
LIGHTLANDS LA
BASS MEAD
BARNFIELD CL
STRANDE VIEW WLK
STRANDE LA
STRAND LA
Strand Water
STRANDE PK
CANNONDOWN RD
SOUTHWOOD GDNS
Cemy
Sutton Farm House
A4094
Lodge
Widbrook House
SUTTON RD
Widbrook Common
White Brook
SL6
HALFWAY HOS
ELMWOOD
OAK HURST
CUBA COTTS
MAIDENHEAD COURT PK
ASHDOWN
HUNGERFORD DR
ABINGDON WLK
BURCOT GDNS
MAPLEDURHAM WLK
WHITCHURCH CL
SHIFFORD CRES
RADCOT CL
HAMBLEDEN WLK
OSNEY RD
GRAFTON CL
CULHAM DR
HOMESIDE CL
LUTMAN LA
WEST MEAD
ALDEBURY RD
PARTRIDGE MEAD
North Town
Sheephouse Farm
FULLERS YD
ASHLEY PK
SHEEPHOUSE RD
THAMES CRES
MAIDENHEAD
SYLVESTER
WHURLEY WAY
CORNWALL CL
WELLHOUSE RD
SANDRINGHAM RD
BROOKDENE CL
GREEN LEYS
SPRING CL
BARN CL
Sch
QUEENSWAY
GLOUCESTER RD
MOFFY HILL
EDINBURGH RD
GARRETTS LA
ATHLONE CL
CONNAUGHT CL
MOORSIDE CL
LAGGAN RD
SAVOY CT
WOODSTOCK CL
NORTH TOWN MOOR
LAKESIDE
SUMMERLEAZE RD
THE PAGODA
HARROW SCHOOL LA
HARROW CL
COOKHAM RD
PEARCE CL
PEARCE RD
LAGGAN SQ
LAKE VIEW
Furze Platt
PO
MOOR LA
SPERLING RD
NORTHFIELD RD
CHESTNUT CL
RAY MILL RD E
BRIDLE RD
HARROW LA
LC
ELLINGTON PK
COLLIER CL
GREEN CL
NORTH TOWN RD
BLACKAMOOR LA
RAY MDW
WHITE ROCK
CAMPER DOWN
RAY PARK
WOODHURST
ADDISON
CALDER CL
BRIDLE CL
BLAKENEY CT
EMILIA CL
CLIVE
DONNINGTON GDNS
A
B
C
3
4
2
1
7
18
84
83
89
30

9
A
B
C
Towing Path
River Thames
Thames Path
White Place Farm
White Brook
Burwood House
TAPLOW COMMON RD
ORKNEY CT
4
PARLIAMENT LA
HUNTSWOOD LA
84
SL1
Green Dr
3
10
Wood
CLIVEDEN RD
Whitebrook Pk
Maidenhead Court
SL6
PARK DR
BATTLEMEAD CL
ISLET
ISLET PK
ISLET PARK HO
HIGH MDWS
ISLET RD
SOMERLEA
COURT DR
HERONS PL
EBSWORTH CL
COURT RD
AMBERLEY CT
2
Hitchambury
HUNT'S LA
LOWER COOKHAM RD
83
Hitchambury Farm
HAZELWOOD CT
MEAD
LOCK MEAD
HAZE MEAD
TUDOR CT
Weir
1
HILL FARM RD
LOCK AVE
HITCHAM LA
HORSHAM REACH
P
BUFFINS
Taplow
1 CHURCH COTTS
2 COLD GROVE COTTS
BOULTERS LA
BOULTERS GDNS
A4094
Boulter's Lock
Taplow Vineyard
DESBOROUGH COTTS
Hill Farm
HITCHAM GRANGE
Jubilee River
HORTON CL
HORTON GRANGE
Taplow Court
19
91
HIGH ST
HILL HO
RECTORY RD
BERRY HILL
CEDAR CHASE
PH
WELLBANK
BOUNDARY RD
LONGWORTH DR
WOODHURST SOUTH
Mill
STOCKWELLS
Poplar Farm

CH
Lambourne Wood
Wymers Wood
Burwood House
TAPLOW COMMON RD
NASHDOM LA
NASHDOM LA
ORKNEY CT
2 NASHDOM
PARLIAMENT LA
ROSE HILL
Rose Hill House
Poyle Cottages
Rose Hill
CHALK PIT LA
HUNTSWOOD LA
Rose Hill Farm
BRICKFIELD LA
Green Dr
Westalls
Hotel
SL1
Hunt's Wood
CH
CLIVEDEN RD
TAPLOW COMMON RD
WYMERS WOOD RD
REDWOOD
BOWMANS CL
ASHCROFT CT
POYLE LA
SL6
PINK LA
WYMERS CL
GRENVILLE CL
Grovefield Hotel
MALLARD CL
NORTH BURNHAM CL
Hitchambury
OXFORD AVE
CAMBRIDGE AVE
WYNDHAM CRES
HUNT'S LA
WILLOW WOOD CL
Hitchambury Farm
Hitcham Park
GREENWAY
TOCKLEY RD
PEPLER WAY
CLONMEL WAY
BREDWARD CL
THE GORE
GORE RD
St Peter's CE Comb Sch
MINNIECROFT RD
HILL FARM RD
HITCHAM LA
HITCHAM LA
HAMILTON GDNS
Hitcham House Farm
BUFFINS
1 CHURCH COTTS
2 COLD GROVE COTTS
CLEARES PASTURE
ACRES
EIGHT ACRES
BURN WLK
DESBOROUGH COTTS
Hill Farm
HITCHAM RD
HITCHAM HO
LENT RISE RD
Lent
HITCHAM GRANGE
LENT GN
LENT GREEN LA
HIGH ST
New Cut
Taplow
20
ALICE LA
ST PETERS
RECTORY RD
PH
Orchardville
WELLBANK
BOUNDARY RD
Poplar Farm
ORCHARDVILLE
A
B
C
84
83
92
9

Dorney Wood
Pumpkin Hill Cottage
Juniper Grove
Pumpkin Hill
Fox Den
Longmead
Snowball Farm
Hunts Wood Farm
ORCHARD BUNGALOW MOBILE HOME PK
High Meadow
CH
SL1
Cant's Hill
Burnham Grove
Burnham
Bottom Waltons
Grove Wood
BOTTOM WALTONS CVN SITE
SL2
Court Farm
Grenville Court
SLOUGH
Lynch Hill Prim Sch
Burnham Gram Sch
THE POUND
Britwell
Liby
The Priory
DROPMORE RD
DORNEY WOOD RD
PUMPKIN HILL
VICTORIA DR
LORD MAYORS DR
HAWTHORN LA
NIGHTINGALE PK
LONGMEAD LA
GROVE RD
GREEN LA
CROW PIECE LA
ALLERDS RD
CHEVELEY GDNS
HAZELHURST RD
BENTLEY PK
LINKSWOOD RD
THE FAIRWAY
WALTON LA
PIPERS CL
PIPERS CT
KIMBERS DR
LONG DR
FAIRFIELD RD
ALMA CT
COURT LA
BRITWELL RD
FARNHAM LA
FARNHAM LA
SAMPSON GN
ROKESBY RD
THE CEDARS
WAVELL GDNS
MASCOLL PATH
DOVE HOUSE CRES
HETHERINGTON CL
ROKESBY RD
PERRYMAN WAY
TRAVIC RD
GAVESTON RD
CALBROKE RD
UMBERVILLE WAY
GOODWIN
SKYDMORE PATH
REEDHAM RD
GREEN LANE CT
JENNERY LA
PENN HO
SEER GREEN HO
DAWES EAST RD
HIGH ST
BEECH
HATCHGATE GDNS
HOGFAIR LA
LINCOLN HATCH LA
LYNCH HILL LA
LOWER BRITWELL RD
STRATFORD CL
NEWPORT RD
GARRARD RD
CECIL WAY
DOWNING PATH
WINTOUN PATH
LONG FURLONG DR
PARKGATE
SANDS FARM DR
BASSETT WAY
VENUS CL
BARTELOTTS RD
COVERDALE WAY
VAUGHAN WAY
EGERTON RD
PEMBERTON RD
MAGPIE WAY
FAIRVIEW RD
FOSTERS PATH
WINDSOR LA
SHENSTONE DR
ST MICHAEL'S CT
RAMSEY CT
HAYMILL RD
WORDSWORTH RD
TENNYSON WAY
KESTREL PATH
TOMLIN RD
VERMONT RD
KINGSLEY PATH
WHITTAKER RD
LOVEGROVE DR
STOMP RD
SHOREHAM RISE
PO
P
A
B
C
1
2
3
4
84
83
94
12
21

Juniper Grove
Pumpkin Hill Cottage
Pumpkin Hill
East Burnham Common
Caldicott Sch
The Stag (PH)
Orchard Bungalow Mobile Home Pk
Hunts Wood Farm
The Crown Inn (PH)
East Burnham Cotts
Leys Farm
East Burnham
SL1
SL2
Cant's Hill
Burnham Grove
East Burnham Park
Bottom Waltons
Allerd's Farm
Grove Wood
Deepwood
Bottom Waltons Cvn Site
B1
1 Wentworth Ind Ct
2 Goodwin Rd
Victoria Dr
Pumpkin Hill
Lord Mayors Dr
Sir Henry Peakes Dr
Bedford Dr
Scotlands Dr
Hawthorn La
Nightingale Pk
Hill Pl
Thompkins La
Crown La
Stoney La
East Burnham La
Grove Rd
Blackpond La
Bybend Cl
Crow Piece La
Allerds Rd
Walton La
Rosken Gr
Devonshire Gn
Cobblers Cl
Farnham La
Kidderminster Rd
Sampsons Gn
Travis Ct
Verdon Ct
Bishops Orch
Doddsfield Rd
Liby
Upper Lees Rd
Beechwood Sch
Dove House Cres
The Cedars
Rokesby Rd
Lilac Ct
Wavell Gdns
Elmar Gn
Woodford Way
Hemming Way
Mascoll Path
The Beeches
Ravensworth Rd
Furzen Cl
Lydsey Cl
St Crayle
Hetherington Cl
Rokesby Rd
Ansculf Rd
Eyre Gn
Aylesworth Ave
Arbour Vale Sch
Perryman Way
Hawkshill Rd
Gaveston Rd
Calbroke Rd
Travic Rd
Marunden Gn
PO
Manfield Cl
Odencroft Rd
Bromycroft Rd
Lower Lees Rd
Lynch Hill Prim Sch
Umberville Way
Goodwin Rd
Wentworth Ave
Lynch Hill La
Chilwick Rd
Monksfield Way
Long Readings La
Bideford Spur
Torquay Spur
Skydmore Path
Claycots Sch
Garrard Rd
Cecil Way
Brighton Spur 1
Newhaven Spur 2
Bridport Way
Penzance Spur
Downing Path
Wintoun Path
Long Furlong Dr
Northcroft
Eastcroft
Bassett Way
Venus Cl
Coverdale Way
Egerton Rd
Pemberton Rd
Magpie Way
Fairview Rd
Britwell
Aldridge Rd
Gascon's Gr
South Croft
Westcroft
Vaughan Way
Kestrel Path
Tomlin Rd
Vermont Rd
SLOUGH
Crofthill Rd
Broomfield Gate
Westfield
Whittaker Rd
Lovegrove Dr
Cowper Rd
Faircroft
End
Sandlers
Newchurch Rd
A
B
C
4
3
2
1
84
83
95
11
22

CENTRE
Liby
VICTORIA RD
SUSSEX HO
READE CT
FORGE DR
ELM CL
A355
BEACONSFIELD RD
Farnham Common
Shakespeare's Way
4
5
A
B
C
Hornbeam Cottage
DUFFIELD LA
NEVILLE CL
ELDERFIELD RD
RICKMAN'S LA
WAKEFIELD CRES
HAZELL WAY
PENNYL GN
BUNBY
ASH GR
Brockhurst Park
Old Orchard Wood
PARSON'S WOOD LA
PURTON LA
PURTON CT
40
Stoke Court
The StokePog Sch
LAKESIDE DR
STOKE COURT DR
GLENFIELDS
ROGERS LA
SEFTON CL
WEST END CT
WEST END LA
ELIZABETH WAY
PENN MDW
84
FARNHAM PARK LA
KEMSLEY CHASE
PARSONAGE LA
Farnham Park
SL2
CH
14
Stoke Poges
Tithe Farm
PARK RD
Farnham Royal
SOSPEL CT
HOME MDW
RECTORY TERR
B416
2
The Clock House
Stoke Park
Mon
MARSH'S PLAIN
83
RECTORY CL
STOKE PARK AVE
1 NORTH COTTS
2 HOWARDS GATE
St Mary's Farnham Royal CE Prim Sch
CHURCH RD
1
Gray's Mon
CHURCH LA
DUFFIELD PK
Stoke Park House (CH)
EAST DR
PARK LAWN
ARDROSSAN CL
P
St Anthony's RC Prim Sch
Penn Wood Prim Sch
WILTSHIRE AVE
CORNWALL AVE
23
97
FIR TREE AVE
STAFFORD AVE
LANCASTER AVE
PENN RD
CAIRNGORM PL
MILTON RD
CUMBERLAND AVE
CANTERBURY AVE
HATTON AVE
NORTHERN RD
ST ELMO CRES
Manor Park
STOKE POGES LA
WARWICK AVE

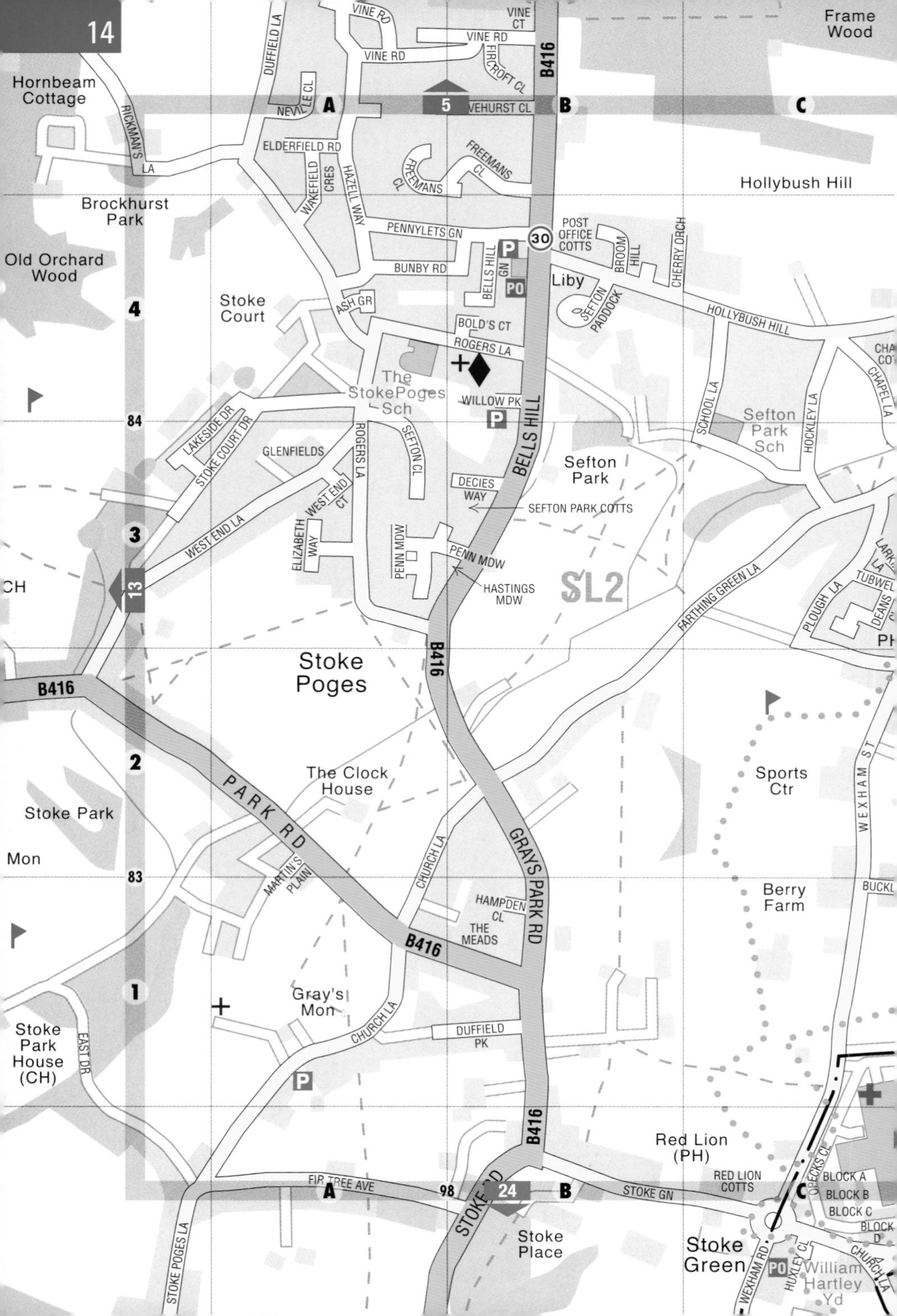
Hornbeam Cottage
Brockhurst Park
Old Orchard Wood
Stoke Court
Frame Wood
Hollybush Hill
Sefton Park
SL2
Stoke Poges
The Clock House
Stoke Park
Mon
Stoke Park House (CH)
Gray's Mon
Sports Ctr
Berry Farm
Red Lion (PH)
Stoke Place
Stoke Green
William Hartley Yd
The StokePoges Sch
Sefton Park Sch
Liby
VINE RD
VINE CT
DUFFIELD LA
NEVILLE CL
VEHURST CL
FIRCROFT CL
ELDERFIELD RD
FREEMANS CL
WAKEFIELD CRES
HAZELL WAY
PENNYLETS GN
BUNBY RD
BELLS HILL GN
POST OFFICE COTTS
BROOM HILL
CHERRY ORCH
SEFTON PADDOCK
HOLLYBUSH HILL
ASH GR
BOLD'S CT
ROGERS LA
WILLOW PK
SCHOOL LA
HOCKLEY LA
CHAPEL LA
LAKESIDE DR
STOKE COURT DR
GLENFIELDS
SEFTON CL
DECIES WAY
SEFTON PARK COTTS
BELLS HILL
WEST END CT
WEST END LA
ELIZABETH WAY
PENN MDW
HASTINGS MDW
FARTHING GREEN LA
PLOUGH LA
TUBWELL
DEANS
B416
PARK RD
MARTIN'S PLAIN
CHURCH LA
GRAYS PARK RD
HAMPDEN CL
THE MEADS
WEXHAM ST
BUCKL
DUFFIELD PK
EAST DR
RICKMAN'S LA
FIR TREE AVE
STOKE RD
STOKE GN
RED LION COTTS
STOKE POGES LA
WEXHAM RD
HUXLEY CL
BLOCK A
BLOCK B
BLOCK C
BLOCK D
CHURCH LA
30
P
PO
A
B
C
5
13
24
84
83
98
1
2
3
4

Mill House Farm

FRAMEWOOD MANOR

A

FRAMEWOOD RD

B

WEXHAM PL

Fulmer Common

FULMER COMMON RD

C

LANGLEY CNR

SL2

Fairfield Lodge

Teikyo Sch (UK)

Upton Wood

Upton Lake

Upton Farm

4

Shakespeare's Way

QUEEN'S DR

84

PH

ONE FARM WAY

Twin Trees Farm

ROWLEY LA

BLACK PARK RD

3

The Thames Valley Nuffield

H

SL3

Wexham Street

Rowley Wood

Iver Heath

RLEY OTTS

CH

Galleons La

Black Park Country Park

P ✕

2

Gallions Wood

Blackpark Lake

Visitor Ctr 83

SAWMILL COTTS

Spring Wood

Rowley Farm

1

Bell Farm

Rowley Lake

A412 LUXBRIDGE RD

A412 Denham

Wexham Park

A

OPAL CT

WEXHAM PARK LA

VALLEY END

LOCK F

B 25 00 **C**

MAIDENHEAD
Ditton House
St Timothee
Pinkneys Court
Pinkneys Green
PINKNEYS FARM
FURZE PLATT RD
A308
LEE LA
DARLING'S LA
PINKNEYS DR
BAKERS ROW
BAKERS LA
MOORLANDS DR
BIX LA
AUSTINSGATE
PH
LIME WLK
THE CONIFERS
COMPTON DR
ARLINGTON CL
HARDWICK CL
BERKLEY CL
GREENWAYS DR
CAMLEY PARK DR
FONTWELL CL
CAMLEY GDNS
ARUNDEL CL
TAVISTOCK CL
SL6
Grays Alley
THICKET GR
HEADINGTON RD
HEADINGTON CL
TRURO CL
FARM CL
FARM RD
CHENISTON GR
1 THE BRYHER
THE FRANTONS
NEWLANDS DR
THE RIDINGS
Sch
ROSELEIGH CL
KENWOOD CL
HOBBIS DR
HIGHWAY AVE
EDITH RD
ST MARGARET'S RD
HAREFIELD RD
PENWOOD CT
THE GARDEN MEWS
Highway
BIRDWOOD RD
TWYNHAM RD
NAPIER RD
ALLENBY RD
WESTFIELD RD
WAVELL RD
HIGHWAY RD
HAVELOCK CRES
HAVELOCK RD
PINE CL
ST MARK'S CRES
ALWYN RD
HIGHFIELD RD
TAYLORS CT
BEECH CL
FIELDING
C3
1 STIRLING PL
2 GREENLANDS CT
3 MERLIN CT
4 WELLINGTON CL
KNOWSLEY CL
ABELL GDNS
CLAREFIELD CL
CLAREFIELD DR
CLAREFIELD RD
CHERINGTON GATE
CRANBROOK DR
BALMORAL
BEVERLEY GDNS
DORCHESTER CL
LYNEHAM GDNS
WINSTON CT
HALIFAX CL
HALIFAX RD
LINCOLN RD
SUNDERLAND RD
HAMPDEN RD
OLDERSHAW MEWS
BLENHEIM RD
VICTOR CL
CAMFIELD CT
LANCASTER RD
HALIFAX WAY
STIRLING GR
PINKNEYS RD
RD
A404 High Wycombe
HENLEY RD
Robin Hood's Arbour
Maidenhead Thicket
A404
9b
A4
A4 Reading
A404(M)
NEWLANDS HO
MONTROSE DR
MARLBOROUGH RD
MARLBOROUGH CL
PO
40
TALBOTS DR
ENDFIELD PL
HAMILTON PK
St Edmund Campion RC Prim Sch
TOLLGATE
SHERWOOD DR
BEECHWOOD DR
HEATHLANDS DR
SANDISPLATT RD
ASHTON PL
CANNON LA
AUTUMN WLK
WOODFIELD DR
Tittle Row
SILVERTREES DR
Altwood CE Sec Sch
ALTWOOD RD
AUDLEY DR
TURPINS GN
GARDEN CL
HOLMWOOD CL
WEBSTER CL
TIMBERS WLK
SILVER CL
BANNARD RD
BLOOMFIELD RD
LEES GDNS
ALTWOOD DR
ALTWOOD CL
Claires Court Sch-Ridgeway
BARLEY MEAD
P
A
B
C
6
26
86
4
82
3
2
81
1

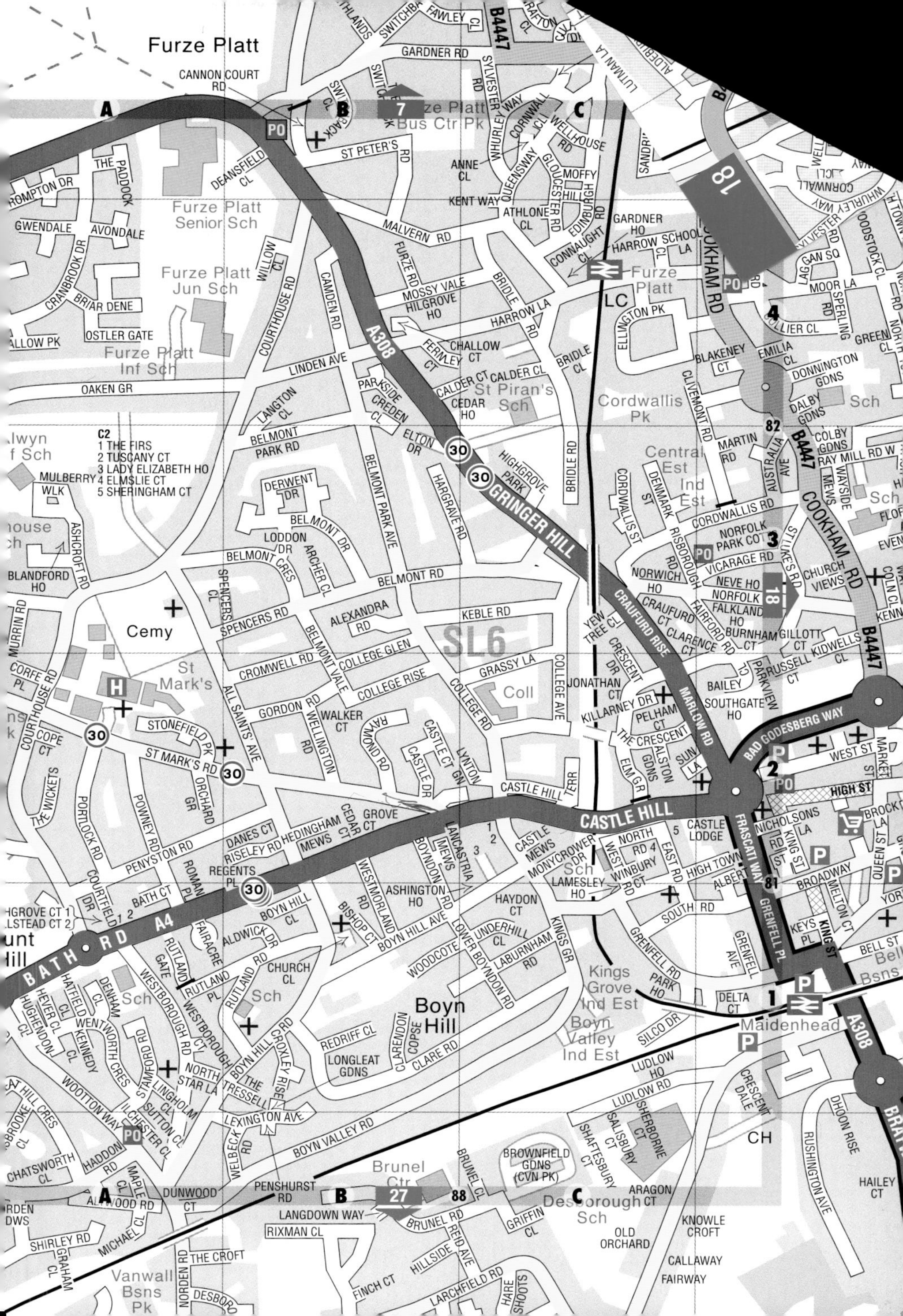
Furze Platt
A
B
C
7
18
4
3
2
1
82
81
88
27
Furze Platt Senior Sch
Furze Platt Jun Sch
Furze Platt Inf Sch
Furze Platt Bus Ctr Pk
Cemy
St Mark's
St Piran's Sch
Cordwallis Pk
Central Est
Ind Est
Furze Platt
Coll
SL6
Boyn Hill
Kings Grove Ind Est
Boyn Valley Ind Est
Maidenhead
Brunel Ctr
Desborough Sch
Vanwall Bsns Pk
C2
1 THE FIRS
2 TUSCANY CT
3 LADY ELIZABETH HO
4 ELMSLIE CT
5 SHERINGHAM CT
A308
A4
B4447
CASTLE HILL
GRINGER HILL
CRAUFURD RISE
MARLOW RD
FRASCATI WAY
BATH RD
COOKHAM RD
BAD GODESBERG WAY
GRENFELL PL
HIGH ST
KING ST
CANNON COURT RD
GARDNER RD
ST PETER'S RD
MALVERN RD
LINDEN AVE
OAKEN GR
BELMONT PARK RD
BELMONT RD
KEBLE RD
CROMWELL RD
COLLEGE RISE
GORDON RD
ST MARK'S RD
PENYSTON RD
BOYN HILL AVE
BOYN HILL RD
BOYN VALLEY RD
LUDLOW RD
SOUTH RD
HARROW LA
COURTHOUSE RD
CAMDEN RD
ALL SAINTS' AVE
COLLEGE AVE
BRIDLE RD
ELLINGTON PK
CORDWALLIS RD
VICARAGE RD
PENSHURST RD
LANGDOWN WAY
RIXMAN CL
BRUNEL RD
OLD ORCHARD
KNOWLE CROFT
CALLAWAY
FAIRWAY
HAILEY CT
RUSHINGTON AVE
DHOON RISE
CRESCENT DALE
CH
LC
PO
H
30

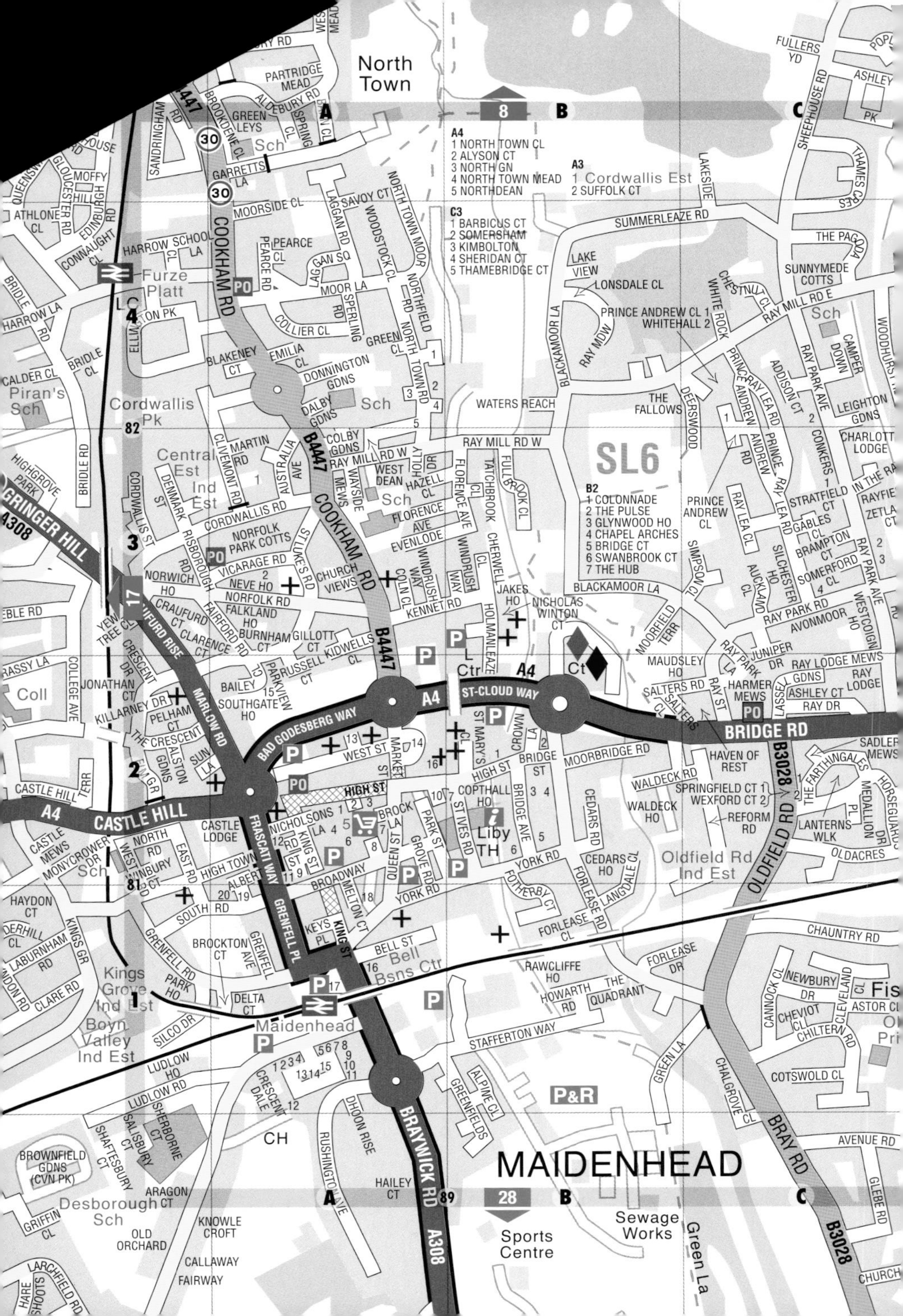
North Town
MAIDENHEAD
SL6
8
28
A
B
C
A4
1 NORTH TOWN CL
2 ALYSON CT
3 NORTH GN
4 NORTH TOWN MEAD
5 NORTHDEAN
A3
1 Cordwallis Est
2 SUFFOLK CT
C3
1 BARBICUS CT
2 SOMERSHAM
3 KIMBOLTON
4 SHERIDAN CT
5 THAMEBRIDGE CT
B2
1 COLONNADE
2 THE PULSE
3 GLYNWOOD HO
4 CHAPEL ARCHES
5 BRIDGE CT
6 SWANBROOK CT
7 THE HUB
PARTRIDGE MEAD
ALDEBURY RD
SPRING CL
GREEN LEYS
BROOKDENE CL
SANDRINGHAM RD
GARRETTS LA
Sch
MOORSIDE CL
COOKHAM RD
B4447
HARROW SCHOOL LA
Furze Platt
PO
LAGGAN RD
SAVOY CT
WOODSTOCK CL
NORTH TOWN MOOR
PEARCE CL
PEARCE RD
LAGGAN SQ
MOOR LA
SPERLING RD
COLLIER CL
NORTHFIELD RD
NORTH TOWN RD
GREEN CL
ELLINGTON PK
BLAKENEY CT
EMILIA CL
DONNINGTON GDNS
DALBY GDNS
COLBY GDNS
Cordwallis Pk
82
MARTIN RD
CLIVEMONT RD
AUSTRALIA AVE
Central Est
Ind Est
DENMARK ST
CORDWALLIS ST
CORDWALLIS RD
RAY MILL RD W
WAYSIDE MEWS
WEST DEAN
HAZELL CL
HOLMWOOD DR
FLORENCE AVE
FLORENCE AVE
EVENLODE
WINDRUSH WAY
TATCHBROOK CL
FULLBROOK CL
CHERWELL CL
WATERS REACH
NORFOLK PARK COTTS
RISBOROUGH RD
ST LUKE'S RD
VICARAGE RD
CHURCH VIEWS
NORWICH HO
NEVE HO
NORFOLK RD
COLN CL
KENNET RD
CRAUFURD CT
FAIRFORD RD
FALKLAND HO
CLARENCE RD
BURNHAM CT
GILLOTT CT
KIDWELLS CL
RUSSELL CT
PARKVIEW
BAILEY CL
SOUTHGATE HO
JAKES HO
NICHOLAS WINTON CT
HOLMANLEAZE
Ctr
GRINGER HILL
A308
17
YEW TREE CL
CRESCENT
COLLEGE AVE
JONATHAN CT
KILLARNEY DR
PELHAM CT
THE CRESCENT
ALSTON GDNS
SUN LA
ELM GR
MARLOW RD
BAD GODESBERG WAY
A4
ST-CLOUD WAY
WEST ST
MARKET ST
ST MARY'S CL
CROWN LA
BRIDGE ST
HIGH ST
Coll
CASTLE HILL TERR
CASTLE HILL
CASTLE MEWS
MONYCROWER DR
NORTH RD
WEST RD
WINBURY CT
EAST RD
CASTLE LODGE
FRASCATI WAY
NICHOLSONS LA
KING ST
BROCK LA
QUEEN ST
GROVE RD
PARK ST
ST IVES RD
COPTHALL HO
BRIDGE AVE
Liby
TH
HIGH TOWN RD
ALBERT ST
BROADWAY
MELTON CT
YORK RD
GRENFELL PL
HAYDON CT
SOUTH RD
KEYS PL
BELL ST
Bell Bsns Ctr
GRENFELL RD
BROCKTON CT
GRENFELL AVE
PARK HO
DELTA CT
Kings Grove Ind Est
Boyn Valley Ind Est
Maidenhead
SILCO DR
LAURELHILL CL
LABURNHAM RD
KINGS GR
CLARE RD
LUDLOW HO
LUDLOW RD
CRESCENT DALE
SHERBORNE CT
SALISBURY CT
SHAFTESBURY CT
CH
BROWNFIELD GDNS (CVN PK)
ARAGON CT
Desborough Sch
GRIFFIN CL
OLD ORCHARD
KNOWLE CROFT
CALLAWAY
FAIRWAY
LARCHFIELD RD
HARE SHOOTS
RUSHINGTON AVE
DHOON RISE
HAILEY CT
BRAYWICK RD
89
A308
Sports Centre
STAFFERTON WAY
ALPINE CL
GREENFIELDS
P&R
Sewage Works
Green La
GREEN LA
YORK RD
FOTHERBY CT
CEDARS RD
CEDARS HO
LANGDALE CL
FORLEASE RD
FORLEASE CL
RAWCLIFFE HO
HOWARTH RD
THE QUADRANT
FORLEASE DR
MOORBRIDGE RD
WALDECK RD
WALDECK HO
SPRINGFIELD CT 1
WEXFORD CT 2
REFORM RD
HAVEN OF REST
Oldfield Rd Ind Est
OLDFIELD RD
B3028
BRIDGE RD
SALTERS RD
SALTERS CL
RAY ST
MAUDSLEY HO
HARMER MEWS
RAY PARK LA
JUNIPER DR
RAY LODGE MEWS
LASSELL GDNS
ASHLEY CT
RAY DR
RAY LODGE
SADLERS MEWS
THE FARTHINGALES
MEDALLION PL
HORSEGUARDS DR
LANTERNS WLK
OLDACRES
CHAUNTRY RD
CANNOCK CL
NEWBURY DR
CLEVELAND
CHEVIOT CL
CHILTERN RD
ASTOR CL
COTSWOLD CL
CHALGROVE CL
BRAY RD
AVENUE RD
GLEBE RD
CHURCH
Fis
LAKESIDE
SUMMERLEAZE RD
LAKE VIEW
LONSDALE CL
PRINCE ANDREW CL 1
WHITEHALL 2
BLACKAMOOR LA
RAY MDW
THE FALLOWS
DEERSWOOD
WHITE ROCK
CHESTNUT CL
RAY MILL RD E
PRINCE ANDREW RD
RAY LEA RD
PRINCE ANDREW CL
RAY LEA CL
ADDISON CT
CONKERS
PRINCE RAY LEA RD
SIMPSON CL
AUCKLAND CL
SILCHESTER HO
GABLES CL
BRAMPTON CT
STRATFIELD CT
SOMERFORD CL
RAY PARK AVE
RAY PARK RD
AVONMOOR
WESTCOIGN HO
MOORFIELD TERR
FULLERS YD
SHEEPHOUSE RD
ASHLEY PK
THAMES CRES
THE PAGODA
SUNNYMEDE COTTS
CAMPER DOWN
LEIGHTON GDNS
CHARLOTT LODGE
IN THE RAY
RAYFIE
ZETLA
Sch
Calder CL
Piran's Sch
BRIDLE CL
BRIDLE RD
HARROW LA
ATHLONE CL
GLOUCESTER RD
EDINBURGH RD
MOFFY HILL
CONNAUGHT RD
HIGHGROVE PARK
30
81
Ct

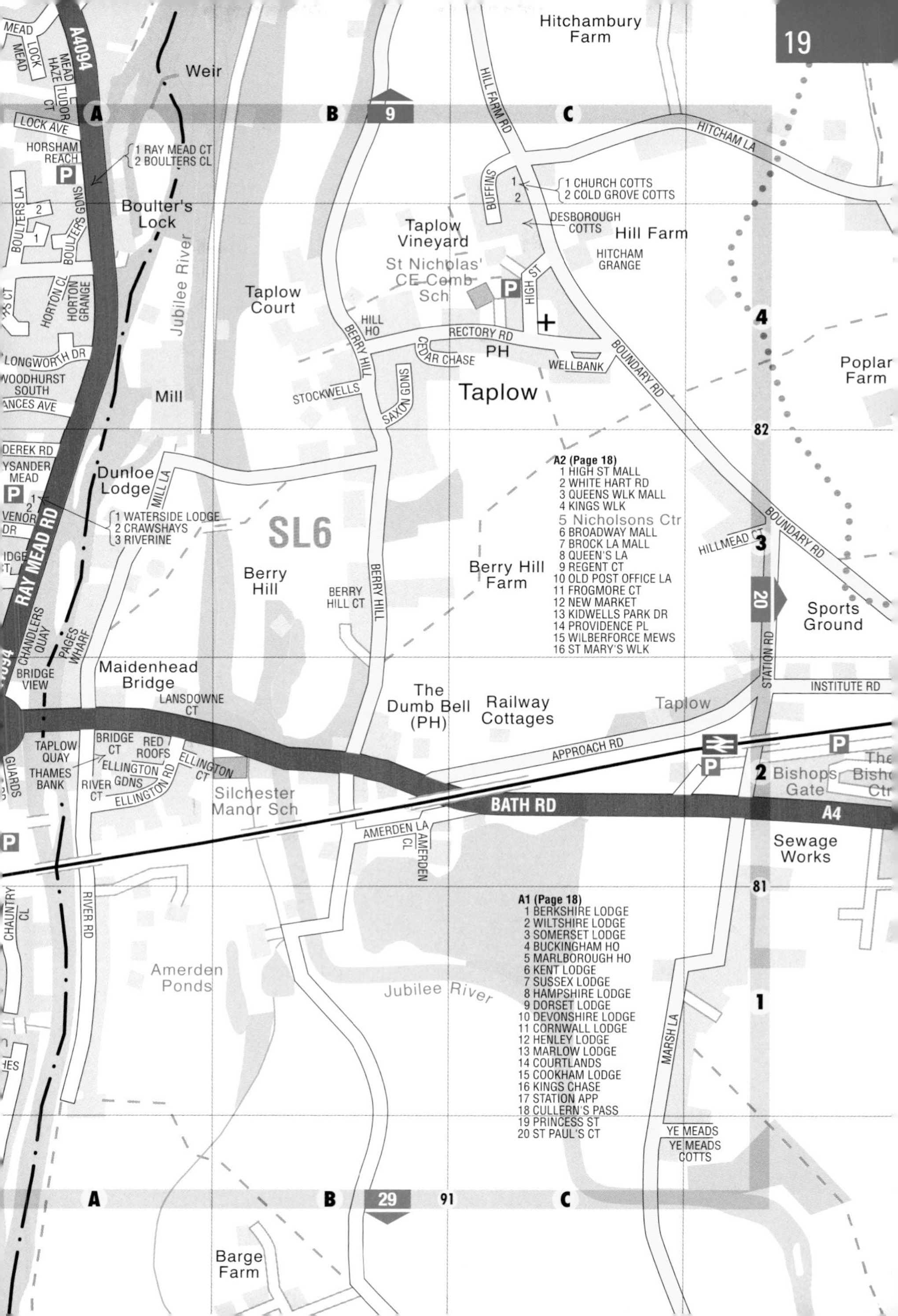

Hitchambury Farm
Weir
A4094
A B C
9
Boulter's Lock
Jubilee River
1 RAY MEAD CT
2 BOULTERS CL
HITCHAM LA
HILL FARM RD
1 CHURCH COTTS
2 COLD GROVE COTTS
DESBOROUGH COTTS
Hill Farm
HITCHAM GRANGE
Taplow Vineyard
St Nicholas' CE Comb Sch
Taplow Court
HIGH ST
BUFFINS
RECTORY RD
CEDAR CHASE
PH
WELLBANK
BOUNDARY RD
Taplow
Poplar Farm
STOCKWELLS
SAXON GDNS
BERRY HILL
HILL HO
Mill
Dunloe Lodge
MILL LA
1 WATERSIDE LODGE
2 CRAWSHAYS
3 RIVERINE
SL6
Berry Hill
BERRY HILL CT
Berry Hill Farm
A2 (Page 18)
1 HIGH ST MALL
2 WHITE HART RD
3 QUEENS WLK MALL
4 KINGS WLK
5 Nicholsons Ctr
6 BROADWAY MALL
7 BROCK LA MALL
8 QUEEN'S LA
9 REGENT CT
10 OLD POST OFFICE LA
11 FROGMORE CT
12 NEW MARKET
13 KIDWELLS PARK DR
14 PROVIDENCE PL
15 WILBERFORCE MEWS
16 ST MARY'S WLK
HILLMEAD CT
20
Sports Ground
STATION RD
INSTITUTE RD
RAY MEAD RD
CHANDLERS QUAY
PAGES WHARF
BRIDGE VIEW
Maidenhead Bridge
LANSDOWNE CT
The Dumb Bell (PH)
Railway Cottages
Taplow
APPROACH RD
TAPLOW QUAY
THAMES BANK
BRIDGE CT
RED ROOFS
ELLINGTON GDNS
ELLINGTON RD
ELLINGTON CT
RIVER CT
Silchester Manor Sch
BATH RD
A4
AMERDEN LA
AMERDEN CL
Bishops Gate
Sewage Works
82
81
4
3
2
1
MEAD
LOCK MEAD
HAZE MEAD
TUDOR CT
LOCK AVE
HORSHAM REACH
BOULTERS LA
BOULTERS GDNS
HORTON CL
HORTON GRANGE
LONGWORTH DR
WOODHURST SOUTH
DEREK RD
GUARDS
CHAUNTRY CL
RIVER RD
Amerden Ponds
Jubilee River
A1 (Page 18)
1 BERKSHIRE LODGE
2 WILTSHIRE LODGE
3 SOMERSET LODGE
4 BUCKINGHAM HO
5 MARLBOROUGH HO
6 KENT LODGE
7 SUSSEX LODGE
8 HAMPSHIRE LODGE
9 DORSET LODGE
10 DEVONSHIRE LODGE
11 CORNWALL LODGE
12 HENLEY LODGE
13 MARLOW LODGE
14 COURTLANDS
15 COOKHAM LODGE
16 KINGS CHASE
17 STATION APP
18 CULLERN'S PASS
19 PRINCESS ST
20 ST PAUL'S CT
MARSH LA
YE MEADS
YE MEADS COTTS
29
91
Barge Farm

Hitchambury Farm
THE GORE
BREDWARD CL
TOCKLEY RD
PEPLER WAY
CLONMEL WAY
GORE RD
St Peter's CE Comb Sch
HILL FARM RD
A
10
B
C
HITCHAM LA
Hitcham House Farm
HAMILTON GDNS
MINNIECROFT RD
OLD F
WILM RD
BURN WLK
CLEARES PASTURE
BUFFINS
EIGHT ACRES
Hill Farm
HITCHAM HO
Lent
LENT RISE RD
LENT GN
LENT GREEN LA
HITCHAM GRANGE
Taplow
New Cut
HIGH ST
P
SL1
4
RECTORY RD
PH
WELLBANK
BOUNDARY RD
Poplar Farm
HITCHAM RD
ALICE LA
Orchardville
ST PE
ORCHARDVILLE
PERRY HO
Burnha Uppe Sch
THE GREEN
BURLINGTON RD
82
Lent Rise
HANBURY CL
BINGHAM RD
BAYLEY CRES
MILNER RD
HARKNESS RD
ALDBOURNE RD
OPENDALE RD
3
HILLMEAD CT
BYWAYS
PO
STOMP RD
Berry Hill Farm
19
EASTFIELD RD
Lent Rise Comb Sch
CHILTERN RD
SOUTHFIE
WENDO RD
Sports Ground
COULSON WAY
COALMANS WAY
MAYPOLE RD
STATION RD
FAIRVIEW RD
WETHER
MIS
INSTITUTE RD
Marshgate Trad Est
Railway Cottages
Taplow
GREEN CL
NURSERY RD
APPROACH RD
P
TAPLOW RD
2
The Bishop Ctr
Bishops Gate
HAG HILL RISE
BRIAR CL
CONWAY RD
HAG HILL LA
RAMBLER CL
MINTON RISE
HURSTFIELD DR
BATH RD
CAVENDISH CL
A4
LAKE END CT
FERN DR
STAFFOR CL
Sewage Works
ABBEY GATE
ROCHFORD WAY
81
SL6
B3026
Superstore
ST JAMES PL
WESTLANDS CL
BURNHAM HTS
OPPIDAN
1
Jubilee River
Pondleys Cottages
MARSH LA
West Town Farm
FARM RD
YE MEADS
YE MEADS COTTS
A
92
30
B
C
LAKE END RD
B3026

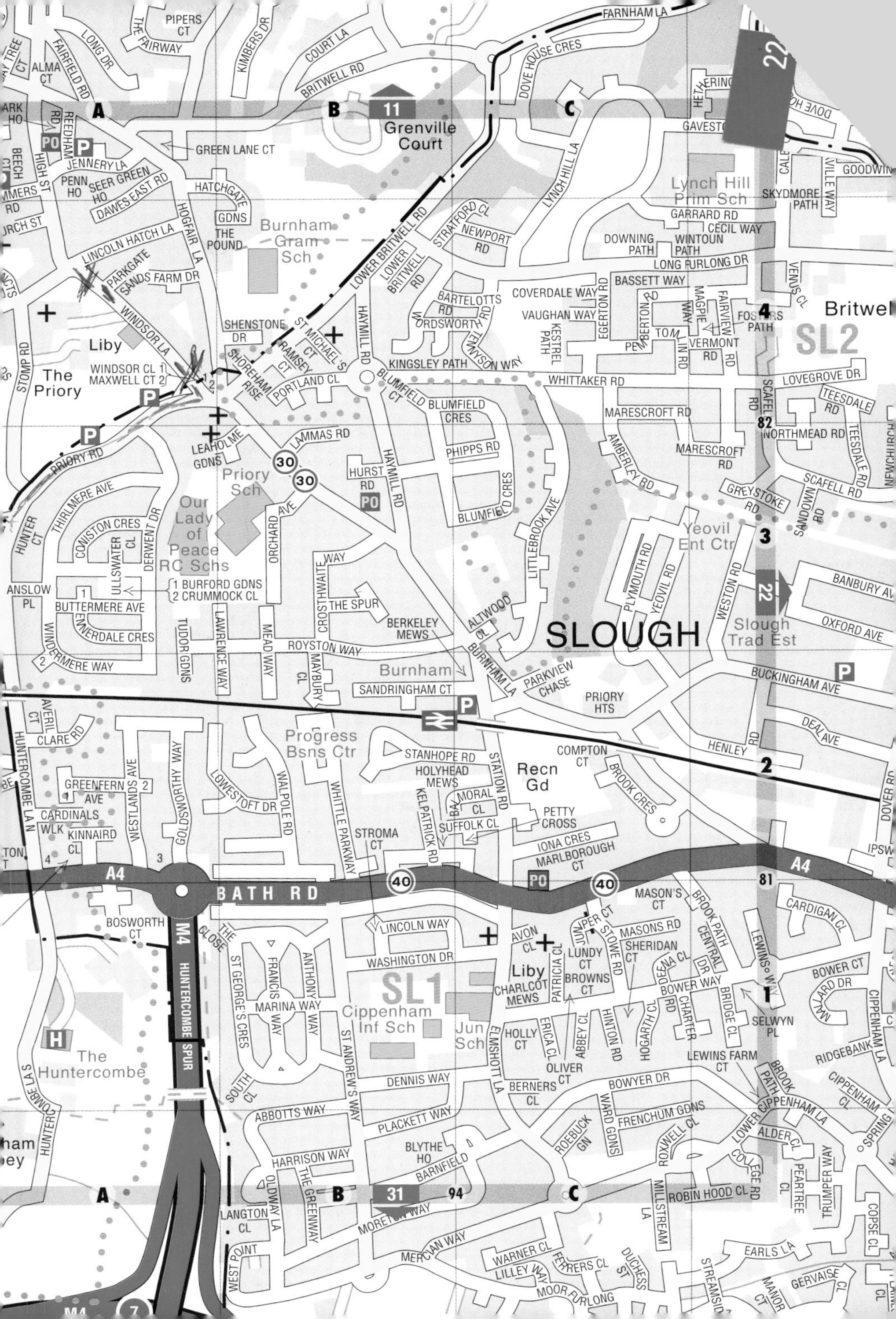

PIPERS CT
THE FAIRWAY
LONG DR
ALMA CT
FAIRFIELD RD
KIMBERS DR
COURT LA
BRITWELL RD
FARNHAM LA
DOVE HOUSE CRES
22
A
B
11
Grenville Court
C
HETHERING
GAVESTO
DOVE HO
REEDHAM RD
PO
P
GREEN LANE CT
JENNERY LA
PENN HO
SEER GREEN HO
DAWES EAST RD
HIGH ST
BEECH
HATCHGATE GDNS
THE POUND
Burnham Gram Sch
HOGFAIR LA
LYNCH HILL LA
Lynch Hill Prim Sch
SKYDMORE PATH
GOODWIN
GARRARD RD
CECIL WAY
DOWNING PATH
WINTOUN PATH
LONG FURLONG DR
STRATFORD CL
NEWPORT RD
LOWER BRITWELL RD
LOWER BRITWELL RD
LINCOLN HATCH LA
PARKGATE
SANDS FARM DR
URCH ST
WINDSOR LA
Liby
The Priory
WINDSOR CL 1
MAXWELL CT 2
STOMP RD
SHENSTONE DR
ST MICHAEL'S CT
RAMSEY CT
SHOREHAM RISE
PORTLAND CL
HAYMILL RD
BARTELOTTS RD
WORDSWORTH RD
TENNYSON WAY
KINGSLEY PATH
COVERDALE WAY
VAUGHAN WAY
KESTREL PATH
EGERTON RD
BASSETT WAY
PEMBERTON RD
MAGPIE WAY
FAIRVIEW RD
FOSTERS PATH
TOMLIN RD
VERMONT RD
VENUS CL
4
Britwel
SL2
WHITTAKER RD
LOVEGROVE DR
BLUMFIELD CT
BLUMFIELD CRES
MARESCROFT RD
SCAFELL RD
TEESDALE RD
82
NORTHMEAD RD
PRIORY RD
LEAHOLME GDNS
LAMMAS RD
30
PHIPPS RD
AMBERLEY RD
MARESCROFT RD
Priory Sch
HURST RD
PO
HAYMILL RD
BLUMFIELD CRES
GREYSTOKE RD
SCAFELL RD
SANDOWN RD
THIRLMERE AVE
CONISTON CRES
DERWENT DR
Our Lady of Peace RC Schs
ORCHARD AVE
ULLSWATER CL
HUNTER CT
LITTLEBROOK AVE
Yeovil Ent Ctr
3
PLYMOUTH RD
YEOVIL RD
WESTON RD
BANBURY AV
1 BURFORD GDNS
2 CRUMMOCK CL
CROSTHWAITE WAY
THE SPUR
ALTWOOD CL
ANSLOW PL
BUTTERMERE AVE
ENNERDALE CRES
WINDERMERE WAY
TUDOR GDNS
LAWRENCE WAY
MEAD WAY
BERKELEY MEWS
ROYSTON WAY
SLOUGH
Slough Trad Est
OXFORD AVE
MAYBURY CL
Burnham
BURNHAM LA
PARKVIEW CHASE
PRIORY HTS
BUCKINGHAM AVE
SANDRINGHAM CT
AVERIL CT
CLARE RD
Progress Bsns Ctr
STANHOPE RD
STATION RD
COMPTON CT
HENLEY RD
DEAL AVE
2
HUNTERCOMBE LA N
GREENFERN AVE
WESTLANDS AVE
GOLDSWORTHY WAY
LOWESTOFT DR
WALPOLE RD
WHITTLE PARKWAY
HOLYHEAD MEWS
BALMORAL CL
Recn Gd
BROOK CRES
DOVER RD
CARDINALS WLK
KINNAIRD CL
KELPATRICK RD
SUFFOLK CL
PETTY CROSS
STROMA CT
IONA CRES
MARLBOROUGH CT
A4
IPSW
BATH RD
40
PO
81
BOSWORTH CT
THE CLOSE
M4
HUNTERCOMBE SPUR
LINCOLN WAY
JUNIPER CT
STOWE RD
MASON'S CT
MASONS RD
BROOK PATH
CENTRAL DR
LEWINS WAY
CARDIGAN CL
ST GEORGE'S CRES
FRANCIS WAY
ANTHONY WAY
WASHINGTON DR
AVON CL
Liby
LUNDY CT
SHERIDAN CT
BROWNS CT
DENA CL
BOWER WAY
BOWER CT
MALLARD DR
SL1
Cippenham Inf Sch
Jun Sch
CHARLCOT MEWS
PATRICIA CL
1
MARINA WAY
HOLLY CT
ERICA CL
ABBEY CL
HINTON RD
HOGARTH CL
CHARTER RD
BRIDGE CL
SELWYN PL
CIPPENHAM LA
H
The Huntercombe
ST ANDREW'S WAY
ELMSHOTT LA
OLIVER CT
LEWINS FARM CT
RIDGEBANK
DENNIS WAY
BERNERS CL
BOWYER DR
BROOK PATH
CIPPENHAM CL
SOUTH CL
ABBOTTS WAY
PLACKETT WAY
WARD GDNS
FRENCHUM GDNS
ROEBUCK GN
ROXWELL CL
LOWER CIPPENHAM LA
ALDER CL
SPRING
HUNTERCOMBE LA S
BLYTHE HO
BARNFIELD
COLLEGE RD
PEARTREE CL
TRUMPER WAY
HARRISON WAY
THE GREENWAY
OLDWAY LA
A
B
31
94
C
ROBIN HOOD CL
MILLSTREAM LA
LANGTON CL
MORETON WAY
COPSE CL
MERCIAN WAY
WEST POINT
WARNER CL
LILLEY WAY
FERRERS CL
DUCHESS ST
EARLS LA
STREAMSIDE
MOOR FURLONG
MANOR
GERVAISE CL
M4
7

FARNHAM
ROKESBY RD
LILAC CT
THE CEDARS
WAVELL GDNS
MASCOLL PATH
THE BEECHES
Liby
RAVENSWORTH RD
DODDSFIELD RD
ELMAR GN
WOODFORD WAY
UPPER LEES RD
Beechwood Sch
HEMMING WAY
HETHERINGTON CL
ROKESBY RD
A
PERRYMAN WAY
12
B
FURZEN CL
LYDSEY CL
EYRE GN
CRAYLE ST
AYLESWORTH AVE
HAWKSHILL RD
C
Arbour Vale Sch
GAVESTON RD
CALBROKE RD
TRAVIC RD
MARUNDEN GN
PO
MANFIELD CL
ODENCROFT RD
BROMYCROFT RD
LOWER LEES RD
LONG READINGS LA
Lynch Hill Prim Sch
LYNCH HILL LA
UMBERVILLE WAY
GOODWIN RD
CHILWICK RD
WENTWORTH AVE
MONKSFIELD WAY
BIDEFORD SPUR
TORQUAY SPUR
SKYDMORE PATH
Claycots Sch
BRIDPORT WAY
PENZANCE SPUR
GARRARD RD
CECIL WAY
BRIGHTON SPUR 1
NEWHAVEN SPUR 2
DOWNING PATH
WINTOUN PATH
LONG FURLONG DR
NORTHCROFT
EASTCROFT
BASSETT WAY
COVERDALE WAY
VAUGHAN WAY
EGERTON RD
4
PEMBERTON RD
MAGPIE WAY
FAIRVIEW RD
FOSTERS PATH
VENUS CL
Britwell
SL2
ALDRIDGE RD
GASCON'S GR
SOUTH CROFT
WESTCROFT
MIDCROFT
CROFTHILL RD
KESTREL PATH
TOMLIN RD
VERMONT RD
NORTHMEAD RD
COWPER RD
FAIRCROFT
END
SANDLERS
BROOMFIELD GATE
WESTFIELD RD
KINGFISHER CT
WHITTAKER RD
LITTLE BROOK AVE
LOVEGROVE DR
SCAFELL RD
TEESDALE RD
NEWCHURCH RD
PENTLAND RD
WILLONERS
TREVOSE HO 1
TYREE HO 2
NORTHBOROUGH RD
MARESCROFT RD
82
AMBERLEY RD
NORTHMEAD RD
TEESDALE RD
NEWCHURCH RD
PENNINE RD
CHATFIELD
THORNDIKE
BELMONT
GREENSIDE
FARADAY RD
FARADAY CL
KINGSWOOD HO 1
BEAUMARIS CT 2
FRANKLIN AVE
FURNIVAL AVE
GREYSTOKE RD
SCAFELL RD
SANDOWN RD
PEVENSEY RD
LITTLEBROOK AVE
3
Yeovil Ent Ctr
DUNDEE RD
BODMIN AVE
LARCH CL
BIRCH GR
ASPEN CL
ROWAN WAY
FEILDVIEW CT
ROSE WLK
21
PLYMOUTH RD
YEOVIL RD
WESTON RD
BANBURY AVE
STIRLING RD
FAIRLIE RD
Perth Trad Est
Slough Trad Est
OXFORD AVE
SYKES RD
PARKVIEW CHASE
P
BUCKINGHAM AVE
DUNDEE RD
DURHAM AVE
GREENOCK RD
EDINBURGH AVE
PRIORY HTS
CAMBRIDGE AVE
30
HARWICH RD
LIVERPOOL RD
Slough Trad Est
STATION RD
Recn Gd
COMPTON CT
2
HENLEY RD
DEAL AVE
FALMOUTH RD
HAMILTON RD
BERKSHIRE AVE
BROOK CRES
BURNHAM LA
SL1
DOVER RD
EASTBOURNE RD
BEDFORD AVE
GRESHAM RD
BRADFORD RD
BUCKINGHAM AVE
ALTONA WAY
IONA CRES
MARLBOROUGH CT
A4
IPSWICH RD
PO
481
MASON'S CT
BROOK PATH
CARDIGAN CL
BERWICK AVE
MALTON AVE
AVON CL
JUNIPER CT
STOWE RD
MASONS RD
CENTRAL DR
LEWINS WAY
WESTGATE CRES
ARGYLL AVE
SHERIDAN CT
DEE NA CL
Liby
LUNDY CT
BROWNS CT
PATRICIA CL
CHARLCOT MEWS
1
BOWER WAY
BOWER CT
MALLARD DR
ABERDEEN AVE
LEIGH RD
AJAX AVE
Sch
ELMSHOTT LA
HOLLY CT
ERICA CL
ABBEY CL
HINTON RD
HOGARTH CL
CHARTER RD
BRIDGE CL
SELWYN PL
CIPPENHAM LA
IVY CRES
Westgate Ret Pk
SLOUGH
OLIVER CT
LEWINS FARM CT
RIDGEBANK
BOARLANDS CL
DUNSTER GDNS
AVEBURY
BERNERS CL
BOWYER DR
BROOK PATH
CIPPENHAM CL
CORFE GDNS
FOTHERINGAY GDNS
WARD GDNS
FRENCHUM GDNS
LOWER CIPPENHAM LA
BRAMBER CT
EGREMONT GDNS
ROEBUCK GN
ROXWELL CL
ALDER CL
SPRING LA
HANOVER GATE
PO
The Westgate Sch
COLLEGE RD
PEARTREE CL
TRUMPER WAY
BENTLEY RD
A4
MILLSTREAM LA
ROBIN HOOD CL
A
95
32
B
OAKFIELD AVE
TWINCHES LA
C
MERCIAN WAY
COPSE CL
LOWER CIPPENHAM LA
Superstores
WARNER CL
LILLEY WAY
FERRERS CL
DUCHESS ST
STREAMSIDE
EARLS LA
AUTUMN CL
RICHARDS WAY
BENNETT'S CL
RALEIGH CL
ADAM CL
GORSE MEADE
CIPPENHAM LA
PEARL GDNS
TOPAZ CL
MOOR FURLONG
MANOR CT
GERVAISE CL
NINE ACRES
PLAINES CL
HARDY CL
30
30

Labels and place names

St Mary's Farnham Royal CE Prim Sch

Stoke Park House (CH)

Stoke Park House (C...

St Anthony's RC Prim Sch

Penn Wood Prim Sch

SL2

Manor Park

FIR TREE AVE

JOURNEYS END

Muddy L...

CH

Crem

Cemy

Baylis Court Sch

Godolphin Inf & Jun Schs

1 DOUGLAS RD
2 MARY MORGAN CT

Herschel Gram Sch

1 CROMER CT
2 GROSVENOR CT
3 REGENT CT
4 BAYLIS PAR
5 RIGBY LODGE
6 OAKWOOD CT

LISMORE PK

Baylis Bsns Ctr

BELGRAVE PAR 1
FRAUNCHIES CT 2
BEAUCHAMP CT 3

Baylis Pond

SL1

Salt Hill

Slough Bsns Ctr

Thames Valley Univ

Slough

Mill West

FOUND...

Street names

CHURCH RD, PARK LAWN, ARDROSSAN, WILTSHIRE AVE, CORNWALL AVE, STAFFORD AVE, BARROW LODGE, LANCASTER AVE, CUMBERLAND AVE, CANTERBURY AVE, HATTON AVE, PENN RD, CAIRNGORM PL, NORTHERN RD, MILTON RD, ST ELMO, BEAUMONT CRES, ST ELMO CL, SALISBURY MEWS, WARWICK AVE, SURREY AVE, SALISBURY GRO, OAK..., VILLIERS RD, BEECHWOOD CRES, LYDFORD AVE, STAUNTON RD, NORTHERN RD, HOWARD AVE, HUNGERFORD AVE, WHITEFORD RD, ESSEX AVE, KENT AVE, BEAUMONT RD, HATTON AVE, GRANVILLE AVE, BRYANT AVE, NORFOLK AVE, HAMPSHIRE AVE, RUTLAND AVE, KIRKWALL SPUR, LERWICK DR, RONALDSAY SPUR, SHERMAN, STEWART AVE, FIRST CRES, SECOND CRES, THIRD CRES, ELY, SUMBURGH WAY, GLOUCESTER AVE, WARRINGTON AVE, WATERBEACH CL, WATERBEACH, CROMWELL DR, HAWTHORNE CRES, CHESTER RD, LEISTON SPUR, SNAPE SPUR, DEVON AVE, COURT CRES, THURSTON RD, MILDENHALL RD, GRANT AVE, BOSTON GR, SHEFFIELD RD, YORK AVE, SYDNEY GR, LITCHAM SPUR, OATLANDS DR, LITTLEPORT SPUR, MUNDESLEY SPUR, MELBOURNE AVE, NORTHAMPTON AVE, BELFAST AVE, BIRLEY RD, STOKE POGES LA, HUGHENDEN RD, ALDBOROUGH SPUR, LODDON SPUR, PURSERS CT, BUCKINGHAM AVE E, AYLESBURY CRES, GODOLPHIN RD, REDWOOD GDNS, WHITBY RD, GODOLPHIN GDNS, OAKLEY CRES, LEEDS RD, PORTSMOUTH CT, ELLIMAN AVE, SCHOOL LA, CHARLOTTE AVE, MYRT... AVE, ALLINGTON CT, WHITEHAVEN, FRANK SUTTON WAY, CARLISLE RD, WOODLAND AVE, CARMARTHEN RD, POOL LA, CARRINGTON RD, NORTH GN, SHACKLETON RD, MONTAGUE RD, KESW..., LAKE AVE, BRADLEY RD, SOUTH GN, RODDELL PL, BELGRAVE RD, QUEENS RD, QUEENS CT, HADLOW CT, BAYLIS RD, GILLIAT RD, PLOUGHLEES LA, GRAYS RD, ST PAUL..., THIRKLEBY CL, PITTS RD, SALT HILL WAY, GRACE CT, WHITE CL, PICKFORDS GDNS, GRAYS PL, SALT HILL AVE, SALT HILL DR, WINDMILL RD, SIMPSONS WAY, BRISTOL WAY, STOKE GDNS, STANLEY COTTS, HARTLAND CL, QUADRIVIUM POINT, CRANRAER SNR, CONEGAR CT, FED CT, BLAIR RD, GATEWICK CL, WILLIAM ST, BRUNEL, RAILWAY TERR, MILL ST, BATH RD, GLENWORTH, CRANBOURNE, HAMBOURNE, A4, A355, A4, B416

Grid references / numbers

24, 13, A, B, C, 4, 82, 3, 2, 1, 81, 30, 33, 97

FARNHAM RD, YARMOUTH RD, WAVERLEY RD, STOKE RD, STOKE POGES LA

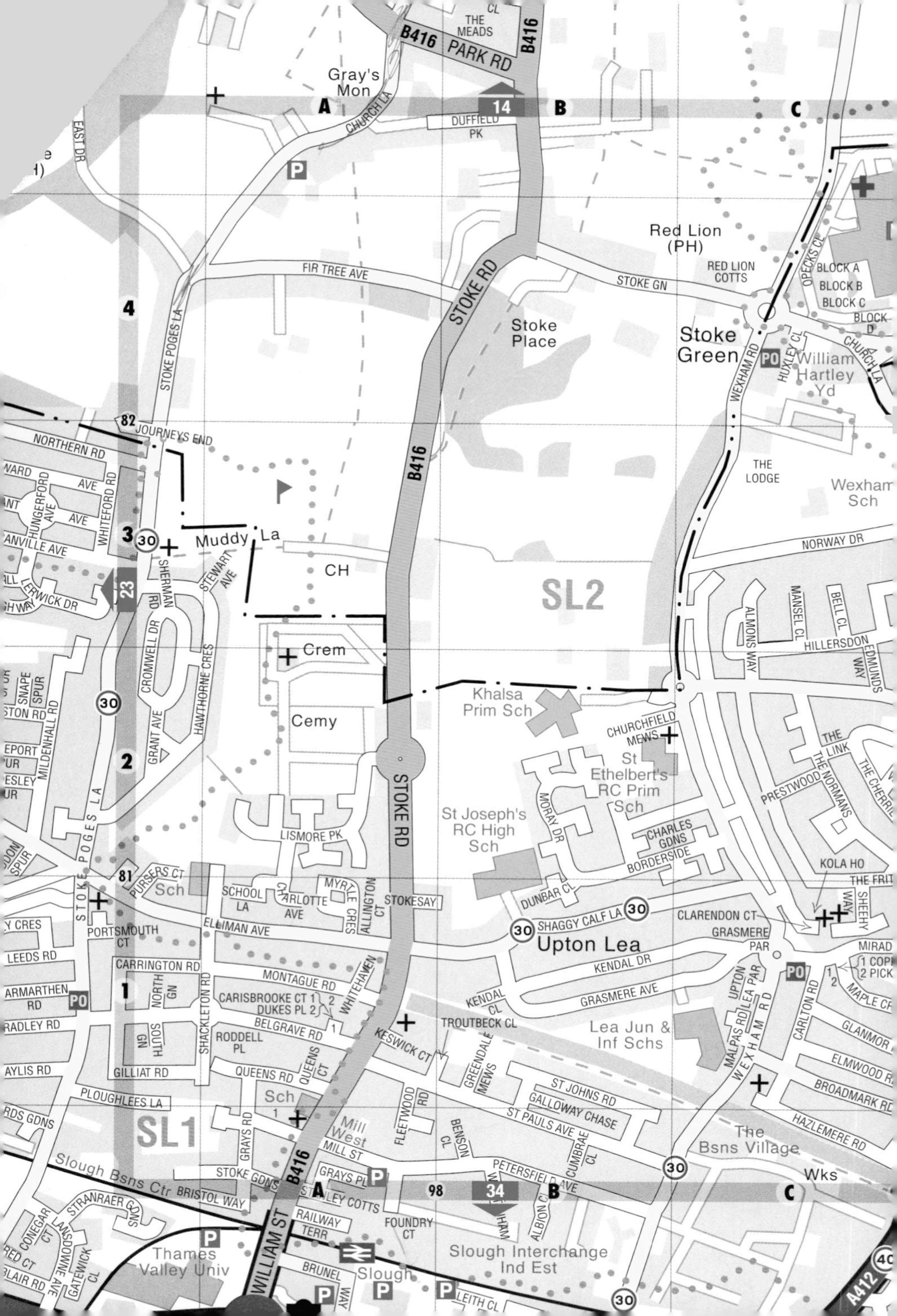

THE MEADS
CL
B416
PARK RD
B416
Gray's Mon
CHURCH LA
14
A
B
C
DUFFIELD PK
EAST DR
P
FIR TREE AVE
STOKE RD
STOKE GN
Red Lion (PH)
RED LION COTTS
OPECKS CL
BLOCK A
BLOCK B
BLOCK C
BLOCK D
CHURCH LA
4
STOKE POGES LA
Stoke Place
Stoke Green
WEXHAM RD
PO
HUXLEY CL
William Hartley Yd
82
JOURNEYS END
NORTHERN RD
WARD
HUNGERFORD AVE
AVE
WHITEFORD RD
AVE
B416
THE LODGE
Wexham Sch
3
30
Muddy La
ANVILLE AVE
SHERMAN
STEWART AVE
CH
NORWAY DR
SL2
23
LERWICK DR
RD
CROMWELL DR
HAWTHORNE CRES
ALMONS WAY
MANSEL CL
BELL CL
HILLERSDON
EDMUNDS WAY
Crem
SNAPE SPUR
STON RD
MILDENHALL RD
30
Cemy
Khalsa Prim Sch
CHURCHFIELD MEWS
GRANT AVE
2
STOKE RD
St Ethelbert's RC Prim Sch
THE LINK
PRESTWOOD
THE NORMANS
THE CHERRIES
MORAY DR
St Joseph's RC High Sch
CHARLES GDNS
BORDERSIDE
SPUR
STOKE POGES LA
LISMORE PK
81
PURSERS CT
Sch
SCHOOL LA
CHARLOTTE AVE
MYRTLE CRES
ALLINGTON CT
STOKESAY
DUNBAR CL
KOLA HO
THE FRITH
SHEEHY WAY
30
SHAGGY CALF LA
CLARENDON CT
GRASMERE PAR
PORTSMOUTH CT
ELLIMAN AVE
30
Upton Lea
CRES
LEEDS RD
CARRINGTON RD
KENDAL DR
MIRADOR
1 COPPER
2 PICKFORD
MONTAGUE RD
WHITEHAVEN
PO
ARMARTHEN RD
PO
1
NORTH GN
CARISBROOKE CT 1
DUKES PL 2
SHACKLETON RD
GRASMERE AVE
KENDAL CL
UPTON LEA PAR
MALPAS RD
CARLTON RD
MAPLE CR
RADLEY RD
SOUTH GN
RODDELL PL
BELGRAVE RD
KESWICK CT
TROUTBECK CL
Lea Jun & Inf Schs
WEXHAM RD
GLANMOR
AYLIS RD
GILLIAT RD
QUEENS RD
QUEENS CT
GREENDALE MEWS
ELMWOOD
BROADMARK RD
PLOUGHLEES LA
Sch
FLEETWOOD RD
ST JOHNS RD
GALLOWAY CHASE
RDS GDNS
SL1
GRAYS RD
Mill West
ST PAULS AVE
CUMBRAE CL
BENSON CL
HAZLEMERE RD
MILL ST
The Bsns Village
PETERSFIELD AVE
30
Slough Bsns Ctr
STOKE GDNS
B416
GRAYS PL
P
Wks
BRISTOL WAY
STANLEY COTTS
98
34
ALBION CL
WHAM
STRANRAER GDNS
CONEGAR CT
LANSDOWNE AVE
GATEWICK CL
RED CT
BLAIR RD
P
Thames Valley Univ
WILLIAM ST
RAILWAY TERR
FOUNDRY CT
Slough Interchange Ind Est
BRUNEL WAY
Slough
P
P
LEITH CL
30
40
A412

Spring Wood
Rowley Farm
A
B
15
C
26
Maidenhead Thicket
Bell Farm
Rowley Lake
Wexham Park
WEXHAM PARK LA
OPAL CT
VALLEY END
4
UXBRIDGE RD
CHURCH GR
WEXHAM WOODS
GRANGEWOOD
82
Stone's Wood
Hotel
A412
3
SL3
ALL SOULS COTTS
Wexham Court Prim Sch
CHURCH LA
LIDSTONE CT
George Green
RIXON CL
OLD HOUSE CT
The Five Rivers (PH)
AUGUST END
CORONATION AVE
DIANA CL
ARMSTRONG HO
KNOLTON WAY
WELDEN
THORN DR
BLINCO LA
AZALEA WAY
BATES CL
SYCAMORE WLK
GRAFTON CL
MOREAU WLK
ALAN WAY
SHORTFERN
POST OFFICE LA
HOMEWOOD
BEAUMONT CT
GEORGE GREEN RD
GEORGE GREEN DR
2
BERRYFIELD
COFTARDS
DAWES MOOR CL
The George (PH)
BROOKSIDE
HARVEY HO
WITHYCROFT
QUINBROOKES
DORNELS
MONTGOMERY PL
81
HOLMEDALE
UXBRIDGE RD
CANNON GATE
SL2
Westfield La
PRESTON RD
BERESFORD AVE
Home Farm
1
MIDDLE GN
40
Nursery
Convent
Middle Green
Trenches Farm
ROCHFORDS GDNS
SERMED CT
ORCHARDS RESIDENTIAL PK
A
B
35
00
C
PICKFORD DR
ORCHARD WAY
FIRS DR
RED LEAF CL
Lavender Farm
THE PINES
BLENHEIM CL
Grand Union Canal Slough Arm
GOODMAN PK
NURSERY LA

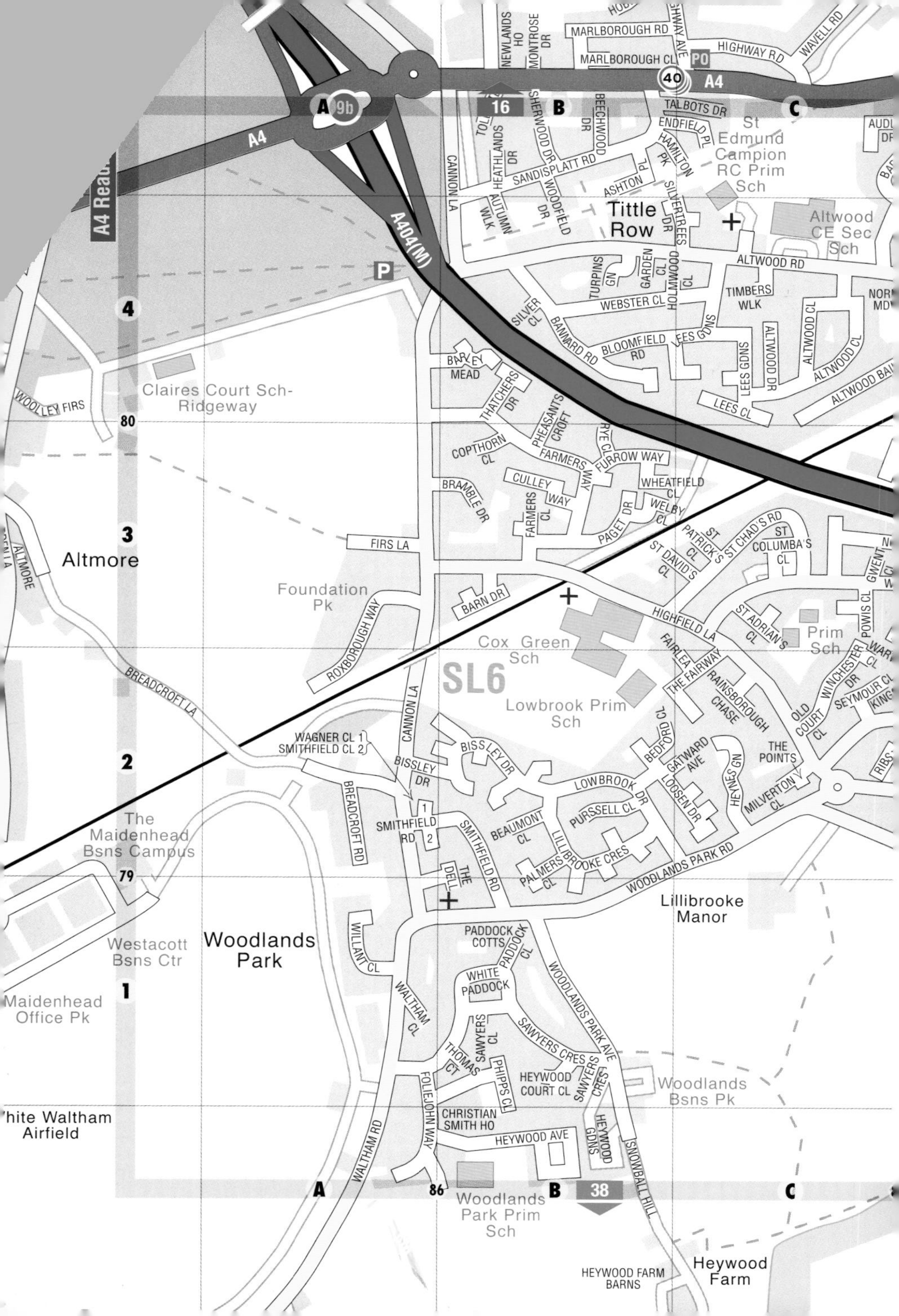

MARLBOROUGH RD
NEWLANDS HO
MONTROSE DR
MARLBOROUGH CL
HIGHWAY RD
WAVELL RD
PO
40
A4
A
9b
16
B
C
TALBOTS DR
ENDFIELD PL
HAMILTON PK
St Edmund Campion RC Prim Sch
A4
A4 Reading
SHERWOOD DR
BEECHWOOD DR
HEATHLANDS DR
SANDISPLATT RD
WOODFIELD DR
CANNON LA
AUTUMN WLK
ASHTON PL
SILVERTREES DR
Tittle Row
Altwood CE Sec Sch
A404(M)
P
ALTWOOD RD
TURPINS GN
GARDEN CL
HOLMWOOD CL
WEBSTER CL
TIMBERS WLK
SILVER CL
BANNARD RD
BLOOMFIELD RD
LEES GDNS
ALTWOOD CL
ALTWOOD DR
ALTWOOD CL
LEES GDNS
LEES CL
ALTWOOD BAILEY
4
BARLEY MEAD
THATCHERS DR
PHEASANTS CROFT
Claires Court Sch-Ridgeway
WOOLLEY FIRS
80
COPTHORN CL
FARMERS WAY
RYE CL
FURROW WAY
CULLEY WAY
WHEATFIELD CL
BRAMBLE DR
FARMERS CL
PAGET DR
WELBY CL
ST PATRICK'S CL
ST CHAD'S RD
ST COLUMBA'S CL
ST DAVID'S CL
GWENT CL
3
Altmore
ALTMORE
FIRS LA
Foundation Pk
BARN DR
HIGHFIELD LA
ST ADRIAN'S CL
Prim Sch
POWIS CL
ROXBOROUGH WAY
Cox Green Sch
FAIRLEA
THE FAIRWAY
WINCHESTER DR
SEYMOUR CL
SL6
BREADCROFT LA
CANNON LA
RAINSBOROUGH CHASE
OLD COURT CL
Lowbrook Prim Sch
WAGNER CL 1
SMITHFIELD CL 2
BISSLEY DR
BEDFORD CL
GATWARD AVE
HEYNES GN
THE POINTS
2
BISSLEY DR
LOWBROOK DR
LOOSEN DR
MILVERTON CL
BREADCROFT RD
SMITHFIELD RD
PURSSELL CL
BEAUMONT CL
LILLIBROOKE CRES
The Maidenhead Bsns Campus
SMITHFIELD RD
PALMERS CL
THE DELL
WOODLANDS PARK RD
79
Lillibrooke Manor
WILLANT CL
PADDOCK COTTS
PADDOCK CL
Westacott Bsns Ctr
Woodlands Park
WHITE PADDOCK
WOODLANDS PARK AVE
1
Maidenhead Office Pk
WALTHAM CL
SAWYERS CL
SAWYERS CRES
THOMAS CT
PHIPPS CL
HEYWOOD COURT CL
SAWYERS CRES
FOLIEJOHN WAY
Woodlands Bsns Pk
White Waltham Airfield
CHRISTIAN SMITH HO
HEYWOOD GDNS
HEYWOOD AVE
WALTHAM RD
SNOWBALL HILL
A
86
B
38
C
Woodlands Park Prim Sch
HEYWOOD FARM BARNS
Heywood Farm

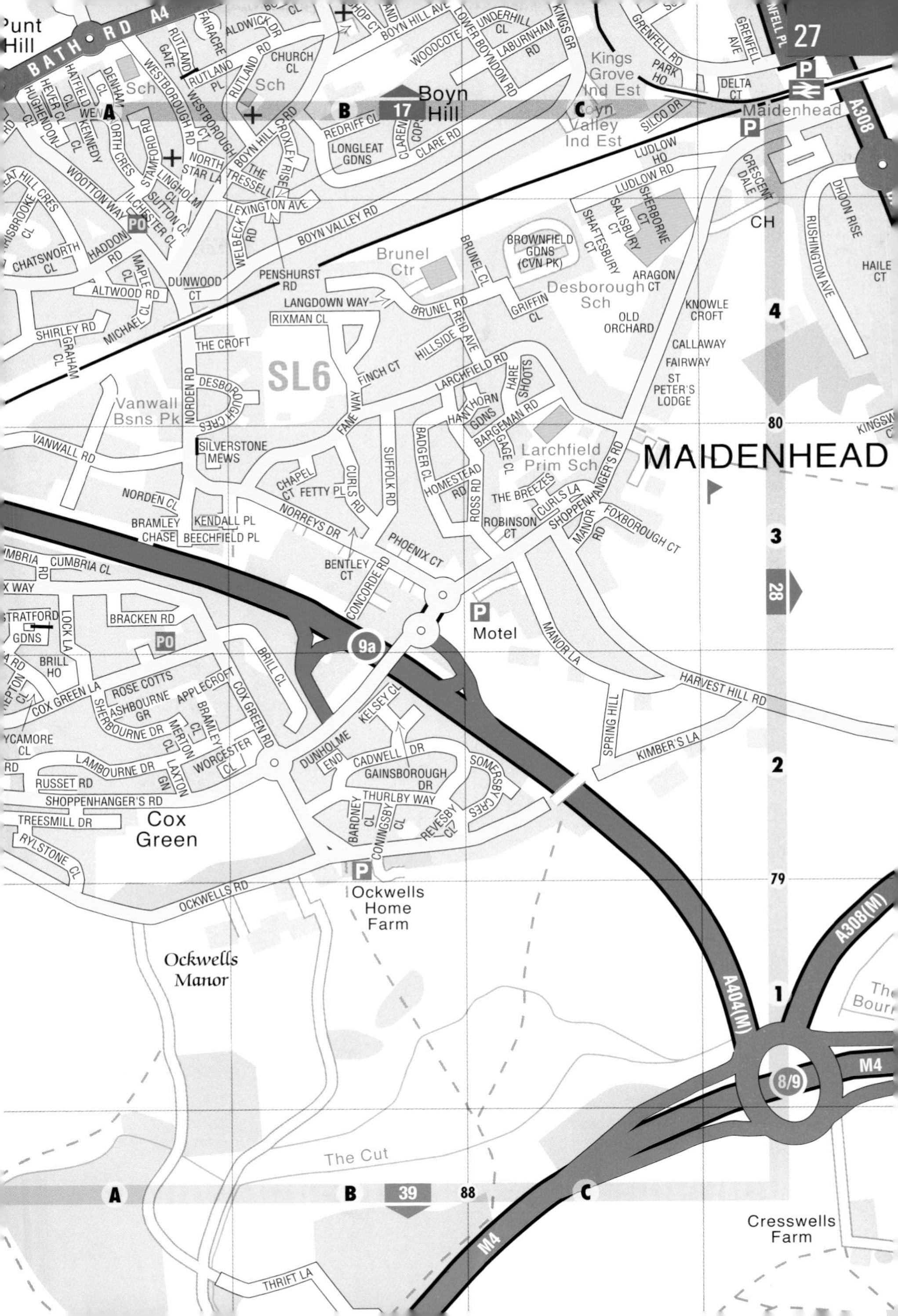

MAIDENHEAD
SL6
Boyn Hill
Cox Green
Ockwells Manor
Ockwells Home Farm
Cresswells Farm
Vanwall Bsns Pk
Brunel Ctr
Desborough Sch
Larchfield Prim Sch
Kings Grove Ind Est
Boyn Valley Ind Est
Maidenhead
Motel
The Cut
BATH RD A4
A308
A308(M)
A404(M)
M4
BOYN VALLEY RD
HARVEST HILL RD
SHOPPENHANGER'S RD
COX GREEN RD
COX GREEN LA
OCKWELLS RD
MANOR LA
THRIFT LA
17
39
28

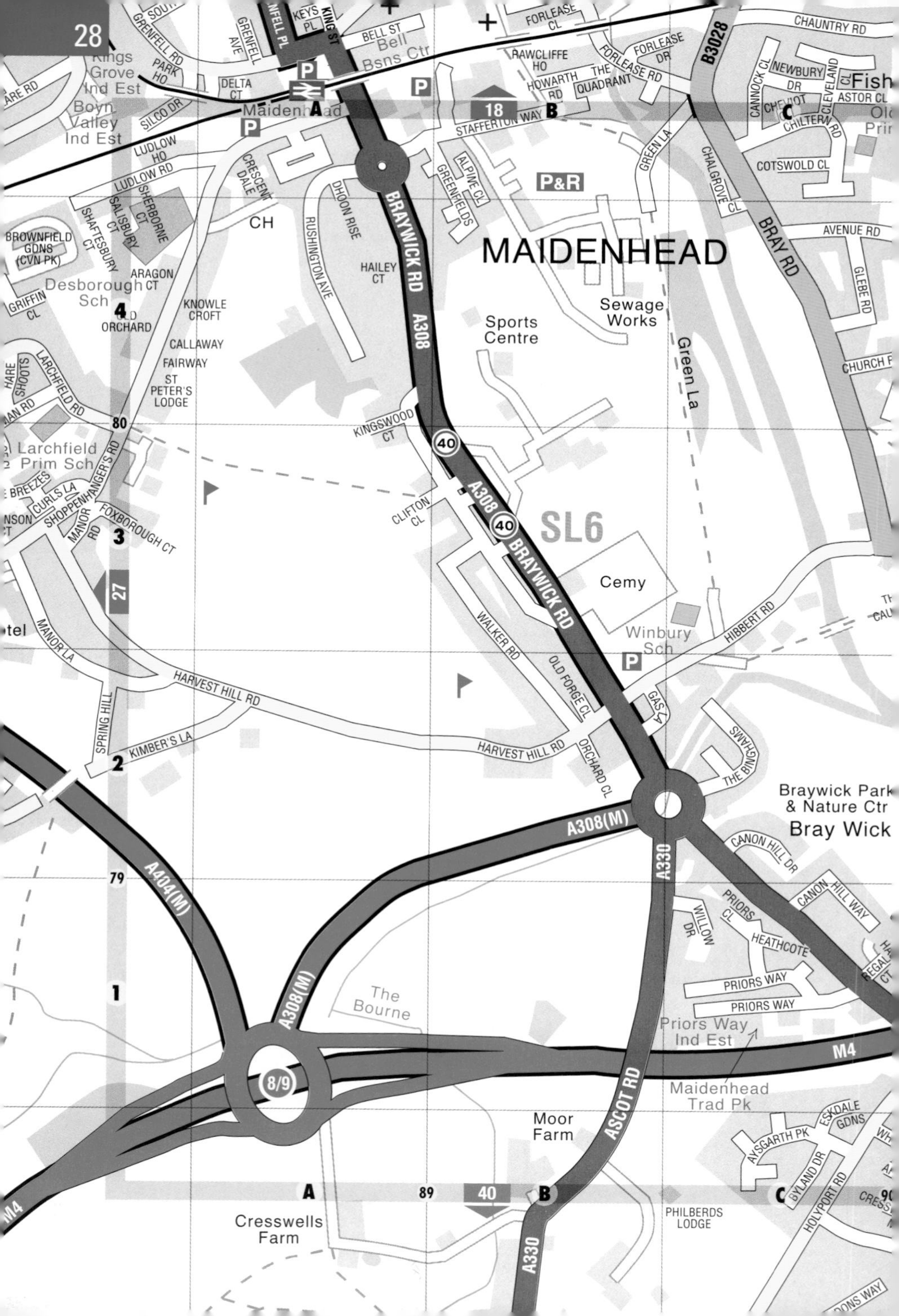
MAIDENHEAD
SL6
BRAYWICK RD
A308
A308(M)
A404(M)
A330
ASCOT RD
M4
8/9
B3028
BRAY RD
Maidenhead
Kings Grove Ind Est
Boyn Valley Ind Est
Bell Bsns Ctr
KEYS PL
KING ST
BELL ST
GRENFELL RD
GRENFELL AVE
PARK HO
DELTA CT
SILCO DR
LUDLOW HO
LUDLOW RD
CRESCENT DALE
FORLEASE CL
FORLEASE DR
FORLEASE RD
RAWCLIFFE HO
HOWARTH RD
THE QUADRANT
STAFFERTON WAY
CHAUNTRY RD
CANNOCK CL
NEWBURY DR
CLEVELAND CL
ASTOR CL
CHEVIOT CL
CHILTERN RD
COTSWOLD CL
CHALGROVE CL
GREEN LA
Green La
AVENUE RD
GLEBE RD
CHURCH RD
P&R
ALPINE CL
GREENFIELDS
DHOON RISE
RUSHINGTON AVE
HAILEY CT
CH
SHERBORNE CT
SALISBURY CT
SHAFTESBURY CT
BROWNFIELD GDNS (CVN PK)
ARAGON CT
Desborough Sch
OLD ORCHARD
GRIFFIN CL
KNOWLE CROFT
CALLAWAY
FAIRWAY
ST PETER'S LODGE
HARE SHOOTS
LARCHFIELD RD
Larchfield Prim Sch
SHOPPENHANGER'S RD
CURLS LA
MANOR RD
FOXBOROUGH CT
MANOR LA
Sports Centre
Sewage Works
KINGSWOOD CT
CLIFTON CL
40
Cemy
Winbury Sch
HIBBERT RD
WALKER RD
OLD FORGE CL
GAS LA
HARVEST HILL RD
ORCHARD CL
SPRING HILL
KIMBER'S LA
THE BINGHAMS
Braywick Park & Nature Ctr
Bray Wick
CANON HILL DR
CANON HILL WAY
PRIORS CL
HEATHCOTE
WILLOW DR
PRIORS WAY
Priors Way Ind Est
Maidenhead Trad Pk
The Bourne
Moor Farm
AYSGARTH PK
ESKDALE GDNS
BYLAND DR
HOLYPORT RD
Cresswells Farm
PHILBERDS LODGE
REGAL
A
B
C
1
2
3
4
18
27
40
79
80
89
90

Amerden Ponds
Jubilee River
A
B
19
C
MARSH LA
YE MEADS
YE MEADS COTTS
4
Barge Farm
80
River Thames
Thames Path
Weir
Bray Lock
Amerden House
OLD MARSH LA
GLEBE CL
M4
3
VICARAGE WLK
VICARAGE DR
CHURCH PATH
FERRY END
CHURCH LA
CHURCH DR
FERRY RD
BETTONEY VERE
BRAYBANK
BEAUFORT PL
RIVER GDNS
OLD MILL LA
AMERDEN PRIORY CVN PK
New Thames Bridge
30
OAK STUBBS LA
MEADOW WAY
WEST CT
HIGH ST
BRAYFIELD RD
BRAY CL
THE TERRACE
Bray
SL6
JESUS HOSPITAL
P
Dorney Sch
HARCOURT CL
HARCOURT RD
Dorney Reach
2
HANOVER MEAD
The Cut
UPPER BRAY RD
DORNEY REACH RD
Monkey Island
CHESTNUT PK
79
MONKEY ISLAND LA
B3028
1
BRAY CT
COURT CL
WINDSOR RD
Marina
Cemy
MOOR END
A
B
41
91
C
Queen's Eyot
LONSDALE WAY
SANDY MEAD
Works
A308
PO
BROADWATER PK
TITHE BARN DR
TITHE CL
40

Jubilee River
A
20
B
C
B3026
Pondley's Cottages
MARSH LA
West Town Farm
FARM RD
YE MEADS
YE MEADS COTTS
4
LAKE END RD
80
OLD MARSH LA
Amerden House
29
GLEBE CL
LAKE END RD
Lake End Farm
PH
3
AMERDEN PRIORY CVN PK
Lake End
New Thames Bridge
MEADOW WAY
OAK STUBBS LA
ASHFORD LA
SL6
M4
Dorney Sch
HARCOURT CL
HARCOURT RD
Dorney Reach
2
MARSH LA
The Palmer Arms (PH)
COURT LA
VILLAGE RD
DORNEY REACH RD
Dorney Court
Monkey Island
79
CHESTNUT PK
Elm View Farm
SL4
MONKEY ISLAND LA
1
P
Marina
Rowing Lake
Queen's Eyot
92
42
Works
BROADWATER PK
TITHE BARN

BOSWORTH CT
M4
HUNTERCOMBE SPUR
THE CLOSE
ST GEORGE'S CRES
FRANCIS WAY
ANTHONY WAY
MARINA WAY
LINCOLN WAY
WASHINGTON DR
AVON CL
Liby
JUNIPER CT
STOWE RD
MASONS RD
LUNDY CT
BROWNS CT
PATRICIA CL
CHARLCOT MEWS
DEENA CL
BOWER WAY
CENTRAL DR
BRIDGE CL
LEWINS WAY
MAYLARD DR
CIPPENHAM LA
A
B
21
C
Jun Sch
HOLLY CT
ERICA CL
ABBEY CL
HINTON RD
HOGARTH CL
CHARTER RD
H
The Huntercombe
HUNTERCOMBE LA S
SOUTH CL
ST ANDREW'S WAY
DENNIS WAY
ELMSHOTT LA
BERNERS CL
BOWYER DR
RIDGEBANK
BROOK PATH
CIPPENHAM CL
ABBOTTS WAY
PLACKETT WAY
WARD GDNS
FRENCHUM GDNS
ROXWELL CL
LOWER CIPPENHAM LA
ALDER CL
SPRING
ROEBUCK GN
BLYTHE HO
BARNFIELD
HARRISON WAY
THE GREENWAY
OLDWAY LA
COLLEGE RD
PEARTREE CL
TRUMPER WAY
SL1
MILLSTREAM LA
ROBIN HOOD CL
LANGTON CL
MORETON WAY
4
COPSE CL
WATERMAN CT
MERCIAN WAY
WARNER CL
FERRERS CL
DUCHESS ST
EARLS LA
WEST POINT
LILLEY WAY
STREAMSIDE
MANOR CT
GERVAISE CL
BOADICEA CL
MOOR FURLONG
1 KENNEDY HO
2 HARBOROUGH CL
7
MOLYNS MEWS
NICHOLAS GDNS
CHAPELS CL
RICHARDS WAY
PALACE CL
COBHAM CL
BIDDLES CL
Recn Gd
TWO MILE DR
HUNTERS WAY
DUPRE CL
GOWINGS GN
Sch
80
1 ORCHARD LODGE
2 SAXON LODGE
3 SHAKESPEARE LODGE
PLUTO CL
NEPTUNE WAY
ELTHAM AVE
MOUNDSFIELD WAY
HOYLAKE CL
PHILBYE MEWS
Cippenham
3
SLOUGH
Roundmoor Ditch
32
M4
Sewage Works
WOOD LA
2
Jubilee River
Dorney
Court Farm
SOUTH FIELD CL
79
Manor Farm
Pigeonhouse Farm
SL4
COMMON RD
COLENORTON CRES
1
NORTHFIELD RD
BOVENEY NEW RD
STOCKDALES RD
MOORES LA
INKERMAN RD
ALMA RD
BELL LA
Riding School
PO
Dorney Common
ETON WICK RD
TILSTONE CL
TILSTONE AVE
LEESON GDNS
VICTORIA RD
CORNWALL CL
QUEENS RD
PRINCES CL
B3026
HAYWARDS
Liby
BOVENEY RD
Elm Farm Bungalow
A
B
43
94
C
Boveney Ditch
Recn Gd
Cress Brook
Eton Wick

MASONS RD
STOWE RD
BROWNS CT
CHARLCOT MEWS
BOWER WAY
BOWER CT
MALLARD DR
WESTGATE CRES
A4
ARGYLL AVE
ABERDEEN AVE
LEIGH RD
BERWICK AVE
AJAX AVE
A
22
B
C
SELWYN PL
IVY CRES
Westgate Ret Pk
TINTAGEL HO 1
SALT HILL MANS 2
LADYDAY PL 3
KINGSMEAD HO 4
HOLLY CT
ERICA CL
ABBEY CL
HINTON RD
HOGARTH CL
CHARTER RD
BRIDGE CL
LEWINS WAY
CIPPENHAM LA
BOARLANDS CL
RIDGEBANK
LEWINS FARM CT
BROOK PATH
DUNSTER GDNS
CORFE GDNS
AVEBURY
FOTHERINGAY GDNS
EGREMONT GDNS
BRAMBER CT
BERNERS CL
BOWYER DR
WARD GDNS
FRENCHUM GDNS
ROXWELL CL
LOWER CIPPENHAM LA
CIPPENHAM CL
SPRING LA
PO
HANOVER GATE
The Westgate Sch
ROEBUCK GN
ALDER CL
COLLEGE RD
PEARTREE CL
TRUMPER WAY
BENTLEY RD
BUNTEN MEADE 1
VANTAGE RD 2
COURT FARM CL 3
STONEY MEADE 4
OAKFIELD AVE
TWINCHES LA
MERCIAN WAY
MILLSTREAM LA
ROBIN HOOD CL
1 ORCHARD LODGE
2 SAXON LODGE
3 SHAKESPEARE LODGE
COPSE CL
AUTUMN CL
LOWER CIPPENHAM LA
Superstores
4
EARLS LA
WARNER CL
FERRERS CL
LILLEY WAY
DUCHESS ST
STREAMSIDE
GERVAISE CL
NINE ACRES
PLAINES CL
RICHARDS WAY
BENNETTS CL
RALEIGH CL
HARDY CL
ADAM CL
GORSE MEADE
CIPPENHAM LA
30
PEARL GDNS
TOPAZ CL
MOOR FURLONG
NICHOLAS GDNS
MANOR CT
RICHARDS WAY
PALACE CL
GLADSTONE WAY
WADE DR
BRUCE
PENDEEN CT
TAMARISK WAY
SPINNEY
SUMMERLEA
WEEKES DR
CRESS RD
80
CHAPELS CL
GOWINGS GN
COBHAM CL
MARCIA CT
Sch
BOULTERS CL
AMERDEN WAY
HUNTERS WAY
DUPRE CL
LUTO CL
GOODWIN VILLAS
Cippenham
BOVENEY CL
FROGMORE CL
ELTHAM AVE
MOUNDSFIELD WAY
HOYLAKE CL
PHILBYE MEWS
BRAEMAR GDNS
JELLICOE CL
Montem Pri Sch
M4
3
SL1
WOOD LA
BADER GDNS
BAIRD CL
HAIG DR
LOCHINVAR CL
MOORE CL
CHARLTON CL
31
Superstore
TELFORD DR
TYNDALE MEWS
Sewage Works
MITCHELL CL
LANCELOT CL
RUBY CL
GARNET CL
COE SPUR
COOPER WAY
BRIDLINGTON SPUR
SCARBOROUGH WAY
FILEY SPUR
STOUR CL
BURGETT RD
COLIN WAY
CHALVEY
WOOD LA
ADELAIDE CL 1
FLAMBOROUGH SPUR 2
GALAHAD CL 3
BANKS SPUR 4
2
M4
Woodpeckers
79
ALMA CT 1
VAUGHAN GDNS 2
BELLSFIELD CT 3
THE WHEATBUTTS 4
NORTHFIELD RD
Manor Farm
North Field
Saddocks Farm
COLENORTON CRES
1
BOVENEY NEW RD
STOCKDALES RD
MOORES LA
INKERMAN RD
BELL LA
COMMON RD
SL4
B3026
ALMA RD
PO
Common Ditch
ETON WICK RD
TILSTONE AVE
TILSTONE CL
LEESON GDNS
VICTORIA RD
CORNWALL CL
QUEENS RD
PRINCES CL
COMMON RD
ALBERT PL
THE WALK
SHEEPCOTE RD
Eton Great Common
Eton Wick CE Fst Sch
Liby
HAYWARDS MEAD
A
95
44
B
C
BUNCES CL
A332
Boveney Ditch
Recn Gd
B3026
ETON WICK RD
Eton Wick

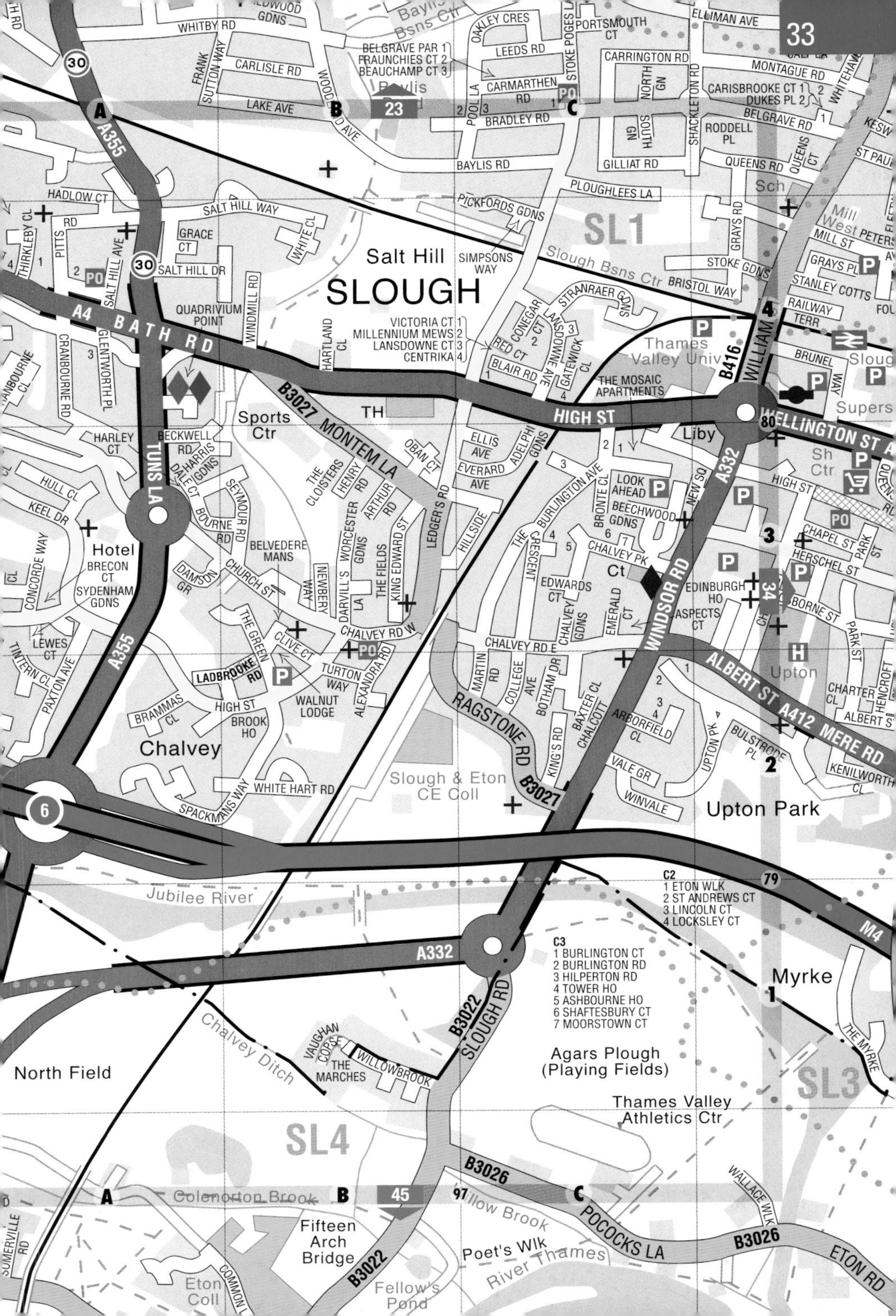
WHITBY RD
GDNS
FRANK SUTTON WAY
CARLISLE RD
WOOD AVE
LAKE AVE
BELGRAVE PAR 1
FRAUNCHIES CT 2
BEAUCHAMP CT 3
OAKLEY CRES
LEEDS RD
CARMARTHEN RD
POOL LA
STOKE POGES LA
PORTSMOUTH CT
ELLIMAN AVE
CARRINGTON RD
MONTAGUE RD
NORTH GN
SOUTH GN
SHACKLETON RD
CARISBROOKE CT 1
DUKES PL 2
BELGRAVE RD
RODDELL PL
QUEENS RD
QUEENS CT
GILLIAT RD
BAYLIS RD
BRADLEY RD
23
A355
30
HADLOW CT
PITTS RD
THIRKLEBY CL
SALT HILL AVE
SALT HILL WAY
GRACE CT
WHITE CL
SALT HILL DR
WINDMILL RD
PICKFORDS GDNS
SIMPSONS WAY
PLOUGHLEES LA
SL1
Salt Hill
SLOUGH
Slough Bsns Ctr
BRISTOL WAY
STOKE GDNS
GRAYS RD
Mill
MILL ST
GRAYS PL
STANLEY COTTS
RAILWAY TERR
QUADRIVIUM POINT
A4 BATH RD
CRANBOURNE RD
GLENTWORTH PL
HARTLAND CL
VICTORIA CT 1
MILLENNIUM MEWS 2
LANSDOWNE CT 3
CENTRIKA 4
RED CT
BLAIR RD
CONEGAR CT
LANSDOWNE AVE
GATEWICK CL
STRANRAER GDNS
Thames Valley Univ
B416
WILLIAM
BRUNEL WAY
THE MOSAIC APARTMENTS
HIGH ST
80
WELLINGTON ST
Liby
Supers
Sports Ctr
TH
B3027 MONTEM LA
HARLEY CT
BECKWELL RD
TUNS LA
HARRIS GDNS
DALE CT
HULL CL
KEEL DR
SEYMOUR RD
BOURNE RD
THE CLOISTERS
HENRY RD
ARTHUR RD
OBAN CT
LEDGER'S RD
ELLIS AVE
EVERARD AVE
ADELPHI GDNS
HILLSIDE
BURLINGTON AVE
THE CRESCENT
BRONTE CL
LOOK AHEAD
BEECHWOOD GDNS
NEW SQ
A332
Sh Ctr
HIGH ST
CHAPEL ST
PARK ST
HERSCHEL ST
Hotel
BRECON CT
CONCORDE WAY
SYDENHAM GDNS
DAMSON GR
CHURCH ST
BELVEDERE MANS
NEWBERY WAY
DARVILL'S LA
WORCESTER GDNS
THE FIELDS
KING EDWARD ST
CHALVEY PK
EDWARDS CT
Ct
CHALVEY GDNS
EMERALD CT
WINDSOR RD
EDINBURGH HO
ASPECTS CT
34
OSBORNE ST
LEWES CT
TINTERN CL
PAXTON AVE
A355
THE GREEN
CLIVE CT
CHALVEY RD W
LADBROOKE RD
TURTON WAY
ALEXANDRA RD
CHALVEY RD E
MARTIN RD
COLLEGE AVE
BOTHAM DR
BAXTER CL
CHALCOTT
ARBORFIELD CL
ALBERT ST A412 MERE RD
PARK ST
Upton
CHARTER CL
HENCROFT
ALBERT ST
BRAMMAS CL
HIGH ST
BROOK HO
WALNUT LODGE
RAGSTONE RD
KING'S RD
UPTON PK
BULSTRODE PL
KENILWORTH CL
Chalvey
WHITE HART RD
SPACKMANS WAY
Slough & Eton CE Coll
B3027
VALE GR
WINVALE
Upton Park
6
Jubilee River
C2
1 ETON WLK
2 ST ANDREWS CT
3 LINCOLN CT
4 LOCKSLEY CT
79
M4
A332
C3
1 BURLINGTON CT
2 BURLINGTON RD
3 HILPERTON RD
4 TOWER HO
5 ASHBOURNE HO
6 SHAFTESBURY CT
7 MOORSTOWN CT
Myrke
THE MYRKE
Chalvey Ditch
VAUGHAN COPSE
THE MARCHES
WILLOWBROOK
B3022 SLOUGH RD
North Field
Agars Plough
(Playing Fields)
Thames Valley
Athletics Ctr
SL3
SL4
B3026
Colenorton Brook
45
97
Willow Brook
POCOCKS LA
B3026
ETON RD
WALLACE WLK
Fifteen
Arch
Bridge
B3022
Poet's Wlk
River Thames
Fellow's Pond
Eton Coll
SUMERVILLE RD
COMMON

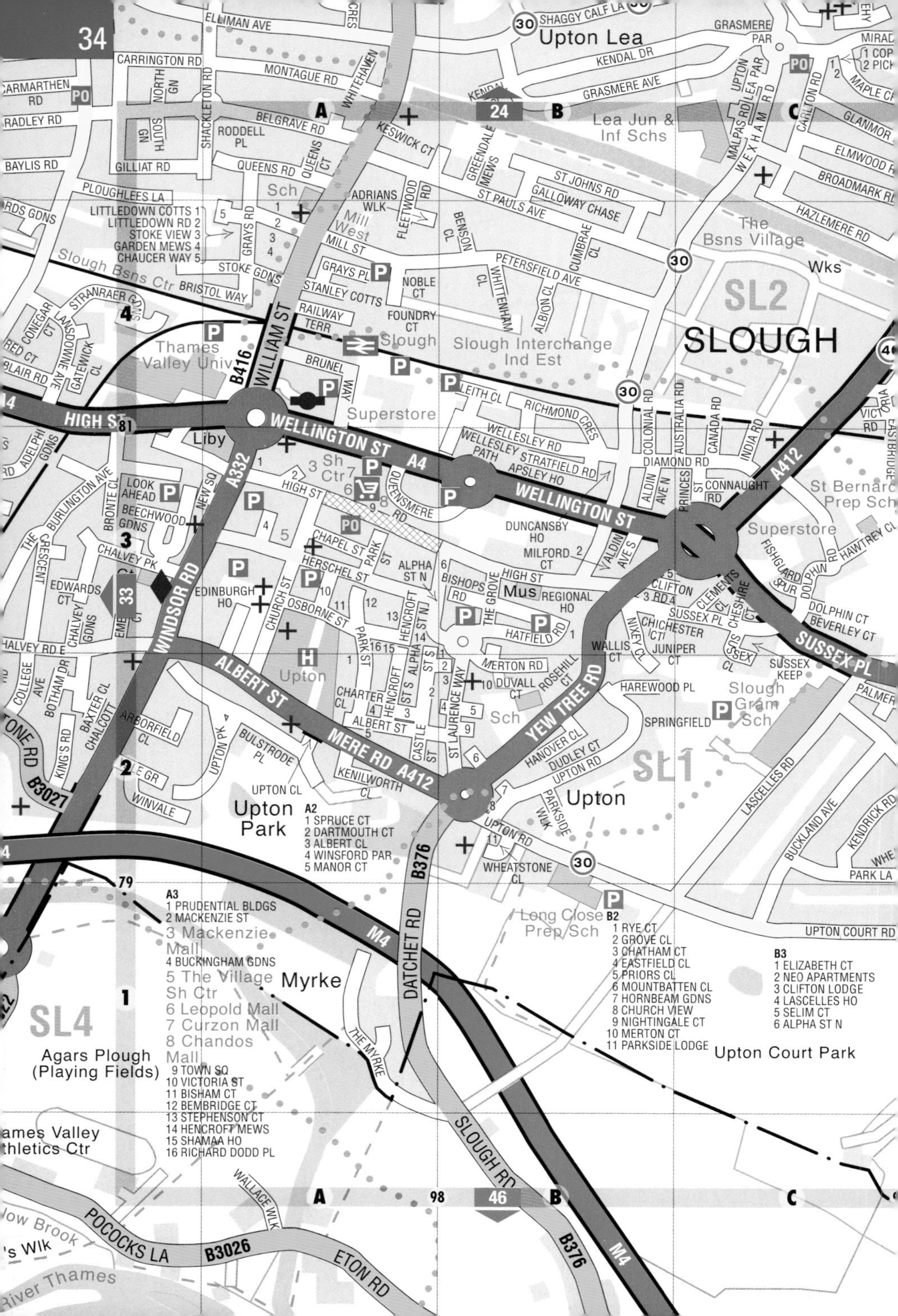

Upton Lea
SHAGGY CALF LA
ELLIMAN AVE
CARRINGTON RD
MONTAGUE RD
WHITEHAVEN
GRASMERE PAR
KENDAL DR
GRASMERE AVE
CARMARTHEN RD
NORTH GN
SOUTH GN
SHACKLETON RD
BRADLEY RD
BELGRAVE RD
KESWICK CT
RODDELL PL
QUEENS RD
QUEENS CT
GILLIAT RD
BAYLIS RD
PLOUGHLEES LA
Lea Jun & Inf Schs
GREENDALE MEWS
ST JOHNS RD
GALLOWAY CHASE
ST PAULS AVE
UPTON LEA PAR
MALPAS RD
WEXHAM RD
CARLTON RD
GLANMOR
ELMWOOD RD
BROADMARK RD
HAZLEMERE RD
MAPLE CR
1 COP
2 PICK
ADRIANS WLK
FLEETWOOD RD
Mill West
MILL ST
BENSON CL
CUMBRAE CL
The Bsns Village
LITTLEDOWN COTTS 1
LITTLEDOWN RD 2
STOKE VIEW 3
GARDEN MEWS 4
CHAUCER WAY 5
GRAYS RD
STOKE GDNS
Slough Bsns Ctr
BRISTOL WAY
GRAYS PL
STANLEY COTTS
NOBLE CT
PETERSFIELD AVE
WHITTENHAM CL
ALBION CL
Wks
SL2
SLOUGH
STRANRAER GDNS
CONEGAR CT
LANSDOWNE AVE
GATEWICK CL
RED CT
BLAIR RD
RAILWAY TERR
FOUNDRY CT
Slough
Slough Interchange Ind Est
Thames Valley Univ
B416
WILLIAM ST
BRUNEL WAY
LEITH CL
RICHMOND CRES
COLONIAL RD
AUSTRALIA RD
CANADA RD
INDIA RD
VICTORIA RD
EASTBRIDGE
HIGH ST
WELLINGTON ST
A4
Superstore
Liby
WELLESLEY RD
WELLESLEY PATH
STRATFIELD RD
APSLEY HO
DIAMOND RD
ALDIN AVE N
PRINCES ST
CONNAUGHT RD
A412
St Bernard's Prep Sch
ADELPHI GDNS
BURLINGTON AVE
BRONTE CL
LOOK AHEAD
NEW SQ
A332
Sh Ctr
QUEENSMERE RD
DUNCANSBY HO
ALDIN AVE S
Superstore
HAWTREY CL
BEECHWOOD GDNS
THE CRESCENT
CHALVEY PK
CHAPEL ST
PARK ST
HERSCHEL ST
ALPHA ST N
MILFORD CT
BISHOPS RD
THE GROVE
HIGH ST
Mus
REGIONAL HO
FISHGUARD SPUR
DOLPHIN RD
DOLPHIN CT
BEVERLEY CT
EDWARDS CT
33
EDINBURGH HO
CHURCH ST
OSBORNE ST
HENCROFT ST N
CLIFTON RD
CLEMENTS CL
CHICHESTER CT
SUSSEX PL
CHESHIRE CT
NIXEY CL
JUNIPER CT
WALLIS CT
CHALVEY GDNS
CHALVEY RD E
WINDSOR RD
COLLEGE AVE
BOTHAM DR
H
Upton
ALBERT ST
MERTON RD
ROSEHILL CT
DUVALL CT
YEW TREE RD
SUSSEX KEEP
SUSSEX PL
PALMER
HAREWOOD PL
Slough Gram Sch
BAXTER CL
CHALCOTT
KING'S RD
CHARTER CL
HENCROFT ST S
ALPHA ST S
CASTLE ST
ST LAURENCE WAY
Sch
SPRINGFIELD
ARBORFIELD CL
UPTON PK
BULSTRODE PL
MERE RD
A412
KENILWORTH CL
HANOVER CL
DUDLEY CT
UPTON RD
SL1
TONE RD
B3027
LE GR
WINVALE
UPTON CL
Upton Park
Upton
PARKSIDE WLK
LASCELLES RD
BUCKLAND AVE
KENDRICK RD
A2
1 SPRUCE CT
2 DARTMOUTH CT
3 ALBERT CL
4 WINSFORD PAR
5 MANOR CT
B376
UPTON RD
WHEATSTONE CL
PARK LA
UPTON COURT RD
79
A3
1 PRUDENTIAL BLDGS
2 MACKENZIE ST
3 Mackenzie Mall
4 BUCKINGHAM GDNS
5 The Village Sh Ctr
6 Leopold Mall
7 Curzon Mall
8 Chandos Mall
9 TOWN SQ
10 VICTORIA ST
11 BISHAM CT
12 BEMBRIDGE CT
13 STEPHENSON CT
14 HENCROFT MEWS
15 SHAMAA HO
16 RICHARD DODD PL
M4
DATCHET RD
Myrke
Long Close Prep Sch
B2
1 RYE CT
2 GROVE CL
3 CHATHAM CT
4 EASTFIELD CL
5 PRIORS CL
6 MOUNTBATTEN CL
7 HORNBEAM GDNS
8 CHURCH VIEW
9 NIGHTINGALE CT
10 MERTON CT
11 PARKSIDE LODGE
B3
1 ELIZABETH CT
2 NEO APARTMENTS
3 CLIFTON LODGE
4 LASCELLES HO
5 SELIM CT
6 ALPHA ST N
Upton Court Park
SL4
Agars Plough (Playing Fields)
THE MYRKE
ames Valley thletics Ctr
SLOUGH RD
WALLACE WLK
98
46
ow Brook
's Wlk
POCOCKS LA
B3026
ETON RD
B376
River Thames

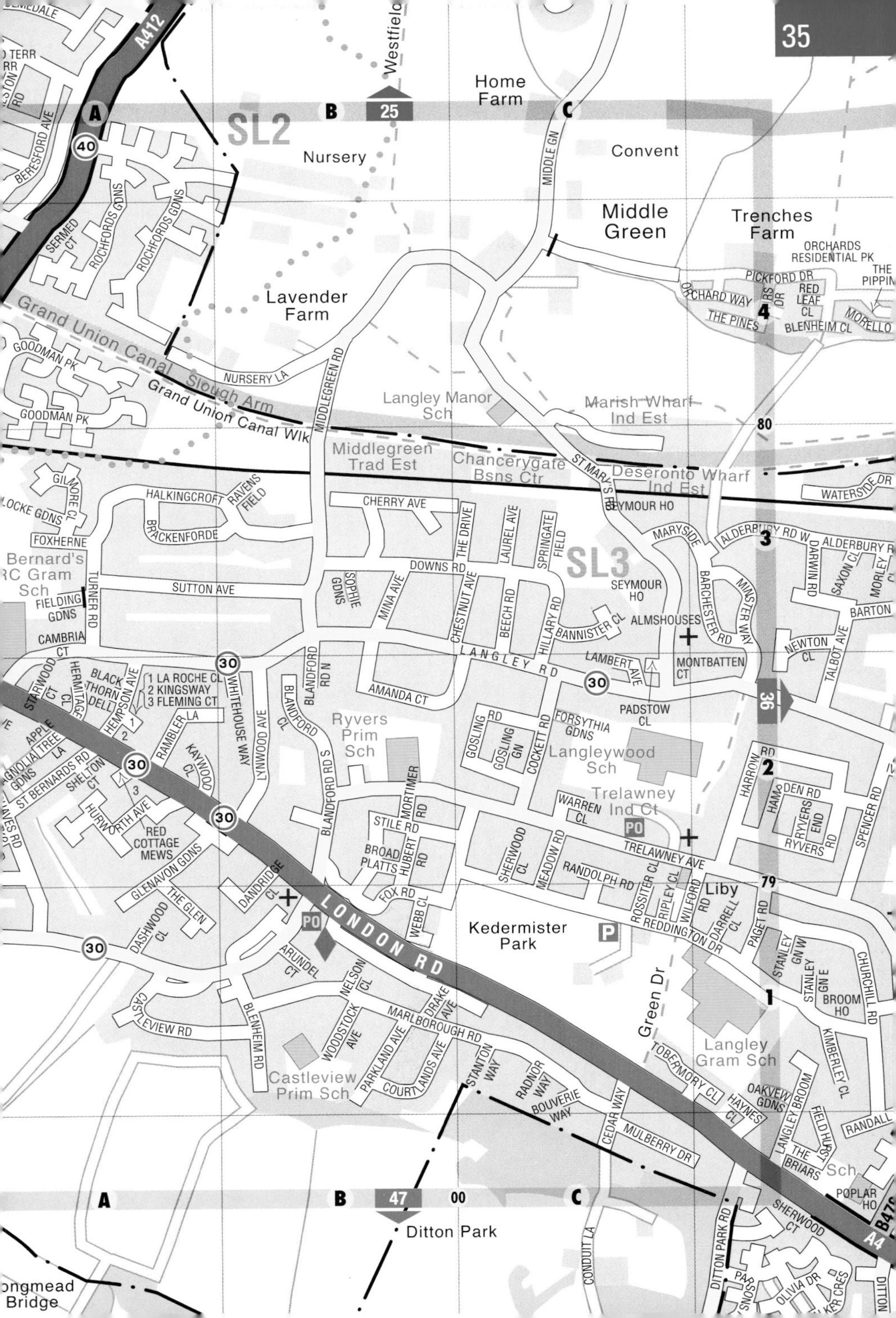

A412
Westfield
Home Farm
25
SL2
Nursery
Convent
Middle Green
Trenches Farm
ORCHARDS RESIDENTIAL PK
Lavender Farm
Grand Union Canal
Grand Union Canal Slough Arm
Grand Union Canal Wlk
NURSERY LA
MIDDLEGREEN RD
MIDDLE GN
Langley Manor Sch
Marish Wharf Ind Est
Middlegreen Trad Est
Chancerygate Bsns Ctr
Deseronto Wharf Ind Est
GOODMAN PK
BERESFORD AVE
ROCHFORDS GDNS
SERMED CT
PICKFORD DR
ORCHARD WAY
RED LEAF CL
THE PINES
BLENHEIM CL
MORELLO
SL3
CHERRY AVE
HALKINGCROFT
RAVENS FIELD
BRACKENFORDE
GILMORE CL
LOCKE GDNS
FOXHERNE
Bernard's RC Gram Sch
FIELDING GDNS
TURNER RD
SUTTON AVE
DOWNS RD
THE DRIVE
LAUREL AVE
SPRINGATE FIELD
SEYMOUR HO
ST MARY'S RD
MARYSIDE
ALDERBURY RD W
ALDERBURY RD
DARWIN RD
SAXON CL
MORLEY
BARTON
SOPHIE GDNS
MINA AVE
CHESTNUT AVE
BEECH RD
HILLARY RD
BANNISTER CL
ALMSHOUSES
BARCHESTER RD
MINSTER WAY
NEWTON CL
TALBOT AVE
CAMBRIA CT
LANGLEY RD
LAMBERT AVE
MONTBATTEN CT
PADSTOW CL
AMANDA CT
BLANDFORD RD N
BLANDFORD CL
BLANDFORD RD S
1 LA ROCHE CL
2 KINGSWAY
3 FLEMING CT
STARWOOD CT
HERMITAGE CL
BLACKTHORN DELL
HEMPSON AVE
WHITEHOUSE WAY
LYNWOOD AVE
RAMBLER LA
KAYWOOD CL
APPLE TREE LA
MAGNOLIA GDNS
ST BERNARDS RD
SHELTON CT
HURWORTH AVE
RED COTTAGE MEWS
Ryvers Prim Sch
GOSLING RD
GOSLING GN
COCKETT RD
FORSYTHIA GDNS
Langleywood Sch
Trelawney Ind Ct
HARROW RD
HAMPDEN RD
RYVERS END
RYVERS RD
SPENCER RD
MORTIMER RD
STILE RD
BROAD PLATTS
HUBERT RD
WARREN CL
SHERWOOD CL
MEADOW RD
TRELAWNEY AVE
RANDOLPH RD
ROSSITER CL
RIPLEY CL
WILFORD RD
DARRELL CL
Liby
PAGET RD
GLENAVON GDNS
THE GLEN
DASHWOOD CL
DANDRIDGE CL
FOX RD
WEBB CL
Kedermister Park
REDDINGTON DR
STANLEY GN W
STANLEY GN E
BROOM HO
CHURCHILL RD
LONDON RD
ARUNDEL CT
NELSON CL
DRAKE AVE
Green Dr
CASTLEVIEW RD
BLENHEIM RD
WOODSTOCK AVE
MARLBOROUGH RD
PARKLAND AVE
COURTLANDS AVE
STANTON WAY
RADNOR WAY
BOUVERIE WAY
Castleview Prim Sch
Langley Gram Sch
TOBERMORY CL
HAYNES CL
OAKVEW GDNS
LANGLEY BROOM
FIELDHURST
KIMBERLEY CL
RANDALL
THE BRIARS
CEDAR WAY
MULBERRY DR
POPLAR HO
SHERWOOD CT
B470
A4
47
00
Ditton Park
Longmead Bridge
CONDUIT LA
DITTON PARK RD
PARSONS
OLIVIA DR
DITTON
36
80
79

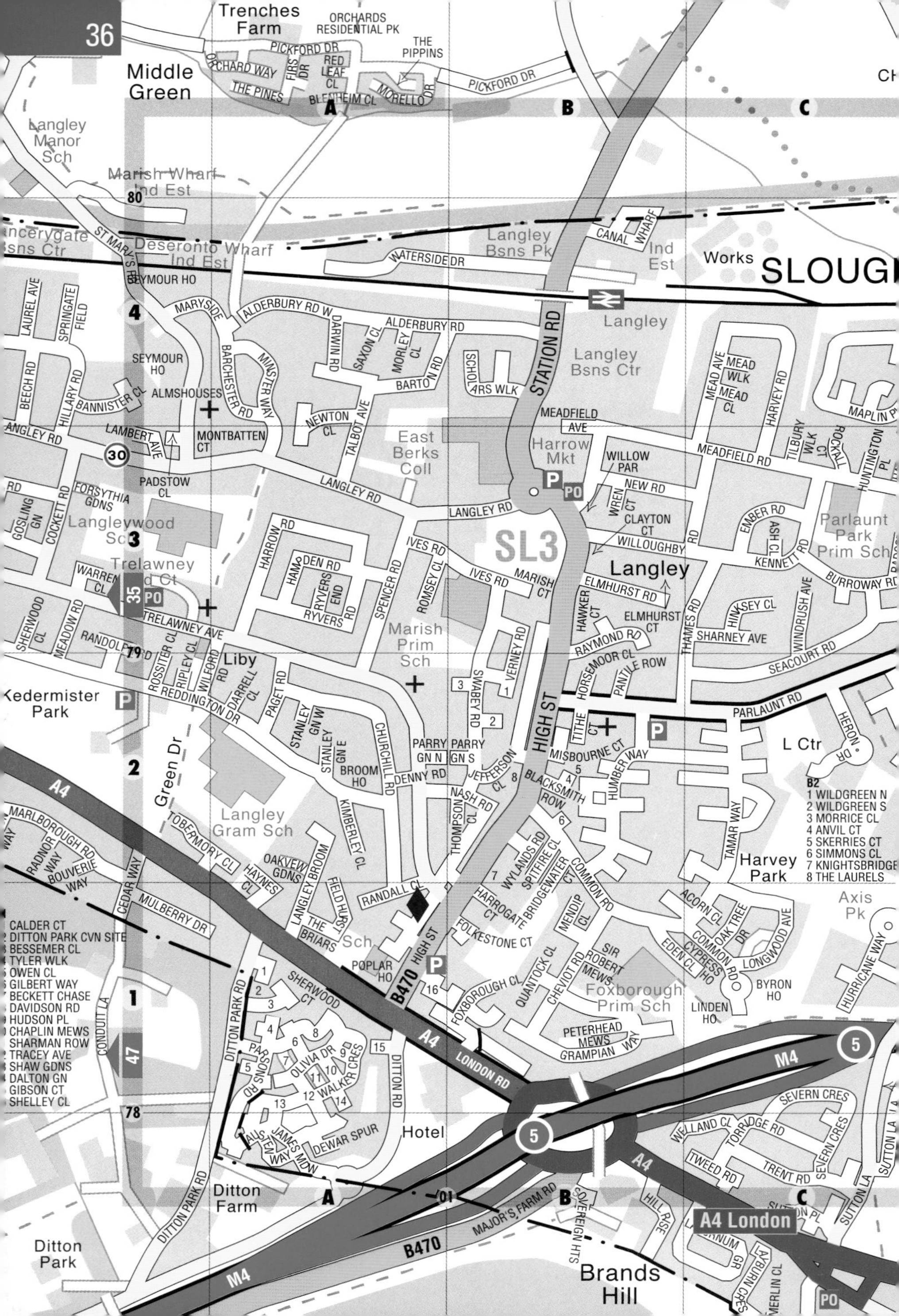
Trenches Farm
ORCHARDS RESIDENTIAL PK
Middle Green
THE PIPPINS
PICKFORD DR
ORCHARD WAY
THE PINES
BLENHEIM CL
MORELLO DR
Langley Manor Sch
Marish Wharf Ind Est
Deseronto Wharf Ind Est
Langley Bsns Pk
CANAL WHARF
Ind Est
Works
SLOUGH
WATERSIDE DR
ST MARY'S RD
SEYMOUR HO
MARYSIDE
ALDERBURY RD W
ALDERBURY RD
STATION RD
Langley
Langley Bsns Ctr
SEYMOUR HO
ALMSHOUSES
BARCHESTER RD
MINSTER WAY
SAXON CL
MORLEY CL
BARTON RD
SCHOLARS WLK
MEADFIELD AVE
MEAD AVE
MEAD WLK
MEAD CL
HARVEY RD
MAPLIN PK
LAUREL AVE
SPRINGATE FIELD
BEECH RD
HILLARY RD
BANNISTER CL
LANGLEY RD
LAMBERT AVE
MONTBATTEN CT
NEWTON CL
TALBOT AVE
East Berks Coll
Harrow Mkt
WILLOW PAR
MEADFIELD RD
TILBURY WLK
ROCKALL CT
HUNTINGTON PL
PADSTOW CL
FORSYTHIA GDNS
NEW RD
WREN CT
CLAYTON CT
WILLOUGHBY RD
EMBER RD
ASH CL
Parlaunt Park Prim Sch
GOSLING GN
COCKETT RD
Langleywood Sch
Trelawney Ind Ct
HARROW RD
HAMPDEN RD
RYVERS END
RYVERS RD
SPENCER RD
IVES RD
ROMSEY CL
MARISH CT
SL3
Langley
ELMHURST RD
KENNETT RD
BURROWAY RD
WARREN CL
TRELAWNEY AVE
SHERWOOD CL
MEADOW RD
RANDOLPH RD
ROSSITER CL
RIPLEY CL
WILFORD RD
Liby
DARRELL CL
PAGET RD
Marish Prim Sch
VERNEY RD
HAWKER CT
ELMHURST CT
RAYMOND RD
HORSEMOOR CL
PANTILE ROW
THAMES RD
HINKSEY CL
SHARNEY AVE
WINDRUSH AVE
SEACOURT RD
Kedermister Park
REDDINGTON DR
STANLEY GN W
STANLEY GN E
CHURCHILL RD
SWABEY RD
HIGH ST
TITHE CT
PARLAUNT RD
HERON DR
L Ctr
Green Dr
BROOM HO
PARRY GN N
PARRY GN S
DENNY RD
JEFFERSON CL
MISBOURNE CT
HUMBER WAY
BLACKSMITH ROW
A4
MARLBOROUGH RD
RADNOR WAY
BOUVERIE WAY
CEDAR WAY
TOBERMORY CL
Langley Gram Sch
KIMBERLEY CL
NASH RD
THOMPSON CL
WYLANDS RD
SPITFIRE CL
BRIDGEWATER CT
COMMON RD
TAMAR WAY
Harvey Park
Axis Pk
B2
1 WILDGREEN N
2 WILDGREEN S
3 MORRICE CL
4 ANVIL CT
5 SKERRIES CT
6 SIMMONS CL
7 KNIGHTSBRIDGE
8 THE LAURELS
MULBERRY DR
HAYNES CL
OAKVEW GDNS
LANGLEY BROOM
FIELD HURST
RANDALL CL
HARROGATE CT
MENDIP CL
ACORN CL
OAK TREE DR
LONGWOOD AVE
HURRICANE WAY
CALDER CT
DITTON PARK CVN SITE
BESSEMER CL
TYLER WLK
OWEN CL
GILBERT WAY
BECKETT CHASE
DAVIDSON RD
HUDSON PL
CHAPLIN MEWS
SHARMAN ROW
TRACEY AVE
SHAW GDNS
DALTON GN
GIBSON CT
SHELLEY CL
THE BRIARS
Sch
POPLAR HO
B470
FOLKESTONE CT
QUANTOCK CL
CHEVIOT RD
SIR ROBERT MEWS
EDEN CL
CYPRESS HO
COMMON RD
BYRON HO
LINDEN HO
Foxborough Prim Sch
DITTON PARK RD
SHERWOOD CT
FOXBOROUGH CL
PETERHEAD MEWS
GRAMPIAN WAY
CONDUIT LA
PARSONS RD
OLIVIA DR
WALKER CRES
DITTON RD
LONDON RD
M4
SEVERN CRES
WELLAND CL
TORRIDGE RD
TWEED RD
TRENT RD
SUTTON LA
Hotel
AUSTEN WAY
JAMES MDW
DEWAR SPUR
Ditton Farm
MAJOR'S FARM RD
SOVEREIGN HTS
HILL RISE
SUTTON PL
A4 London
Ditton Park
B470
LABURNUM GR
AYLBURN CRES
MERLIN CL
Brands Hill
DITTON PARK RD

MANSION LA
A
B
C
Grand Union Canal
Grand Union Canal Wlk
Caravan Park
Caravan Park
Works
80
Iver
BUCKFIELD CT
WELLESLEY CT
THORNEY LA S
BATHURST WLK
PO
Liby
BATHURST CL
CHEQUERS BRIDGE COTTS
Withy Bridge
SLO
ST JAMES WLK
SYKE CLUAN
SYKE INGS
WELLESLEY AVE
SOMERSET WAY
MARKET LA
Richings Park
Sports Ground
RICHINGS PL
RICHINGS WAY
ST LEONARDS WLK
WOODLAND GRANGE
MAIN DR
NORTH PK
Thorney House
79
FORMBY CL
DEVERILLS WAY
KEMPE CL
STORNAWAY RD
THE POYNINGS
SL3
CH
Old Slade Farm
OLD SLADE LA
Home Wood
SUTTON LA
LITTLE SUTTON LA
Sutton
M4 London (A4)
Oak Plantation
M4
Old Wood
Sewage Works
78
03
Gravel Pit

Westacott Bsns Ctr
Maidenhead Office Pk
WOODLANDS PARK RD
WILLANT CL
PADDOCK COTTS
PADDOCK CL
WHITE PADDOCK
WALTHAM CL
WOODLANDS PARK AVE
Lillibrooke Manor
A
26
B
C
Woodlands Park
SAWYERS CRES
SAWYE CL
THOMAS CT
PHIPPS CL
HEYWOOD COURT CL
SAWYERS CRES
Woodlands Bsns Pk
FOLIEJOHN WAY
CHRISTIAN SMITH HO
HEYWOOD AVE
HEYWOOD GDNS
SNOWBALL HILL
WALTHAM RD
White Waltham Airfield
Woodlands Park Prim Sch
4
HEYWOOD FARM BARNS
Heywood Farm
78
Sewage Works
SL6
3
SNOWBALL HILL
M4
White Waltham
Waltham Place
2
77
B3024
Paley Street Farm
PALEY ST
1
Littlefield Green
Whitehouse Farm
LITTLEFIELD GN
B3024
Whites Farm
Great Wood
A
86
B
Duell Farm
C
M4 Reading (A33)
Littlefield Farm
HOW LANE FARM
GREEN LA
The Royal Oak (PH)

Ockwells Manor
Ockwells Home Farm
A
B
27
C
A404(M)
A308(M)
The Bourne
M4
8/9
The Cut
Cresswells Farm
4
THRIFT LA
78
THRIFT LA
Belmont Farm
MEADOW VIEW LA
3
Thimble Farm
STURT GN
ROLLS LA
40
SL6
A330
Stud Green
ASCOT RD
addock Wood
2
Foxley Green Farm
Holyport Manor Sch
77
The Jolly Gardener (PH)
A330
B3024
FOREST GREEN RD
1
Longchase Farm
Little Foxley
Gadbridge Farm
Highfield Farm
LONG LA
Touchen-end
B3024
A
B
88
C
A330 Bracknell (A3095)
Paley Street
SHEEPCOTE LA
A330
The Bourne

A404(M)
A308(M)
The Bourne
28
A
B
C
A330
Priors Way Ind Est
Maidenhead Trad Pk
M4
8/9
Moor Farm
ASCOT RD
Cresswells Farm
PHILBERDS LODGE
HEARNE DR
HOLYPORT ST
ELM COTTS
MANOR WAY
HOLYPORT RD
Holyport CE Prim Sch
PO
LYNDEN CL
STOMPITS RD
NEW RD
STROUD FARM RD
THE BRAMBLES
LANGWORTHY END
LANGWORTHY LA
PETERS LA
GAYS LA
LINDORES RD
LINDORES HO
TRENCHARD RD
REEVE RD
HENDONS WAY
AYSGARTH PK
ESKDALE GDNS
BYLAND DR
HOLYPORT RD
FIRFIELD 1
LARKFIELD 2
HEATHCOTE
PRIORS WAY
WILLOW DR
A308
Belmont Farm
MEADOW VIEW LA
ROLLS LA
39
PAMELA ROW
PH
John Gays House
Holyport
SL6
Stud Green
Bartletts La
BARTLETTS LA
THE FIELDINGS
DAIRY CT
MONEYROW GN
IVY CL
Primrose La
Moneyrow Green
Holyport Manor Sch
The Jolly Gardener (PH)
B3024
FOREST GREEN RD
Old Beams
Gadbridge Farm
Little Foxley
LONG LA
FOREST GN
Blackbird La
The Rising Sun (PH)
89
The Bourne
Mount Scipett Copse
1
2
3
4
77
78

M4
B3028
A
B
29
C
P
WINDSOR RD
BRAY CT
COURT CL
Marina
Cemy
MOOR END
LONSDALE WAY
SANDY MEAD
TITHE CL
BUCKLEBURY CL
Works
Queen's Eyot
4
PO
TITHE BARN DR
BROADWATER PK
TITHE BARN DR
40
HUXTABLE GDNS
A308
WESTBROOK
LYNGFIELD PK
MONKEY ISLAND LA
MONKEY ISLAND LA
78
MONKEY ISLAND CT
BUILDER'S CROSS
WINDSOR RD
Water Oakley
3
WATER OAKLE FARM COTTS
WATER OAKLEY COTTS
42
A308
SL6
FERNDALE PK CVN PK
The Guild House
The Queen's Head (PH)
Stroud Farm
SL4
2
FIFIELD RD
THE RETREAT
The Retreat Farm
MANOR GR
77
Fifield
GREEN LA
Coningsby Farm
CONINGSBY LA
FIFIELD WAY COTTS
MEADOW WAY
1
STEWART CL
Grove House
Pond Farm
FOREST VIEW COTTS
Fifield House
FOREST GREEN RD
Ledger Farm
LEDGER LA
FIFIELD COTTS
91
Braywood CE Fst Sch
OAKLEY GREEN RD
B3024
Banham Farm
Kimber Farm

30
A
B
C
MONKEY ISLAND LA
Marina
Rowing Lake
Queen's
Eyot
Works
4
SL6
BROADWATER PK
TITHE BARN DR
WESTBROOK
78
MONKEY ISLAND LA
A308
MONKEY
ISLAND
CT
BUILDER'S
CROSS
3
Water Oakley
WINDSOR RD
WATER OAKLEY
FARM COTTS
WATER
OAKLEY
COTTS
DOWN PL
Dorney Lake
Park
Hotel
41
FERNDALE PK
CVN PK
The Queen's Head
(PH)
Down
Place
Farm
A308
WINDSOR RD
2
SL4
Oak View
Farm
Cemy
OAKLEY
GREEN RD
The Retreat
Farm
77
1
Bishops
Farmhouse
BISHOPS FARM CL
ffield
House
Braywood
CE Fst
Sch
Kimbers
Lane
Farm
Oakley
Place
Farm
A
92
B
C
B3024
OAKLEY GREEN RD
B3024
Kimbers
Farm
BRAYWOOD
COTTS
OAKLEY GREEN RD
Oakley
Green

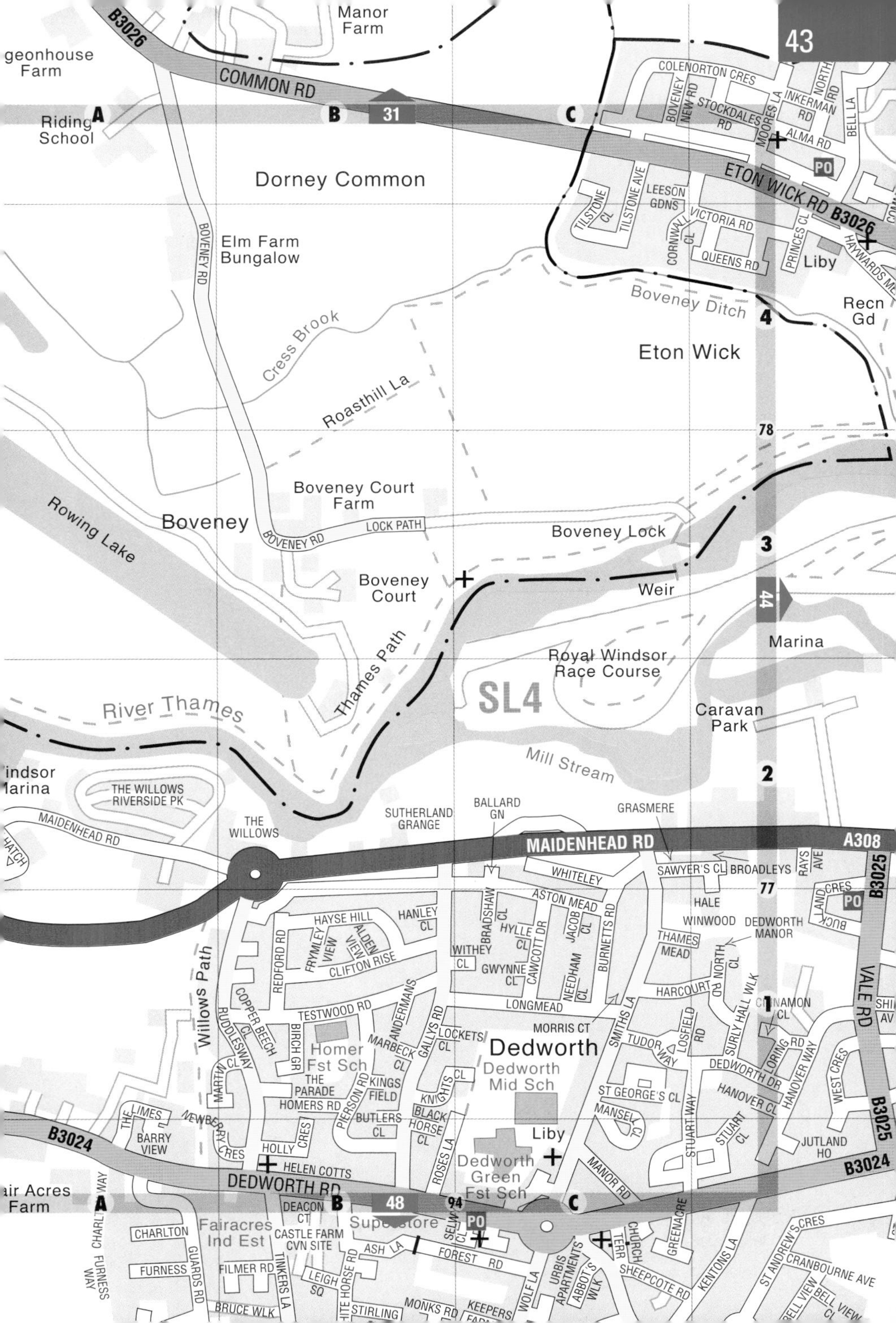
Manor Farm
B3026
geonhouse Farm
COMMON RD
Riding School
A
B
31
C
Dorney Common
COLENORTON CRES
BOVENEY NEW RD
STOCKDALES RD
MOORES LA
INKERMAN RD
NORTH RD
BELL LA
ALMA RD
PO
ETON WICK RD B3026
TILSTONE CL
TILSTONE AVE
LEESON GDNS
CORNWALL CL
VICTORIA RD
QUEENS RD
PRINCES CL
HAYWARDS MEAD
Liby
BOVENEY RD
Elm Farm Bungalow
Boveney Ditch
Recn Gd
Cress Brook
4
Eton Wick
Roasthill La
78
Boveney Court Farm
Rowing Lake
Boveney
LOCK PATH
BOVENEY RD
Boveney Lock
3
Boveney Court
Weir
44
Thames Path
Marina
Royal Windsor Race Course
SL4
River Thames
Caravan Park
Mill Stream
Windsor Marina
2
THE WILLOWS RIVERSIDE PK
MAIDENHEAD RD
THE WILLOWS
SUTHERLAND GRANGE
BALLARD GN
GRASMERE
MAIDENHEAD RD
A308
WHITELEY
SAWYER'S CL
BROADLEYS
RAYS AVE
B3025
77
ASTON MEAD
HALE
BUCKLAND CRES
PO
HANLEY CL
HAYSE HILL
BRADSHAW CL
HYLLE CL
JACOB CL
BURNETTS RD
WINWOOD
DEDWORTH MANOR
REDFORD RD
FRYMLEY VIEW
ALDEN VIEW
CLIFTON RISE
WITHEY CL
CAWCOTT DR
GWYNNE CL
NEEDHAM CL
THAMES MEAD
NORTH CL
VALE RD
Willows Path
COPPER BEECH CL
TESTWOOD RD
ANDERMANS
LONGMEAD
HARCOURT RD
SURLY HALL WLK
CINNAMON CL
RUDDLESWAY
BIRCH GR
GALLYS RD
LOCKETS CL
MORRIS CT
SMITHS LA
LOSFIELD RD
1
LORING RD
HANOVER WAY
MARBECK CL
Homer Fst Sch
Dedworth
TUDOR WAY
DEDWORTH DR
WEST CRES
MARTIN CL
THE PARADE
PIERSON RD
KINGS FIELD
KNIGHTS CL
Dedworth Mid Sch
ST GEORGE'S CL
HANOVER CL
B3025
THE LIMES
NEWBERRY CRES
HOMERS RD
BLACK HORSE CL
BUTLERS CL
MANSEL CL
STUART WAY
STUART CL
JUTLAND HO
B3024
BARRY VIEW
HOLLY CRES
Liby
HELEN COTTS
ROSES LA
Dedworth Green Fst Sch
MANOR RD
B3024
DEDWORTH RD
Fair Acres Farm
CHARLTON WAY
A
DEACON CT
B
48
94
C
GREENACRE
Superstore
PO
SELWYN CL
Fairacres Ind Est
CHARLTON
CASTLE FARM CVN SITE
ASH LA
FOREST RD
URBIS APARTMENTS
ABBOT'S WLK
CHURCH TERR
KENTONS LA
ST ANDREW'S CRES
CRANBOURNE AVE
FURNESS
GUARDS RD
FILMER RD
TINKERS LA
LEIGH SQ
WHITE HORSE RD
WOLF LA
SHEEPCOTE RD
BELL VIEW
BELL VIEW CL
FURNESS WAY
BRUCE WLK
STIRLING
MONKS RD
KEEPERS FARM

Saddocks Farm
Manor Farm
North Field
32
A
B
C
COLENORTON CRES
BOVENEY NEW RD
STOCKDALES RD
MOORES LA
INKERMAN
NORTHFIELD RD
BELL LA
ALMA RD
COMMON RD
B3026
Common Ditch
PO
ETON WICK RD
TILSTONE CL
TILSTONE AVE
LEESON GDNS
CORNWALL CL
VICTORIA RD
QUEENS RD
PRINCES CL
Liby
HAYWARDS MEAD
COMMON RD
ALBERT PL
THE WALK
SHEEPCOTE RD
Eton Great Common
Eton Wick CE Fst Sch
CLIFTON LODGE
Recn Gd
Boveney Ditch
4
Eton Wick
ETON WICK RD
BUNCES CL
A332
STONEBRIDGE
BROKEN
THE SANDLES
South Field
78
Boveney Lock
3
Royal Windsor Race Course
Weir
43
SL4
A332
Marina
Caravan Park
Mill Stream
2
THE RIVERBANK
WHITE LILIES ISLAND
THE MOORINGS
CLEWER PK
Windsor L Ctr
Clewer Village
MILL LA
CLEWER COURT RD
STEPHENSON DR
SWAN TERR
STOVELL RD
A308
MAIDENHEAD RD
40
VILLIERS CT
B3025
RAYS AVE
SAWYER'S CL
BROADLEYS
WHITELEY
77
BRADSHAW CL
ASTON MEAD
HYLLE CL
CAWCOTT DR
JACOB CL
GWYNNE CL
NEEDHAM CL
BURNETTS RD
HALE
WINWOOD
DEDWORTH MANOR
BUCKLAND CRES
PO
Cemy
THAMES MEAD
NORTH CL
A308
MAIDENHEAD RD
WELLS CL
ERRINGTON DR
St Edward's Royal Free Ecumenical Mid Sch
St Edward's RC Fst Sch
The Windsor Boys' Sch
WELLESLEY HO
VANSITTART RD
RUTHERFORD CL
VALE RD
HARCOURT RD
SURLY HALL WLK
CINNAMON CL
SHIRLEY AVE
LONGMEAD
1
MORRIS CT
SMITHS LA
LOSFIELD RD
LORING RD
HANOVER WAY
CHANTRY CL
PARSONAGE LA
RECTORY CL
MAYNARD CT
SIR SYDNEY CAMM HO
ALBERT ST
CLARENCE CT
Dedworth
Dedworth Mid Sch
TUDOR WAY
DEDWORTH DR
WEST CRES
EAST CRES
Recn Gd
HASLEMERE RD
TERRENT CT
OAK LA
ORCHARD AVE
HELSTON LA
PETWORTH CT
THE PAVILIONS
CLARENCE RD
FAWCETT
CHILTERN CT
CLARENDON CT
COURT M
ST GEORGE'S CL
HANOVER CL
B3025
B3024
CLARENCE RD
A308
GOSLAR WAY
MANSELL CL
STUART WAY
STUART CL
JUTLAND HO
Liby
Dedworth Green Fst Sch
MANOR RD
DEDWORTH RD
CROSS OAK
CARTER CL
ST JOHNS RD
NEW TOWN
TREVELYAN CT
IMPERIAL RD
ALMOND CL
GREEN LA
CLEWER AVE
B3024
A
95
49
B
C
BRIDGEMAN DR
BIRCHINGTON RD
WINDMILL CL
YORK RD
B3024
GREENACRE
CHURCH TERR
URBIS APARTMENTS
ABBOT'S WLK
SHEEPCOTE RD
KENTONS LA
ST ANDREW'S CRES
ST ANDREW'S AVE
CRANBOURNE AVE
ST JOHNS DR
CONVENT RD
HATCH LA
Clewer New Town
COMBERMERE CL
Oakfield Fst Sch
PO
SPRINGFIELD CL
YORK AVE
BELL VIEW
BELL VIEW CL
BAILEY CL
FOREST RD

A332
Myrke
A
B
33
C
B3022
SLOUGH RD
Chalvey Ditch
VAUGHAN
CORSE
THE MARCHES
WILLOWBROOK
North Field
SL4
Agars Plough
(Playing Fields)
THE MYRKE
SL3
Thames Valley
Athletics Ctr
B3026
Colenorton Brook
Willow Brook
WALLACE WK
Fifteen
Arch
Bridge
POCOCKS LA
4
ETON RD
B3026
Poet's Wlk
River Thames
COMMON LA
Eton
Coll
Fellow's
Pond
JUDY'S PAS
B3026
B3022
Lock Cut
78
WILLOW PL
ETON WICK RD
SLOUGH RD
Jubilee River
COMMON LA
Weir
River Thames
HIGH ST
BALDWIN'S SHORE
Eton
Coll
Mus
KEATS LA
GULLIVER'S
JOURDELAY'S PAS
Eton Porny
CE Fst Sch
3
The Home Park
ETON
Liby
SUNBURY RD
TANGIER LA
SL3
SOUTH MEADOW LA
PO
SUN CL
P&R
Recn Gd
46
VICARAGE FLATS
Weir
ROMNEY LOCK RD
KING EDWARD VII AVE
TURKS HEAD CT 1
THE ALMSHOUSES 2
CHANTRY PL 3
ATHERTON CT 4
WIGGINGTON HO 5
CHURCH CL
1 TANGIER CT
2 SUNBURY CT
B470
MEADOW LA
ETON SQ
ETON CT
KING STABLE ST
Windsor & Eton
Riverside
PRINCE ALBERT'S WLK
The Brocas
ETON RIVERSIDE
B3022
Slopes
Lodge
Thames Path
BROCAS TERR
EMLYN BLDGS
BROCAS ST
THAMES SIDE
FARM YD
DATCHET RD
6 RIVERSIDE WLK
7 GEORGE V PL
8 THE CLOISTERS
WINDSOR
2
The
Windsor
Bsns Ctr
River
Thames
St George's
Sch
BARRY AVE
RIVER ST
THAMES AVE
THAMES ST
CHAPTER MEWS
NORTH TERR
B1
1 CASTLEVIEW HO
2 HORSESHOE CLOISTERS
3 LODGINGS OF THE MILITARY KNIGHTS
4 HENRY III TWR
5 Windsor Royal Sta
6 KING EDWARD CT
7 AMBERLEY PL
8 MARKET ST
9 CHURCH ST
10 QUEEN CHARLOTTE ST
11 CHURCH LA
12 ST ALBANS CL
13 RED BRICK COTTS
14 BURFORD HO
15 COPPERFIELD HO
16 PEASCOD PL
17 MELLOR WLK
18 ROYAL FREE CT
19 SUN PAS
20 HIBBERT'S ALLEY
21 CHARIOTT'S PL
22 ELLISON HO
23 SHENSTON CT
24 WESSEX CT
25 RALSTON CT
Vansittart
Est
Windsor & Eton
Central
LOWER WARD
Windsor
Castle
LIME AVE
77
BRIDGEWATER WAY
BRIDGEWATER TERR
CHAPEL HILL
EAST TERR
CHALK HILL
GOSWELL RD
CASTLE HILL
SOUTH TERR
ARTHUR RD
ROYAL MEWS
SL4
GOSWELL HILL
ST ALBAN'S ST
ADELAIDE RD
ATHLONE SQ
HIGH ST
PEASCOD ST
QUEEN VICTORIA'S WLK
HUNTERS MEWS
ACRE PAS
GUARDS VIEW
1
CLARENCE CRES
CHARLES ST
OXFORD RD E
WILLIAM ST
Liby
B470
PARK ST
Princess
Christians
JAMES ST
ACRE
BACHELORS
COBURG HO
A1
1 CAMBRIDGE HO
2 WARD ROYAL PAR
3 CHRISTIAN SQ
4 CRESCENT VILLAS
5 WARD ROYAL
6 BOWES-LYON CL
7 MOUNTBATTEN SQ
8 CHARLES HO
9 QUEEN ANNE'S CT
VICTORIA ST
BARRACK LA
REGENT CT
SHEET ST
Adelaide
Cottage
ALMA RD
DORSET RD
TRINITY PL
SPINNERS WLK
RUSSELL ST
Victoria
Barracks
CLAREMONT RD
ALBANY RD
KEPPEL ST
DAGMAR RD
BROOK ST
QUEEN ELIZABETH'S WLK
HAMTREY RD
TEMPLE RD
TEMPLE GATE
ALEXANDRA RD
CORONATION AV
Coll
DEVEREUX RD
HELENA RD
PARK CL
ST MARK'S RD
A
B
50
97
C
The Home Park
ST MARK'S PL
LEONARD'S AVE
ST LEONARD'S
GROVE RD
PRINCE CONSORT COTTS
QUEENS RD
LAMMAS CT
FRANCES RD
ADELAIDE SQ
KINGS RD
FROGMORE DR
OSBORNE MEWS
BEAUMONT RD
FAIRLIGHT AVE
GLOUCESTER PL
Frogmore
Frogmore
Cottages
Sch

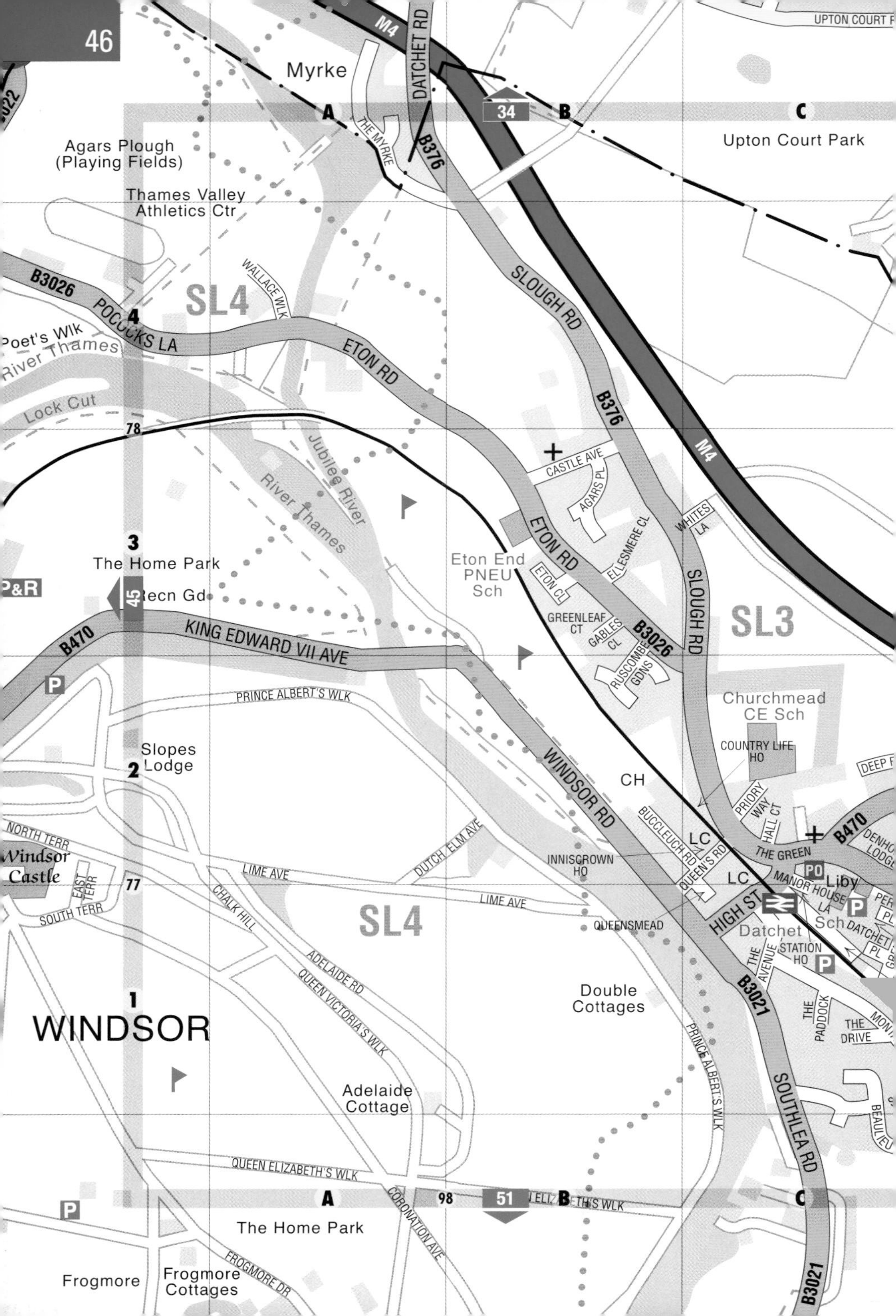

M4
DATCHET RD
UPTON COURT P
Myrke
34
A
B
C
THE MYRKE
B376
Upton Court Park
Agars Plough
(Playing Fields)
Thames Valley
Athletics Ctr
B3026
WALLACE WLK
SL4
POCOCKS LA
4
Poet's Wlk
River Thames
ETON RD
SLOUGH RD
Lock Cut
78
B376
M4
CASTLE AVE
AGARS PL
Jubilee River
River Thames
WHITES LA
ELLESMERE CL
ETON RD
3
The Home Park
Eton End
PNEU
Sch
ETON CL
SLOUGH RD
SL3
P&R
45
Recn Gd
GREENLEAF CT
GABLES CL
B3026
B470
KING EDWARD VII AVE
RUSCOMBE GDNS
P
PRINCE ALBERT'S WLK
Churchmead
CE Sch
COUNTRY LIFE HO
Slopes
Lodge
2
WINDSOR RD
CH
DEEP F
PRIORY WAY
HALL CT
B470
NORTH TERR
DUTCH ELM AVE
BUCCLEUCH RD
LC
THE GREEN
DENHO LODGE
Windsor
Castle
LIME AVE
INNISCROWN HO
QUEEN'S RD
PO
LC
EAST TERR
77
SOUTH TERR
CHALK HILL
LIME AVE
MANOR HOUSE LA
Liby
HIGH ST
Sch
SL4
QUEENSMEAD
Datchet
DATCHET PL
ADELAIDE RD
THE AVENUE
STATION HO
P
QUEEN VICTORIA'S WLK
B3021
Double
Cottages
1
WINDSOR
PRINCE ALBERT'S WLK
THE PADDOCK
THE DRIVE
SOUTHLEA RD
Adelaide
Cottage
BEAULIEU
QUEEN ELIZABETH'S WLK
A
98
51
B
C
ELIZABETH'S WLK
P
CORONATION AVE
The Home Park
FROGMORE DR
Frogmore
Frogmore
Cottages
B3021

Kedermister Park
REDDINGTON DR
DARREL CL
PAGET RD
ARUNDEL CT
NELSON CL
DRAKE AVE
A4
CASTLEVIEW RD
BLENHEIM RD
WOODSTOCK AVE
PARKLAND AVE
COURTLANDS AVE
35
LONDON RD
Green Dr
Langley Gram Sch
BROOM HO
KIMBERLEY CL
TOBERMORY CL
HAYNES CL
OAKVIEW GDNS
LANGLEY BROOM
FIELD HURST
RANDALL CL
Castleview Prim Sch
STANTON WAY
RADNOR WAY
BOUVERIE WAY
CEDAR WAY
MULBERRY DR
THE BRIARS
Sch
POPLAR HO
B470
SHERWOOD CT
Ditton Park
CONDUIT LA
DITTON PARK RD
PARSONS RD
36
OLIVIA DR
WALKER CRES
DITTON RD
ngmead Bridge
78
AUSTEN WAY
JAMES MDW
DEWAR SPUR
Ditton Farm
M4
RIDING CT
Riding Court Farm
Mast
SL3
Ditton Park
B470
RIDING COURT RD
MAJOR'S FARM RD
LONDON RD
FAIRFIELD AVE
FAIRFIELD CL
MONTROSE AVE
JUBILEE WAY
CORNERWAYS
LAWN CL
SATIS HO
LINK RD
MONTROSE WAY
DITTON RD
Cemy
CEDAR CT
THE LAWN
LINCHFIELD RD
30
1 FLEETBROOK HO
2 BROOKFIELD HO
NT VILLAS EST
rtland ns Ctr
PENN RD
NEW RD
The Queen Mother Reservoir
atchet
Recn Gd
TALBOT PL
HOLMLEA RD
HOLMLEA WLK
HORTON RD
The Rising Sun (PH)
ELMCROFT
MARSHFIELD
COBB CL
Datchet Common
MILL PL
MILL PLACE CVN PK
00
Pumping Station
B376

A308
Willows Path
B3383
B3024
Bishops Farmhouse
BISHOPS FARM CL
PH
Fair Acres Farm
A4
1 GUARDS WLK
2 CHARLTON PL
3 CHARLTON WLK
4 CHARLTON SQ
5 CHARLTON ROW
6 FURNESS SQ
7 FURNESS WLK
8 FURNESS PL
9 FURNESS ROW
10 KENNEALLY WLK
11 KENNEALLY CL
12 KENNEALLY PL
13 KENNEALLY ROW
14 LIDDELL SQ
LIDDELL PL 1
LIDDELL WAY 2
NICHOLLS WLK 3
LYELL PL E 4
LYELL WLK E 5
LYELL WLK W 6
LYELL PL W 7
WRIGHT WAY 8
WRIGHT SQ 9
Oakley Green
Ye Old Red Lion (PH)
Gale House Farm
Tarbay Farm
TARBAY LA
Alexander Fst Sch
SL4
Darkhole Bridge
St Leonard's Farm
St Leonard's
Legoland Windsor
Darkhole Ride
High Standinghill Woods
Forbe's Fields
ST LEONARD'S RD
Queen Adelaide's Ride
B3022
WINKFIELD
Forest Park
Clewer Green
P&R
Dedworth
Homer Fst Sch
Dedworth Mid Sch
Liby
Dedworth Green Fst Sch
Superstore
PO
FIVEWAYS
DEDWORTH RD
Fairacres Ind Est
CASTLE FARM CVN SITE
DEACON CT
43
TESTWOOD RD
CLIFTON RISE
LONGMEAD
REDFORD RD
FRYMLEY VIEW
ALDEN VIEW
WITHEY CL
GWYNNE CL
HYLLE CL
CAWCOTT DR
NEEDHAM CL
BURNETTS
SMITHS LA
TUDOR
ST GEORGE'S
MANSELL CL
MANOR RD
CHURCH TERR
SHEEPCOTE
ABBOT'S WLK
URBIS APARTMENTS
FUZZENS WLK
FOSTER AVE
BURTON WAY
LODGE WAY
PARK CNR
KEELER CL
CAMM AVE
LUFF CL
WASHINGTON DR
ILLINGWORTH
TURNOAK PK
ST LEONARD'S HILL
FAIRLAWN PK
DOWER PK
COOMBE HILL CT
SNOWDEN CL
WILTON CRES
HEMWOOD RD
BRYER PL
GILMAN CRES
FRANKLYN CRES
BENNING CL
STROUD CL
ROWLAND CL
DUNCANNON CRES
BASFORD WAY
TOZER WLK
LOVEJOY LA
BRUCE WLK
FILMER RD
TINKERS LA
LEIGH SQ
WINCH TERR
MERWIN WAY
WHITE HORSE RD
STIRLING CL
BURNHAM CL
DEAN CL
WYATT RD
PRIORS RD
POOLMANS RD
WOLF LA
MONKS RD
KEEPERS FARM CL
IRVING HO
LESLIE DUNNE HO
PINER COTTS
FOREST RD
ASH LA
SELWYN CL
HELEN COTTS
HOLLY CRES
BUTLERS CL
BLACK HORSE CL
ROSES LA
KNIGHTS CL
LOCKETS CL
GALLYS RD
MARBECK CL
ANDERMANS
PIERSON RD
KINGS FIELD
THE PARADE
HOMERS RD
MARTIN CL
RUDDLESWAY
COPPER BEECH CL
CH GR
NEWBERRY CRES
THE LIMES
BARRY VIEW
CHARLTON WAY
FURNESS WAY
CHARLTON
FURNESS
KENNEALLY
GUARDS RD
LIDDELL
NICHOLLS
LYELL RD
SIDNEY RD
WRIGHT
A
B
C
1
2
3
4
75
76
93
94

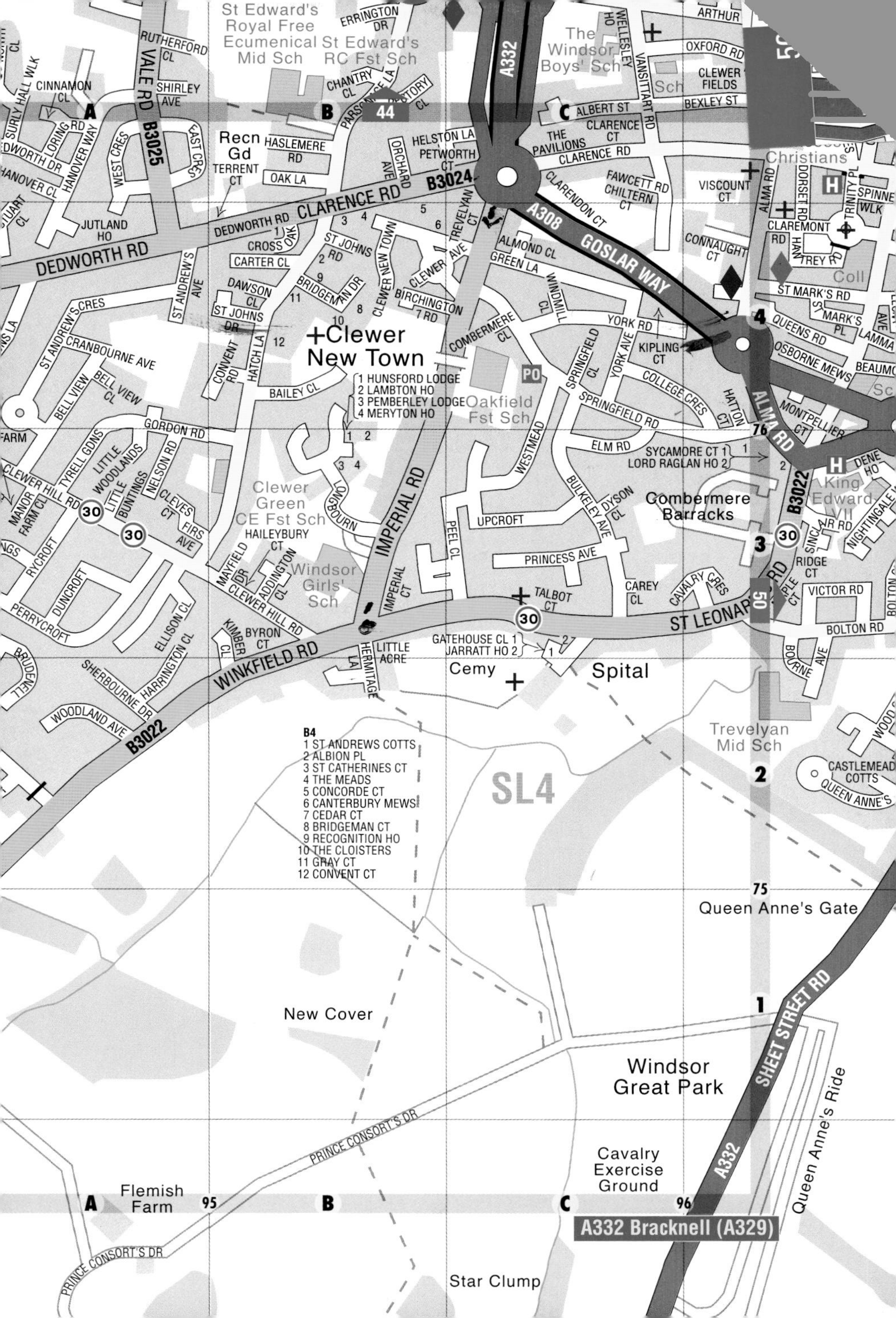

St Edward's Royal Free Ecumenical Mid Sch
St Edward's RC Fst Sch
The Windsor Boys' Sch
Recn Gd
Clewer New Town
Oakfield Fst Sch
Clewer Green CE Fst Sch
Windsor Girls' Sch
Combermere Barracks
King Edward VII
Cemy
Spital
Trevelyan Mid Sch
Christians
Coll
SL4
Queen Anne's Gate
New Cover
Windsor Great Park
Cavalry Exercise Ground
Flemish Farm
Star Clump
Queen Anne's Ride
A332 Bracknell (A329)
DEDWORTH RD
CLARENCE RD
GOSLAR WAY
WINKFIELD RD
IMPERIAL RD
ALMA RD
SHEET STREET RD
ST LEONARDS RD
PRINCE CONSORT'S DR
1 HUNSFORD LODGE
2 LAMBTON HO
3 PEMBERLEY LODGE
4 MERYTON HO
SYCAMORE CT 1
LORD RAGLAN HO 2
GATEHOUSE CL 1
JARRATT HO 2
B4
1 ST ANDREWS COTTS
2 ALBION PL
3 ST CATHERINES CT
4 THE MEADS
5 CONCORDE CT
6 CANTERBURY MEWS
7 CEDAR CT
8 BRIDGEMAN CT
9 RECOGNITION HO
10 THE CLOISTERS
11 GRAY CT
12 CONVENT CT
44
50

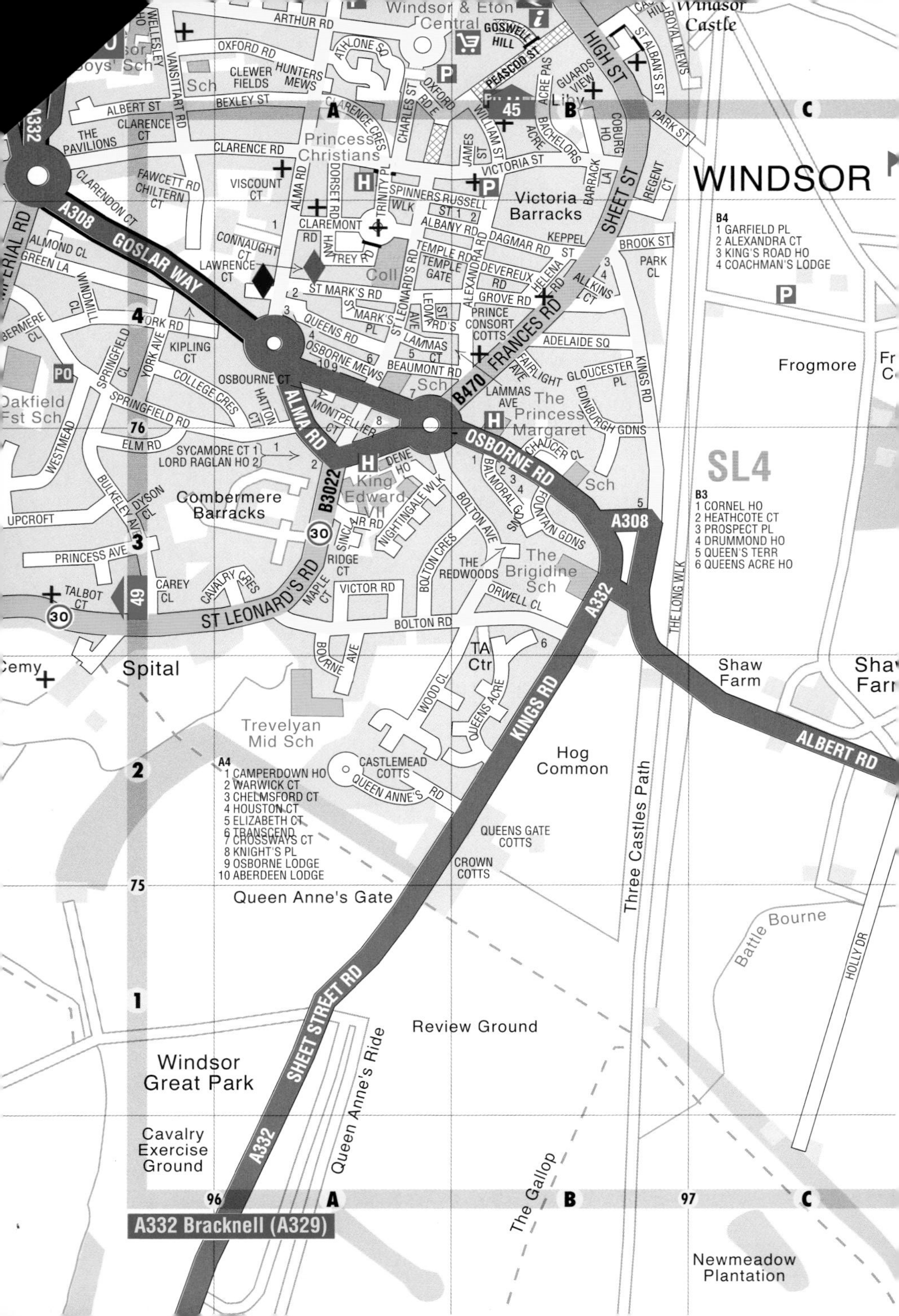

Windsor & Eton Central
Windsor Castle
ARTHUR RD
GOSWELL HILL
PEASCOD ST
HIGH ST
ST ALBAN'S ST
ROYAL MEWS
WELLESLEY
OXFORD RD
ATHLONE SQ
VANSITTART RD
CLEWER FIELDS
HUNTERS MEWS
Boys' Sch
Sch
ALBERT ST
BEXLEY ST
CLARENCE CT
CLARENCE CRES
CHARLES ST
OXFORD RD E
ACRE PAS
GUARDS VIEW
Liby
45
WILLIAM ST
BACHELORS ACRE
COBURG HO
PARK ST
A332
THE PAVILIONS
CLARENCE RD
Princess Christians
DORSET RD
JAMES ST
BARRACK LA
REGENT CT
WINDSOR
VICTORIA ST
FAWCETT RD
CHILTERN CT
VISCOUNT CT
ALMA RD
TRINITY PL
SPINNERS WLK
RUSSELL ST
Victoria Barracks
SHEET ST
CLARENDON CT
A308
GOSLAR WAY
IMPERIAL RD
ALMOND CL
GREEN LA
CONNAUGHT CT
CLAREMONT RD
HAWTREY RD
ALBANY RD
DAGMAR RD
KEPPEL ST
BROOK ST
PARK CL
B4
1 GARFIELD PL
2 ALEXANDRA CT
3 KING'S ROAD HO
4 COACHMAN'S LODGE
LAWRENCE CT
Coll
TEMPLE RD
TEMPLE GATE
DEVEREUX RD
HELENA RD
ALEXANDRA RD
ATKINS CT
WINDMILL CL
ST MARK'S RD
ST MARK'S PL
ST LEONARD'S AVE
LEONARD'S ST
GROVE RD
PRINCE CONSORT COTTS
FRANCES RD
ADELAIDE SQ
COMBERMERE CL
YORK RD
YORK AVE
SPRINGFIELD CL
QUEENS RD
OSBORNE RD
LAMMAS CT
KIPLING CT
OSBORNE MEWS
BEAUMONT RD
B470
FAIRLIGHT AVE
GLOUCESTER PL
KINGS RD
Frogmore
PO
COLLEGE CRES
OSBOURNE CT
HATTON CT
Sch
LAMMAS AVE
The Princess Margaret
Oakfield Fst Sch
SPRINGFIELD RD
ALMA RD
MONTPELLIER CT
EDINBURGH GDNS
76
WESTMEAD
ELM RD
SYCAMORE CT 1
LORD RAGLAN HO 2
DENE HO
CHAUCER CL
OSBORNE RD
SL4
BULKELEY AVE
DYSON CL
Combermere Barracks
King Edward VII
NIGHTINGALE WLK
BALMORAL GDNS
BOLTON AVE
FOUNTAIN GDNS
Sch
B3
1 CORNEL HO
2 HEATHCOTE CT
3 PROSPECT PL
4 DRUMMOND HO
5 QUEEN'S TERR
6 QUEENS ACRE HO
UPCROFT
B3022
SINCLAIR RD
A308
PRINCESS AVE
30
RIDGE CT
BOLTON CRES
THE REDWOODS
The Brigidine Sch
TALBOT CT
49
CAREY CL
CAVALRY CRES
MAPLE CT
VICTOR RD
ORWELL CL
A332
THE LONG WLK
ST LEONARD'S RD
BOLTON RD
Cemy
Spital
BOURNE AVE
TA Ctr
Shaw Farm
WOOD CL
QUEENS ACRE
KINGS RD
ALBERT RD
Trevelyan Mid Sch
Hog Common
A4
1 CAMPERDOWN HO
2 WARWICK CT
3 CHELMSFORD CT
4 HOUSTON CT
5 ELIZABETH CT
6 TRANSCEND
7 CROSSWAYS CT
8 KNIGHT'S PL
9 OSBORNE LODGE
10 ABERDEEN LODGE
CASTLEMEAD COTTS
QUEEN ANNE'S RD
QUEENS GATE COTTS
CROWN COTTS
Three Castles Path
75
Queen Anne's Gate
Battle Bourne
HOLLY DR
SHEET STREET RD
Review Ground
Queen Anne's Ride
Windsor Great Park
A332
Cavalry Exercise Ground
The Gallop
96
97
A
B
C
A332 Bracknell (A329)
Newmeadow Plantation

Datchet
Double Cottages
46
Adelaide Cottage
Home Park
Royal Mausoleum
Prince Consort's Home Farm
Windsor Hall
Royal Gardens
River Thames
Thames Path
Albert Bridge
Battle Bourne
Weir
Southlea Farm
SL3
Datchet
Recn Gd
Manor Farm
Moram Lodge
Dunboyne Pl
New Cut
Ham Bridge
SL4
1 Victoria Ho
2 The Tapestries
3 Tapestries Hall
4 Stanley Ho
5 Wheatsheaf Par
6 Croft Cnr
7 Shaw Ct
Liby
Clayhall Farm
Old Windsor Lock
The Manor
The Priory
White Hermitage
Tileplace Farm
Old Windsor
Recn Gd
Peter's Hill
St Peter's CE Mid Sch
52
B3021
A308
Datchet Rd
Southlea Rd
Straight Rd
Church Rd
St Luke's Rd
Ham La
Ham Island
Clayhall La
Queen Elizabeth's Wlk
Coronation Ave
Evergreen Oak Ave
Mulberry Ave
Prince Albert's Wlk
Queen Victoria's Wlk
Adelaide Rd
Frogmore Dr
Frogmore Flats
Montagu Rd
The Drive
Elmcroft
Saffron Cl
Beaulieu Cl
Marshfield
Holmlea Wlk
The Avenue
The Paddock
Datchet Pl
Green La
Manor Farm Cotts
Albany Rd
Tyle Pl
William Ellis Cl
Miller's La
Lyndwood Dr
Robin Willis Way
Queen's Cl
St Peter's Cl
Glebe Rd
The Avenue
Cell Farm Ave
Cell Farm
Meadow Cl
Meadow Way
Follett Cl
Pollard Cl
The Grange
Saxon Way
Ricardo Rd
Gregory Dr
Nursery Pl
Newton La
Kingsbury Dr
Cornwell Rd
Crimp Hill
St Andrew's Cl
The Friary
Friary Rd
Farm Dr
King John's Cl
A B C
1 2 3 4
75 76
98 99
40

A308
MANOR FARM COTTS
Liby
51
CLAYHALL LA
TYLE PL
ALBANY RD
A
B
C
B3021
POLLARD CL
THE GRANGE
Old Windsor Lock
The Manor
CHURCH RD
GLEBE RD
ST PETER'S CL
QUEEN'S CL
CELL FARM AVE
CELL FARM
WHITE HERMITAGE
The Priory
WILLIAM ELLIS CL
ST LUKE'S RD
STRAIGHT RD
THE AVENUE
MEADOW CL
LYNDWOOD DR
MILLER'S LA
Tileplace Farm
ROBIN WILLIS WAY
Recn Gd
MEADOW WAY
FOLLETT CL
ST ANDREW'S CL
1 LYNDWOOD PAR
2 RANDALL CT
3 HARTLEY COPSE
4 CROFTERS
5 NEWTONSIDE
40
RICARDO RD
SAXON WAY
GREGORY DR
CORNWELL RD
KINGSBURY DR
NURSERY PL
Peter's Hill
St Peter's CE Mid Sch
CRIMP HILL
BURFIELD RD
NEWTON CT
NEWTON LA
PO
THE FRIARY
FRIARY RD
NEWTON SIDE ORCH
FARM DR
ORCHARD RD
A308
74
KINGSBURY DR
WARRINGTON SPUR
SAGE CT
FRIARY ISLAND
GILSON CT
Cemy
King's Court Fst Sch
ASHBROOK RD
MILLS SPUR
MALT HOUSE CL
LIME TREE CT
AYLESWORTH SPUR
WALPOLE RD
THE MOORINGS
RIVERSIDE
HARWOOD GDNS
GROVE CL
GROVE HO
BEARS RAILS PK
Old Windsor
3
BRINKWORTH PL
KEPPEL SPUR
TUDOR LA
Woodside Farm
OUSELEY RD
THE EMBANKMENT
PELLING HILL
OUSELEY LODGE
The Dower House
SL4
2
Runnymede House
Woodside
Beaumont
73
South Lodge Farm
Wild Boar Enclosure
Beaumont Farm
PRIEST HILL
1
St John's Beaumont Sch
TW20
A328
Cookes Hill
OAK LA
98
99
RIDGEMEAD RD
A328 Englefield Green
Park Place
THE DELL
Bishopsgate Sch
BISHOPSGATE RD
RICHARDSON HO
The Fox & Hounds (PH)

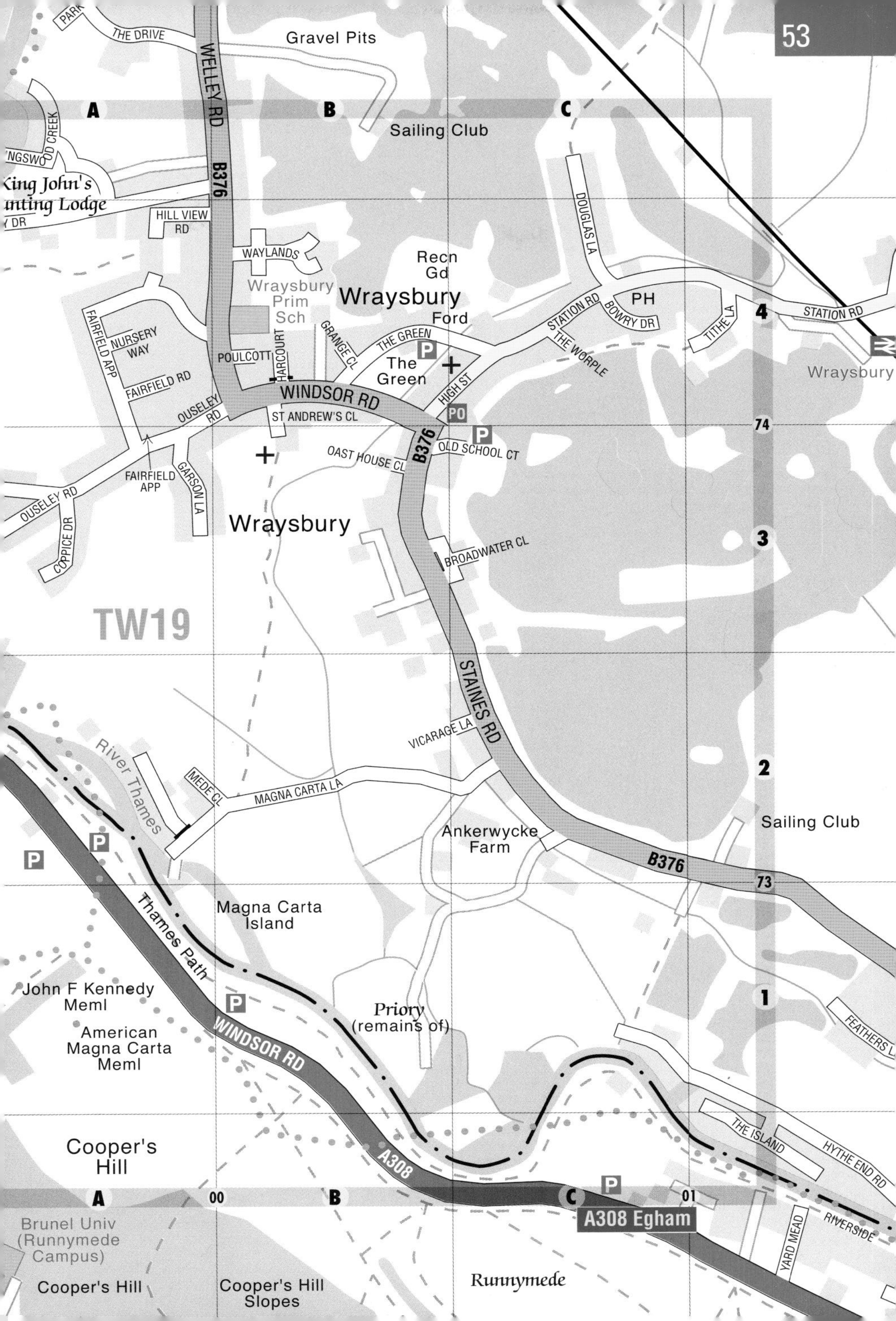
53
Gravel Pits
THE DRIVE
PARK
WELLEY RD
B376
A
B
C
Sailing Club
OD CREEK
NGSWO
King John's
unting Lodge
Y DR
HILL VIEW RD
WAYLANDS
DOUGLAS LA
Recn Gd
Wraysbury Prim Sch
Wraysbury
Ford
PH
STATION RD
BOWRY DR
TITHE LA
4
STATION RD
Wraysbury
FAIRFIELD APP
NURSERY WAY
GRANGE CL
THE GREEN
THE WORPLE
POULCOTT
HARCOURT
The Green
HIGH ST
FAIRFIELD RD
WINDSOR RD
PO
OUSELEY RD
ST ANDREW'S CL
74
B376
OLD SCHOOL CT
OAST HOUSE CL
FAIRFIELD APP
GARSON LA
OUSELEY RD
COPPICE DR
Wraysbury
3
BROADWATER CL
TW19
STAINES RD
VICARAGE LA
River Thames
MEDE CL
MAGNA CARTA LA
2
Sailing Club
Ankerwycke Farm
B376
73
Thames Path
Magna Carta Island
John F Kennedy Meml
1
Priory (remains of)
American Magna Carta Meml
WINDSOR RD
FEATHERS LA
THE ISLAND
HYTHE END RD
Cooper's Hill
A308
A
00
B
C
01
A308 Egham
RIVERSIDE
YARD MEAD
Brunel Univ (Runnymede Campus)
Cooper's Hill
Cooper's Hill Slopes
Runnymede

Index

Street names are listed alphabetically and show the locality, the Postcode district, the page number and a reference to the square in which the name falls on the map page

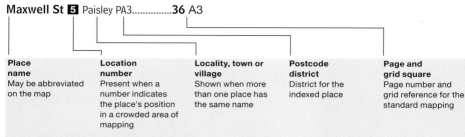

Maxwell St **5** Paisley PA3..............**36** A3

Place name	Location number	Locality, town or village	Postcode district	Page and grid square
May be abbreviated on the map	Present when a number indicates the place's position in a crowded area of mapping	Shown when more than one place has the same name	District for the indexed place	Page number and grid reference for the standard mapping

Towns and villages are listed in CAPITAL LETTERS
Public and commercial buildings are highlighted in magenta. **Places of interest** are highlighted in blue with a star★

Abbreviations used in the index

Acad	**Academy**	Ct	**Court**	Hts	**Heights**	Pl	**Place**
App	**Approach**	Ctr	**Centre**	Ind	**Industrial**	Prec	**Precinct**
Arc	**Arcade**	Ctry	**Country**	Inst	**Institute**	Prom	**Promenade**
Ave	**Avenue**	Cty	**County**	Int	**International**	Rd	**Road**
Bglw	**Bungalow**	Dr	**Drive**	Intc	**Interchange**	Recn	**Recreation**
Bldg	**Building**	Dro	**Drove**	Junc	**Junction**	Ret	**Retail**
Bsns, Bus	**Business**	Ed	**Education**	L	**Leisure**	Sh	**Shopping**
Bvd	**Boulevard**	Emb	**Embankment**	La	**Lane**	Sq	**Square**
Cath	**Cathedral**	Est	**Estate**	Liby	**Library**	St	**Street**
Cir	**Circus**	Ex	**Exhibition**	Mdw	**Meadow**	Sta	**Station**
Cl	**Close**	Gd	**Ground**	Meml	**Memorial**	Terr	**Terrace**
Cnr	**Corner**	Gdn	**Garden**	Mkt	**Market**	TH	**Town Hall**
Coll	**College**	Gn	**Green**	Mus	**Museum**	Univ	**University**
Com	**Community**	Gr	**Grove**	Orch	**Orchard**	Wk, Wlk	**Walk**
Comm	**Common**	H	**Hall**	Pal	**Palace**	Wr	**Water**
Cott	**Cottage**	Ho	**House**	Par	**Parade**	Yd	**Yard**
Cres	**Crescent**	Hospl	**Hospital**	Pas	**Passage**		
Cswy	**Causeway**	HQ	**Headquarters**	Pk	**Park**		

Index of towns, villages, streets, hospitals, industrial estates, railway stations, schools, shopping centres, universities and places of interest

Abb–Alt

A

Abbey Cl SL1 .....**21** C1
Abbey Gate SL6 ...**20** B2
Abbot's Wlk SL4 ..**48** C4
Abbotts Way SL1..**21** B1
Abell Gdns SL6 ...**16** C4
Aberdeen Ave
  SL1 ....**22** B1
Aberdeen Lodge **10**
  SL4 ....**50** A4
Abingdon Wlk SL6 .**7** C2
Acorn Cl SL3......**36** C1
Acre Pas SL4 .....**45** B1
Adam Cl SL1......**32** B4
Addington Cl SL4 .**49** B3

Addison Ct SL6 ...**18** C4
Adelaide Cl SL1 ...**32** B3
Adelaide Rd SL4 ..**46** A1
Adelaide Sq SL4 ..**50** B4
Adelphi Gdns SL1 .**33** C3
Adrians Wlk SL2 ..**34** A4
Agars Pl SL3......**46** B3
Ajax Ave SL1......**22** C1
Alan Way SL3 .....**25** C2
Albany Rd
  Old Windsor SL4 ..**51** B1
  Windsor SL4 ......**50** B4
Albert Cl SL1 **3** ..**32** A2
Albert Pl SL4 .....**44** B4
Albert Rd SL4......**50** C2
Albert St
  Maidenhead SL6 ...**18** A2
  Slough SL1.......**34** A2
  Windsor SL4 ......**44** C1
Albion Cl SL2 .....**34** B4

Albion Cotts SL6 ...**2** A2
Albion Pl **2** SL4 ..**49** B4
Aldborough Spur
  SL1 ....**23** C2
Aldbourne Rd
  SL1 ....**20** C3
Aldebury Rd SL6 ...**8** A1
Alden View SL4 ...**43** B1
Alderbury Rd SL3 .**36** A4
Alderbury Rd W
  SL3 ....**36** A4
Alder Cl SL1 ......**32** A4
Aldin Ave N SL1...**34** B3
Aldin Ave S SL1 ..**34** B3
Aldridge Rd SL2 ..**22** B4
Aldwick Dr SL6 ...**17** B1
Alexander Fst Sch
  SL4 ....**48** A3
Alexandra Ct **2**
  SL4 ....**50** B4

Alexandra Rd
  Maidenhead SL6 ...**17** B3
  Slough SL1.......**33** B2
  Windsor SL4 ......**50** B4
Alice La SL1 ......**20** C4
Allenby Rd SL6....**16** C2
Allerds Rd SL2 ....**12** B3
Alleyns La SL6 ....**2** B3
Allington Ct SL2 ..**24** A1
Allkins Ct SL4.....**50** B4
All Saints Ave SL6 **17** B2
All Saints CE Jun Sch
  SL6 ....**17** A1
All Souls Cotts
  SL3 ....**25** C3
Alma Ct
  Burnham SL1......**11** A1
  Eton SL4 ....**32** A1
Alma Rd
  Eton SL4 ....**32** A1

Alma Rd continued
  Windsor SL4 ......**50** A4
Almond Cl SL4....**49** C4
Almond Rd SL1 ...**11** A1
Almons Way SL2 ..**24** C3
Almshouses SL3 ..**35** C3
Almshouses The
  SL4 ....**45** B2
Alpha St N **6** SL1 .**34** B3
Alpha St S SL1 ....**34** A2
Alpine Cl SL6......**18** B1
Alston Gdns SL6 ..**17** C2
Altona Way SL1 ...**22** C2
Altwood Bailey
  SL6 ....**26** C4
Altwood CE Sec Sch
  SL6 ....**26** C4
Altwood Cl
  Maidenhead SL6 ...**26** C4
  Slough SL1.......**21** C3

Altwood Dr SL6 . . . 26 C4
Altwood Rd SL6 . . . 26 C4
Alvista Ave SL6 . . . 20 C2
Alwyn Inf Sch SL6 . . . 17 A3
Alwyn Rd SL6 . . . 16 C3
Alyson Ct 2 SL6 . . 18 A4
Amanda Ct SL3 . . . 35 B2
Amberley Ct SL6 . . . 9 A2
Amberley Pl 7 SL4 . . . 45 B1
Amberley Rd SL2 . . 21 C3
Amerden Cl SL6 . . 19 B2
Amerden La SL6 . . 19 B2
Amerden Priory Cvn Pk SL6 . . . 29 C3
Amerden Way SL1 . . . 32 B3
American Magna Carta Meml* TW20 . . . 53 A1
Anchor Ct SL6 . . . 3 A2
Andermans SL4 . . . 43 B1
Anne Cl SL6 . . . 7 C1
Ansculf Rd SL2 . . . 12 B1
Anslow Pl SL1 . . . 21 A3
Anthony Way SL1 . 21 B1
Anvil Ct 4 SL3 . . . 36 B2
Applecroft SL6 . . . 27 A2
Appletree La SL3 . . 35 A2
Approach Rd SL6 . 19 C2
Apsley Cotts SL6 . . . 2 C2
Apsley Ho SL1 . . . 34 B3
Aragon Ct SL6 . . . 27 C4
Arborfield Cl SL1 . 33 C2
Arbour Vale Sch SL2 . . . 12 C1
Archer Cl SL6 . . . 17 B3
Ardrossan Cl SL2 . . 23 A4
Argyll Ave SL1 . . . 22 B1
Arkley Ct SL6 . . . 41 A4
Arlington Cl SL6 . . 16 B3
Armstrong Ho SL2 . . . 25 A2
Arthur Rd
Slough SL1 . . . 33 B3
Windsor SL4 . . . 45 A1
Arundel Cl SL6 . . . 16 B3
Arundel Ct SL3 . . . 35 B1
Ascot Rd SL6 . . . 40 B3
Ashbourne Gr SL6 . . . 27 A2
Ashbourne Ho 5 SL1 . . . 33 C3
Ashbrook Rd SL4 . . 52 B3
Ash Cl SL3 . . . 36 C3
Ashcroft Ct SL1 . . . 10 C2
Ashcroft Rd SL6 . . . 17 A3
Ashdown SL6 . . . 8 C2
Ashenden Wlk SL2 . 4 C3
Ashford La SL4 . . . 30 C3
Ash Gr SL2 . . . 14 A4
Ashgrove Ct SL6 . . 17 A1
Ashington Ho SL6 17 C1
Ash La SL4 . . . 48 B4
Ashley Ct SL6 . . . 18 C2
Ashley Pk SL6 . . . 8 C1
Ashton Pl SL6 . . . 16 B1
Aspects Ct SL1 . . . 33 C3
Aspen Cl SL2 . . . 22 C3
Aston Mead SL4 . . 43 C1
Astonville SL2 . . . 4 B3
Astor Cl SL6 . . . 18 C1
Atherton Ct SL4 . . . 45 B2
Athlone Cl SL6 . . . 17 C4
Athlone Sq SL4 . . . 45 A1
Auckland Cl SL6 . . 18 C3
Audley Dr SL6 . . . 16 C1
August End SL3 . . . 25 C2
Austinsgate SL6 . . 16 A3
Australia Ave SL6 . 18 A3
Australia Rd SL1 . . 34 C3
Autumn Cl SL1 . . . 32 A4
Autumn Wlk SL6 . . 26 B4
Avebury SL1 . . . 22 B1
Avenue Rd SL6 . . . 28 C4
Avenue The
Datchet SL3 . . . 46 C1
Farnham Common SL2 . . . 4 A3
Maidenhead SL6 . . . 9 A2
Old Windsor SL4 . . . 51 C1
Averil Ct SL6 . . . 21 A2
Avon Cl SL1 . . . 21 C1
Avondale SL6 . . . 17 A4
Avonmoor SL6 . . . 18 C3
Axis Pk SL3 . . . 36 C1
Aylesbury Cres SL1 . . . 23 B2
Aylesworth Ave SL2 . . . 12 C1
Aylesworth Spur SL4 . . . 52 B3
Aysgarth Pk SL6 . . 40 C4
Azalea Way SL3 . . . 25 C2

B

Bachelors Acre SL4 . . . 45 B1
Bader Gdns SL1 . . . 32 B3
Badger Cl SL6 . . . 27 B3
Badgers Wood SL2 . 4 B2
Bad Godesberg Way SL6 . . . 18 A2
Badminton Rd SL6 . . . 16 C1
Bailey Cl
Maidenhead SL6 . . . 18 A2
Windsor SL4 . . . 49 B4
Baird Cl SL1 . . . 32 C3
Bakers La SL6 . . . 16 A3
Bakers Row SL6 . . . 16 A3
Baldwin Pl SL6 . . . 17 A2
Baldwin Rd SL1 . . . 11 A1
Baldwin's Shore SL4 . . . 45 B3
Ballard Gn SL4 . . . 43 C2
Balmoral SL6 . . . 16 C4
Balmoral Cl SL1 . . . 21 C2
Balmoral Gdns SL4 . . . 50 B3
Banbury Ave SL1 . . 22 A3
Banks Spur SL1 . . . 32 C3
Bannard Rd SL6 . . . 26 B4
Bannister Cl SL3 . . 35 C3
Barbicus Ct 1 SL6 . . . 18 C3
Barchester Rd SL3 . . . 36 A4
Bardney Cl SL6 . . . 27 B2
Bargeman Rd SL6 27 C4
Barley Mead SL6 . . 26 B4
Barn Cl
Farnham Common SL2 . . . 4 A3
Maidenhead SL6 . . . 8 A1
Barn Dr SL6 . . . 26 B3
Barnfield SL1 . . . 31 B4
Barnfield Cl SL6 . . . 8 A4
Barrack La SL4 . . . 45 B1
Barrow Lodge SL2 . . . 23 A4
Barr's Rd SL6 . . . 20 C2
Barry Ave SL4 . . . 45 A2
Barry View SL4 . . . 48 A4
Bartelotts Rd SL2 . 21 C4
Bartletts La SL6 . . . 40 B2
Barton Rd SL3 . . . 36 A4
Basford Way SL4 . . 48 B3
Bassett Way SL2 . . 21 C4
Bass Mead SL6 . . . 8 A4
Bates Cl SL3 . . . 25 C2
Bath Ct SL6 . . . 17 A1
Bath Rd
Maidenhead SL6 . . . 17 A1
Slough, Cippenham SL1, SL6 . . . 21 B1
Slough SL1, SL6 . . . 21 B1
Battlemead Cl SL6 . 9 A2
Baxter Cl SL1 . . . 33 C2
Baybrook SL6 . . . 3 A1
Bayley Cres SL1 . . . 20 B3
Baylis Bsns Ctr SL1 . . . 23 B1
Baylis Court Sch SL1, SL2 . . . 23 B3
Baylis Par SL1 . . . 23 C2
Baylis Rd SL1 . . . 23 C1
Bay Tree Ct SL1 . . . 11 A1
Beaconsfield Rd SL2 . . . 4 B1
Beauchamp Ct SL1 . . . 23 C1
Beaufort Pl SL6 . . . 29 B3
Beaulieu Cl SL3 . . . 51 C4
Beaumaris Ct SL1 23 A3
Beaumont Cl SL6 . 26 B2
Beaumont Ct SL3 . 25 B2
Beaumont Rd
Slough SL2 . . . 23 B3
Windsor SL4 . . . 50 A4
Beckett Chase 7 SL3 . . . 36 A1
Beckwell Rd SL1 . . 33 A3
Bedford Ave SL1 . . 22 B2
Bedford Cl SL6 . . . 26 B2
Bedford Dr SL2 . . . 4 A1
Beech Cl SL6 . . . 16 C3
Beech Ct SL1 . . . 11 A1
Beeches Dr SL2 . . . 4 A2
Beeches Rd SL2 . . . 4 A2
Beeches The SL2 . . 12 A1
Beechfield Pl SL6 27 A3
Beech Rd SL3 . . . 35 C3
Beechwood Dr SL6 . . . 16 B1
Beechwood Gdns SL1 . . . 33 C3
Beechwood Rd SL2 . . . 23 B3
Beechwood Sch SL2 . . . 12 C1
Belfast Ave SL1 . . . 23 B2
Belgrave Par SL1 . 23 C1
Belgrave Rd SL1 . . 24 A1
Bell Bsns Ctr SL6 . 18 A1
Bell Cl SL2 . . . 24 C3
Bell La SL4 . . . 32 A1
Bellsfield Ct SL4 . . 32 A1
Bells Hill SL2 . . . 14 B3
Bells Hill Gn SL2 . . 14 B4
Bell St SL6 . . . 18 A1
Bell View SL4 . . . 49 A4
Bell View Cl SL4 . . . 49 A4
Belmont SL2 . . . 22 B3
Belmont Cres SL6 17 B3
Belmont Dr SL6 . . . 17 B3
Belmont Park Ave SL6 . . . 17 B3
Belmont Park Rd SL6 . . . 17 B3
Belmont Rd SL6 . . . 17 B3
Belmont Vale SL6 . 17 B3
Belvedere Mans SL1 . . . 33 B3
Bembridge Ct 12 SL1 . . . 34 A3
Bennetts Cl SL1 . . . 32 B4
Benning Cl SL4 . . . 48 B3
Benson Cl SL2 . . . 34 B4
Bentley Ct SL6 . . . 27 B3
Bentley Pk SL2 . . . 11 B2
Bentley Rd SL1 . . . 32 B4
Beresford Ave SL2 . . . 25 A1
Berkeley Mews SL1 . . . 21 C2
Berkley Cl SL6 . . . 16 B3
Berkshire Ave SL1 . . . 22 C2
Berkshire Lodge 1 SL6 . . . 18 A1
Berners Cl SL1 . . . 21 C1
Berries Rd SL6 . . . 3 B3
Berryfield SL2 . . . 25 A2
Berry Hill SL6 . . . 19 B2
Berry Hill Ct SL6 . . 19 B3
Berwick Ave SL1 . . 22 C1
Bessemer Cl 3 SL3 . . . 36 A1
Bestobell Rd SL1 . . 23 A2
Bettoney Vere SL6 . . . 29 A3
Beverley Ct SL1 . . . 34 C3
Beverley Gdns SL6 . . . 16 C4
Bexley St SL4 . . . 45 A1
Biddles Cl SL1 . . . 31 C4
Bideford Spur SL2 . . . 12 C1
Bingham Rd SL1 . . 20 B3
Binghams The SL6 . . . 28 C2
Birch Gr
Slough SL2 . . . 22 C3
Windsor SL4 . . . 43 B1
Birchington Rd SL4 . . . 49 B4
Birdwood Rd SL6 . 16 C2
Birley Rd SL1 . . . 23 B2
Bisham Ct 11 SL1 . 34 A3
Bishop Ct SL6 . . . 17 B1
Bishop Ctr The SL6 . . . 20 A2
Bishops Farm Cl SL4 . . . 42 C1
Bishops Gate SL6 . 20 A2
Bishops Orch SL2 . 12 C1
Bishops Rd SL1 . . . 34 B3
Bissley Dr SL6 . . . 26 B2
Bix La SL6 . . . 16 A3
Blackamoor La SL6 . . . 18 B3
Black Butt Cotts SL6 . . . 3 C2
Black Horse Cl SL4 . . . 48 B4
Black Park Rd SL3 . . . 15 C3
Blackpond La SL2 12 C3
Blacksmith Row SL3 . . . 36 B2
Blackthorn Dell SL3 . . . 35 A2
Blair Rd SL1 . . . 33 C4
Blakeney Ct SL6 . . . 18 A4
Blandford Cl SL3 . . 35 B2
Blandford Ho SL6 . 17 A3
Blandford Rd N SL3 . . . 35 B2
Blandford Rd S SL3 . . . 35 B2
Blenheim Rd
Maidenhead SL6 . . . 16 C3
Slough SL3 . . . 35 B1
Blinco La SL3 . . . 25 C2
Block A SL2 . . . 24 C4
Block B SL2 . . . 24 C4
Block C SL2 . . . 24 C4
Block D SL2 . . . 24 C4
Block F SL2 . . . 25 A4
Bloomfield Rd SL6 . . . 26 B4
Blumfield Cres SL1 . . . 21 C3
Blumfield Ct SL1 . . 21 B4
Blunden Dr SL3 . . . 37 A2
Blythe Ho SL1 . . . 31 B4
Boadicea Cl SL1 . . 31 C4
Boarlands Cl SL1 . . 22 A1
Bodmin Ave SL2 . . 22 B3
Bold's Ct SL2 . . . 14 B4
Bolton Ave SL4 . . . 50 B3
Bolton Cres SL4 . . . 50 A3
Bolton Rd SL4 . . . 50 A3
Borderside SL2 . . . 24 B2
Boston Gr SL1 . . . 23 A2
Bosworth Ct SL1 . . 21 A1
Botham Dr SL1 . . . 33 C2
Bottom Waltons Cvn Site SL2 . . . 12 A2
Boulters Cl
Maidenhead SL6 . . . 19 A4
Slough SL1 . . . 32 B3
Boulters Ct SL6 . . . 19 A4
Boulters Gdns SL6 . . . 19 A4
Boulters La SL6 . . . 19 A4
Boundary Rd SL1, SL6 . . . 20 A3
Bourne Ave SL4 . . . 50 A2
Bourne Rd SL1 . . . 33 B3
Bouverie Way SL3 . . . 35 C1
BOVENEY . . . 43 A3
Boveney Cl SL1 . . . 32 B3
Boveney New Rd SL4 . . . 31 C1
Boveney Rd SL4 . . . 43 A4
Bower Ct SL1 . . . 22 A1
Bower Way SL1 . . . 21 C1
Bowes-Lyon Cl 6 SL4 . . . 45 A1
Bowmans Cl SL1 . . 10 C2
Bowry Dr TW19 . . . 53 C4
Bowyer Dr SL1 . . . 21 C1
Boyndon Rd SL6 . . 17 B2
Boyne Hill CE Inf Sch SL6 . . . 17 B1
BOYN HILL . . . 17 B1
Boyn Hill Ave SL6 . 17 B1
Boyn Hill Cl SL6 . . . 17 B1
Boyn Hill Rd SL6 . . 17 B1
Boyn Valley Ind Est SL6 . . . 17 C1
Boyn Valley Rd SL6 . . . 27 B4
Bracken Cl SL2 . . . 4 C3
Brackenforde SL3 35 A3
Bracken Rd SL6 . . . 27 A3

Bradcutts La SL6...2 C3
Bradford Rd SL1 ..22 B2
Bradley Rd SL1 ...23 C1
Bradshaw Cl SL4..43 C1
Braemar Gdns
SL1 ....32 B3
Bramber Ct SL1...32 B4
Bramble Dr SL6...26 B3
Brambles The
SL6 ....40 C3
Bramley Chase
SL6 ....27 A3
Bramley Cl SL6 ...27 A2
Brammas Cl SL1 ..33 A2
Brampton Ct SL6..18 C3
BRAY 29 B2
Braybank SL6.....29 B3
Bray Cl SL6.......29 A3
Bray Ct SL6.......29 A1
Brayfield Rd SL6..29 A3
Bray Rd SL6 ......28 C4
BRAY WICK 28 C2
Braywick Park &
Nature Ctr*
SL6 ....28 C2
Braywick Rd SL6..28 B3
Breadcroft Rd
SL6 ....26 A2
Brecon Ct SL1 ....33 A3
Bredward Cl SL1 ..10 C1
Breezes The SL6 ..27 C3
Briar Cl SL6.......20 C2
Briar Dene SL6 ...17 A4
Briar Glen SL6 ....2 C1
Briars The SL3 ....36 A1
Briar Way SL2 ....22 C3
Brickfield La SL1..10 C3
Bridge Ave
Cookham Rise SL6...2 C1
Maidenhead SL6 ...18 B2
Bridge Cl SL1.....22 A1
Bridge Ct
⑤ Maidenhead
SL6................18 B2
Taplow SL6 ....19 A2
Bridgeman Ct ⑧
SL4.............49 B4
Bridgeman Dr
SL4.............49 B4
Bridge Rd SL6 ....18 C2
Bridge St SL6.....18 B2
Bridge View SL6 ..19 A2
Bridgewater Ct
SL3................36 B2
Bridgewater Terr
SL4.............45 B1
Bridgewater Way
SL4.............45 B1
Bridle Cl SL1 .....17 C4
Bridle Rd SL6.....17 C4
Bridlington Spur
SL1 ....32 C3
Bridport Way SL2 .22 C4
Brighton Spur
SL2................22 C4
Brigidine Sch The
SL4.............50 B3
Brill Cl SL6 ....27 B2
Brill Ho SL6.......27 A2
Brinkworth Pl
SL4.............52 B3
Bristol Way SL1...23 B2
BRITWELL 22 A4
Britwell Rd SL1...11 B1

Broadleys SL4 ....44 A2
Broadmark Rd
SL2 ....24 C1
Broad Oak SL2....23 A4
Broad Oak Ct SL2 .23 A4
Broad Platts SL3 ..35 B2
Broadwater Cl
TW19............53 B3
Broadwater Pk
SL6 ....41 C4
Broadway SL6 ....18 A2
Broadway Mall ⑥
SL6 ....18 A2
Broadway The SL2 .4 B1
Brocas St SL4.....45 B2
Brocas Terr SL4...45 B2
Brock La SL6 .....18 A2
Brock Lane Mall ⑦
SL6 ....18 A2
Brockton Ct SL6 ..18 A1
Broken Furlong
SL4 ....44 C4
Brompton Dr SL6 ..7 A1
Bromycroft Rd
SL2 ....12 B1
Bronte Cl SL1.....33 C3
Brook Cres SL1 ...21 C2
Brookdene Cl SL6..8 A1
Brookfield Ho
SL3................47 B1
Brook Ho SL1.....33 B2
Brook Path SL1 ...22 A1
Brookside SL3 ....25 C2
Brook St SL4......50 B4
Broomfield Gate
SL2................22 C4
Broom Hill
Cookham Rise SL6...2 C1
Stoke Poges SL2 ...14 B4
Broom Ho SL3 ....36 A2
Brownfield Gdns
(Cvn Pk) SL6 .....27 C4
Browns Ct SL1 ...21 C1
Bruce Cl SL1......32 B4
Bruce Wlk SL4....48 B4
Brudenell SL4 ....49 A2
Brunel Cl SL6.....27 C4
Brunel Dr SL6.....27 B4
Brunel Rd SL6 ....27 B4
Brunel Way SL1...34 A4
Bryant Ave SL2...23 C3
Bryer Pl SL4......48 B3
Bryher The SL6 ...16 B2
Buccleuch Rd SL3 46 B2
Buckingham Ave
SL1 ....22 C2
Buckingham Ave E
SL1 ....23 A2
Buckingham Gdns ④
SL1 ....34 A3
Buckingham Ho ④
SL6 ....18 A1
Buckland Ave SL2 34 C2
Buckland Cres
SL4 ....44 A1
Buckland Gate
SL3................14 C1
Bucklebury Cl
SL6 ....41 A4
Buffins SL6 ....9 C1
Builder's Cross
SL6 ....14 C3
Bulkeley Ave SL4..49 C3
Bulstrode Pl SL1..34 A2
Bunby Rd SL2.....14 A4
Bunces Cl SL4 ....44 C4

Bunten Meade
SL1 ....32 C4
Burcot Gdns SL6...7 C2
Burfield Rd SL4...52 B3
Burford Gdns SL1 .21 A3
Burford Ho ⑭
SL4 ....45 B1
Burgett Rd SL1 ...32 C2
Burlington Ave
SL1 ....33 C3
Burlington Ct ①
SL1 ....33 C3
Burlington Rd
Burnham SL1......20 C4
② Slough SL1....33 C3
Burnetts Rd SL4 ..43 C1
BURNHAM.......11 A2
Burnham Cl SL4 ..48 B4
Burnham Ct SL6 ..18 A3
Burnham Gram Sch
SL1 ....21 B4
Burnham Hts SL1 .21 A2
Burnham La SL1 ..21 C2
Burnham Sta SL1 .21 B2
Burnham Upper Sch
SL1 ....20 C3
Burnt Oak SL6 ....3 A2
Burn Wlk SL1.....10 C1
Burroway Rd SL3..36 C3
Burton Way SL4...48 C3
Business Village The
SL2................34 C4
Butlers Cl SL4 ....43 B1
Buttermere Ave
SL1 ....21 A3
Bybend Cl SL2....12 C3
Byland Dr SL6 ....40 C4
Byron Ct SL4......49 B3
Byron Ho SL3.....36 C1
Byways SL1.......20 B3

C

Cadogan Cl SL6...40 B3
Cadwell Dr SL6 ...27 B2
Cages Wood Dr
SL2 ....4 A3
Cairngorm Pl SL2 .23 B4
Calbroke Rd SL2 ..12 A1
Calder Cl SL6 .....17 C4
Calder Ct
Maidenhead SL6 ...17 B4
① Slough SL3....36 A1
Caldicott Sch SL2 .12 C4
Callaway SL6 .....27 C4
Cambria Ct SL3 ...35 A3
Cambridge Ave
Burnham SL1......10 C2
Slough SL1.......22 B2
Cambridge Ho ①
SL4 ....45 A1
Camden Rd SL6...17 B4
Camfield Ct SL6...16 B3
Camley Gdns SL6 .16 B3
Camley Park Dr
SL6 ....16 A3
Camm Ave SL4....48 C3
Camperdown SL6 .18 C4
Camperdown Ho ①
SL4 ....50 A4
Canada Rd SL1....34 C3
Canal Wharf SL3 ..36 B4
Cannock Cl SL6 ...18 C1
Cannon Court Rd
SL6 ....7 B2
Cannondown Rd
SL6 ....7 C4

Cannon Gate SL2 .25 A1
Cannon Hill Cl
SL6 ....29 A1
Cannon La SL6....26 A2
Canon Hill Dr SL6 28 C2
Canon Hill Way
SL6 ....28 C2
Canterbury Ave
SL2 ....23 A4
Canterbury Mews ⑥
SL4 ....49 B4
Cardigan Cl SL1...22 A1
Cardinals Wlk
SL6 ....21 A2
Carey Cl SL4......49 C3
Carisbrooke Cl
SL6 ....17 A1
Carisbrooke Ct
SL1 ....24 A1
Carlisle Rd SL1 ...23 B1
Carlton Rd SL2....24 C1
Carmarthen Rd
SL1 ....23 C1
Carrington Rd
SL1 ....23 C1
Carter Cl SL4 .....49 B4
Castle Ave SL3 ...46 B3
Castle Cl SL6.....17 B2
Castle Dr SL6.....17 B2
Castle Farm Cvn Site
SL4 ....48 B4
Castle Hill
Maidenhead SL6 ...17 C2
Windsor SL4 .....45 B1
Castle Hill Terr
SL6 ....17 C2
Castle Lodge SL6 .18 A2
Castlemead Cotts
SL4 ....50 A2
Castle Mews SL6..17 C2
Castle St SL4......34 A2
Castleview Ho ①
SL4 ....45 B1
Castleview Prim Sch
SL3................35 B1
Castleview Rd
SL3................35 A1
Causeway The
SL6 ....29 A3
Cavalry Cres SL4..50 A3
Cavendish Cl SL6 .20 B2
Cawcott Dr SL4 ..43 C1
Cecil Way SL2 ....22 A4
Cedar Chase SL6..19 B4
Cedar Ct
Datchet SL3......47 A1
Maidenhead SL6 ...17 B2
⑦ Windsor SL4...49 B4
Cedar Dr SL6 .....3 B2
Cedar Ho SL6.....17 B4
Cedars Ho SL6....18 B2
Cedars Rd SL6....18 B2
Cedars The SL2 ...12 A1
Cedar Way SL3...35 C1
Cell Farm SL4.....51 C1
Cell Farm Ave
SL4 ....51 C1
Central Dr SL1....22 A1
Central Est SL6 ...17 C3
Centre The SL2 ...4 B1
Centrika SL1......33 C4
Chalcott SL1......33 C2
Chalgrove Cl SL6..18 C1
Chalk Hill SL4.....46 A1
Chalk Pit La SL1...10 C3
Challow Ct SL6 ...17 B4
CHALVEY 33 A2

Chalvey Gdns SL1 33 C3
Chalvey Gr SL1....32 C3
Chalvey Pk SL1 ...33 C3
Chalvey Rd E SL1..33 C3
Chalvey Rd W SL1 33 B3
Chancerygate Bsns
Ctr SL3 ....35 C3
Chandlers Quay
SL6 ....19 A3
Chandos Mall ⑧
SL1 ....34 A3
Chantry Cl SL4....44 B1
Chantry Pl SL4....45 B2
Chapel Arches ④
SL6 ....18 B2
Chapel Cotts SL2..14 C4
Chapel Ct SL6....27 B2
Chapel Hill SL4 ...45 B1
Chapel La SL2 ....14 C4
Chapels Cl SL1....35 C1
Chapel St SL1.....34 A3
Chaplin Mews ⑩
SL3 ....36 A1
Chapter Mews
SL4 ....45 B2
Chariott's Pl ㉑
SL4 ....45 B1
Charlcot Mews
SL1 ....21 C1
Charles Gdns SL2 24 B2
Charles Ho ⑧
SL4 ....45 A1
Charles St SL4....45 A1
Charlotte Ave SL2 24 A1
Charlotte Lodge
SL6 ....18 C3
Charlton SL4......48 A4
Charlton Cl SL1...32 C3
Charlton Pl ②
SL4 ....48 A4
Charlton Row ⑤
SL4 ....48 A4
Charlton Sq ④
SL4 ....48 A4
Charlton Way SL4 48 A4
Charlton Wlk ③
SL4 ....48 A4
Charter Cl SL1....34 A4
Charter Rd SL1 ...21 C1
Chase The SL6....7 A2
Chatfield SL1.....22 B3
Chatham Ct ③
SL1 ....34 B2
Chatsworth Cl
SL6 ....27 A4
Chaucer Cl SL4...50 B3
Chaucer Way SL1 34 A4
Chauntry Cl SL6...19 A1
Chauntry Rd SL6..18 C1
Chelmsford Ct ③
SL4 ....50 A4
Cheniston Gr SL6 .16 A2
Chequers Bridge
Cotts SL0 ....37 A4
Cherington Gate
SL6 ....16 C4
Cherries The SL2..24 C2
Cherry Ave SL3 ...35 B3
Cherry Orch SL2 ..14 B4
Cherry Tree Rd
SL2 ....13 A4
Cherwell Cl SL6...18 B3
Cheshire Rd SL1...34 C3
Chester Rd SL1...23 B2
Chestnut Ave SL3 .23 B2
Chestnut Cl SL6...18 C4
Chestnut Dr SL4 ..49 A2

Chestnut Pk SL6 . . 29 C2
Cheveley Gdns
SL1 . . . . 11 A2
Cheviot Cl SL6 . . . . 18 C1
Cheviot Rd SL3 . . 36 B1
Chichester Ct SL1 34 C3
Chiltern Court Mews
SL4 . . . . 44 C1
Chiltern Ct SL4 . . . 44 C1
Chiltern Rd
Burnham SL1. . . . . . 20 C3
Maidenhead SL6 . . . 18 C1
Chilton Ct SL6 . . . . 21 A2
Chilwick Rd SL2 . . 22 A4
Choke La SL6 . . . . . . 6 C3
Christian Smith Ho
SL6 . . . . 38 B4
Christian Sq 3
SL4 . . . . 45 A1
Christmas La SL2 . . 4 B4
Christopher Ho
SL2 . . . . 4 B2
Church Cl
Eton SL4 . . . . 45 B3
Maidenhead SL6 . . . 18 C1
Church Cotts SL6 . . 9 C1
Church Dr SL6 . . . . 29 A3
Churchfield Mews
SL2 . . . . 24 C2
Church Gr SL3 . . . . 25 A3
Churchill Rd SL3 . . 36 A2
Church La
Bray SL6 . . . . 29 A3
Slough SL2, SL3. . . . 25 A3
Stoke Poges SL2 . . . 14 A1
11 Windsor SL4. . . . 45 B1
Churchmead CE Sch
SL3 . . . . 46 C2
Church Path SL6 . . 29 A3
Church Rd
Farnham Royal
SL2. . . . . 13 A1
Maidenhead SL6 . . . 28 C4
Old Windsor SL4 . . . 51 C1
Church St
Burnham SL1. . . . . . 21 A4
Slough SL1. . . . . . . 33 B3
Slough, Upton Park
SL1. . . . . 34 A3
9 Windsor SL4. . . . 45 B1
Church Terr SL4 . . 48 C4
Church View 8
SL1 . . . . 34 B2
Church Views
SL6 . . . . 18 A3
Cinnamon Cl SL4. . 44 A1
CIPPENHAM 32 A3
Cippenham Cl
SL1 . . . . 22 A1
Cippenham Inf Sch
SL1 . . . . 21 B1
Cippenham Jun Sch
SL1 . . . . 21 C1
Cippenham La
SL1 . . . . 32 C4
Claires Court Sch
(Senior Boys)
SL6 . . . . 18 C4
Claires Court Schs-
The College & Sixth
Form SL6 . . . . 17 C2
Clappers Mdw
SL6 . . . . 19 A4
Clare Dr SL2 . . . . . . 4 A3
Clarefield Cl SL6 . 16 C4
Clarefield Dr SL6. 16 B4
Clarefield Rd SL6 . 16 C4

Claremont Rd
SL4 . . . . 50 A4
Clarence Cres
SL4 . . . . 45 A1
Clarence Ct
Maidenhead SL6 . . . 17 C3
Windsor SL4 . . . . . . 44 C1
Clarence Rd SL4 . . 44 C1
Clarendon Copse
SL6 . . . . 17 B1
Clarendon Ct
Slough SL2. . . . . . . 24 C1
Windsor SL4 . . . . . . 44 C1
Clare Rd
Maidenhead SL6 . . . 17 B1
Slough SL6. . . . . . . 21 A2
Claycots Sch SL2. 12 B1
CLAYHALL FARM . 50 C1
Clayhall La SL4 . . . 51 A1
Clayton Ct SL3 . . . . 36 B3
Cleares Pasture
SL1 . . . . 10 C1
Clements Cl SL1 . . 34 C3
Clevehurst Cl SL2. . 5 C1
Cleveland Cl SL6. 18 C1
Cleves Ct SL4 . . . . . 49 A3
Clewer Ave SL4 . . . 49 B4
Clewer Court Rd
SL4 . . . . 44 C2
Clewer Fields SL4 45 A1
CLEWER GREEN . . 48 C2
Clewer Green CE Fst
Sch SL4 . . . . 49 B3
Clewer Hill Rd
SL4 . . . . 49 A3
CLEWER NEW
TOWN 49 B4
Clewer New Town
SL4 . . . . 49 B4
Clewer Pk SL4 . . . . 44 B2
CLEWER
VILLAGE 44 B2
Clifton Cl SL6 . . . . . 28 B3
Clifton Lodge
Eton SL4 . . . . 44 B4
8 Slough SL1. . . . . 34 B3
Clifton Rd SL1 . . . . 34 C3
Clifton Rise SL4. . 43 B1
Clive Ct SL1 . . . . . . 33 B3
Cliveden Mead SL6 9 A1
Cliveden Rd SL6 . . 9 C3
Clivemont Rd SL6 18 A3
Cloisters The
Eton SL4 . . . . 45 B2
Slough SL1. . . . . . . 33 B3
10 Windsor SL4. . . 49 B4
Clonmel Way SL1 .10 C1
Close The SL1. . . . . 21 B1
Coachman's Lodge 4
SL4 . . . . 50 B4
Coalmans Way SL1,
SL6 . . . . 20 B3
Cobb Cl SL3 . . . . . . 47 B1
Cobblers Ct SL2. . 12 C2
Cobham Cl SL1 . . . 32 A4
Coburg Ho SL4 . . . 45 B1
Cockett Rd SL3 . . 35 C2
Coe Spur SL1 . . . . 32 C2
Coftards SL2. . . . . 25 A2
Colby Gdns SL6 . . 18 A3
Cold Grove Cotts
SL6 . . . . 9 C1
Colenorton Cres
SL4 . . . . 31 C1
Colinswood SL2. . . 4 A4
Colin Way SL1 . . . . 32 C2

College Ave
Maidenhead SL6 . . . 17 C2
Slough SL1. . . . . . . 33 C2
College Cres SL4. . 49 C4
College Glen SL6 . 17 B2
College Rd
Maidenhead SL6 . . . 17 C2
Slough SL1. . . . . . . 32 A4
College Rise SL6 . . 17 B2
Colley Hill La SL2 . . 5 B4
Collier Cl SL6 . . . . . 18 A4
Collinswood Rd
SL2 . . . . 4 B3
Collum Green Rd
Fulmer SL2 . . . . 5 C3
Stoke Poges SL2 . . . . 5 A4
Coln Cl SL6 . . . . . . 18 A3
Colonial Rd SL1. . 34 B3
Colonnade 1 SL6 18 B2
Combermere Cl
SL4 . . . . 49 C4
Common La SL4 . . 45 B4
Common Rd
Dorney SL4 . . . . 31 B1
Eton SL4 . . . . 32 B1
Slough SL3. . . . . . . 36 B1
Common Wood
SL2 . . . . 4 B3
Compton Ct SL1 . . 21 C2
Compton Dr SL6 . 16 B3
Concorde Ct 5
SL4 . . . . 49 B4
Concorde Rd SL6 . 27 B3
Concorde Way
SL1 . . . . 33 A3
Conduit La SL3 . . 47 C4
Conegar Ct SL1 . . 33 C4
Conifers The SL6. 16 B3
Coningsby Cl SL6 . 27 B2
Coningsby La SL6 41 A1
Coniston Cres
SL1 . . . . 21 A3
Conkers SL6 . . . . . 18 C3
Connaught Cl SL6 17 C4
Connaught Ct
SL4 . . . . 50 A4
Connaught Rd
SL1 . . . . 34 C3
Convent Ct 12
SL4 . . . . 49 B4
Convent Rd SL4 . . 49 B4
Conway Rd SL6 . . 20 C2
COOKHAM 3 C2
Cookham Dean
Bottom SL6. . . . . . . 2 A3
Cookham Lodge 15
SL6 . . . . 18 A1
Cookham Montessori
Sch SL6 . . . . 3 A2
Cookham Rd SL6. 18 A4
COOKHAM RISE . . 2 C1
Cookham Rise Prim
Sch SL6 . . . . 2 C1
Cookham Sta SL6 . 3 A2
Coombe Hill Ct
SL4 . . . . 48 B3
Cooper Way SL1 . 32 C2
Cope Ct SL6 . . . . . 17 A2
Copper Beech Cl
SL4 . . . . 43 B1
Copperfield Ho 15
SL4 . . . . 45 B1
Copperfield Terr
SL2 . . . . 24 C1
Coppice Dr TW19 .53 C4
Copse Ct SL1 . . . . 32 A4
Copthall Ho SL6 . 18 B2

Copthorn Cl SL6 . . 26 B3
Cordwallis Est 1
SL6 . . . . 18 A3
Cordwallis Pk
SL6 . . . . 17 C3
Cordwallis Rd
SL6 . . . . 18 A3
Cordwallis St SL6 .17 C3
Corfe Gdns SL1 . . 22 B1
Corfe Pl SL6 . . . . . 17 A2
Cornel Ho 1 SL4 . 50 B3
Cornerways SL3 . . 47 A2
Cornwall Ave SL2 .23 A4
Cornwall Cl
Eton SL4 . . . . 43 C4
Maidenhead SL6 . . . 7 C1
Cornwall Lodge 11
SL6 . . . . 18 A1
Cornwell Rd SL4 . . 52 A4
Coronation Ave
Slough SL3. . . . . . . 25 C2
Windsor SL4 . . . . . . 51 A4
Cotswold Cl
Maidenhead SL6 . . . 18 C1
Slough SL1. . . . . . . 32 C2
Coulson Way SL1 . 20 C2
Country Life Ho
SL3 . . . . 46 C2
Court Cl SL6 . . . . . 29 A1
Court Cres SL1. . . . 23 B2
Court Dr SL6. . . . . . 9 A2
Court Farm Cl
SL1 . . . . 32 C4
Courtfield Dr SL6 .17 A1
Courthouse Jun Sch
SL6 . . . . 16 C3
Courthouse Rd
SL6 . . . . 17 A3
Court La
Burnham SL1. . . . . . 11 B1
Dorney SL4 . . . . 30 C2
Courtlands 14
SL6 . . . . 18 A1
Courtlands Ave
SL3 . . . . 35 B1
Court Rd SL6 . . . . . 9 A2
Coverdale Way
SL2 . . . . 21 C4
Cowper Rd SL2 . . 22 B4
Coxborrow Cl SL6. . 2 C2
COX GREEN 27 A2
Cox Green La SL6 .27 A2
Cox Green Rd SL6 27 B2
Cox Green Sch
SL6 . . . . 26 B3
Cranbourne Ave
SL1 . . . . 49 A4
Cranbourne Cl
SL1 . . . . 33 A4
Cranbourne Rd
SL1 . . . . 33 A4
Cranbrook Dr SL6 17 A4
Craufurd Ct SL6. . 17 C3
Craufurd Rise
SL6 . . . . 17 C3
Crawshays SL6 . . . 19 A3
Crayle St SL2 . . . . 12 C1
Creden Cl SL6 . . . . 17 B4
Crescent Dale
SL6 . . . . 18 A1
Crescent Dr SL6 . 17 C2
Crescent The
Maidenhead SL6 . . . 17 C2
Slough SL1. . . . . . . 33 C3
Crescent Villas 4
SL4 . . . . 45 A1
Cress Rd SL1 . . . . 32 C3

Che – Dav 57

Cresswells Mead
SL6 . . . . 41 A4
Crimp Hill SL4,
TW20. . . . . 52 A1
Crispin Way SL2 . . 4 C3
Croft Cnr SL4 . . . . 51 B1
Crofters SL4. . . . . . 52 A4
Crofthill Rd SL2. . 22 C4
Croft The SL6 . . . . 27 A4
Cromer Ct SL1 . . . 23 C2
Cromwell Dr SL1. 23 C3
Cromwell Rd SL6 . 17 B2
Cross Oak SL4 . . . 49 B4
Crossways Ct 7
SL4 . . . . 50 A4
Crosthwaite Way
SL1 . . . . 21 B3
Crown Cotts SL4 . 50 B2
Crown La
Farnham Royal
SL2. . . . . 12 B3
Maidenhead SL6 . . . 18 B2
Crow Piece La
SL2 . . . . 12 A3
Croxley Rise SL6 . 17 B1
Crummock Cl SL1 21 A2
Cuba Cotts SL6 . . 8 C2
Culham Dr SL6. . . . 7 C1
Cullen's Pass 18
SL6 . . . . 18 A1
Culley Way SL6 . . 26 B3
Cumberland Ave
SL2 . . . . 23 A4
Cumbrae Cl SL2. . 34 B4
Cumbria Cl SL6 . . 27 A3
Curls La SL6 . . . . . 27 C3
Curls Rd SL6. . . . . 27 B3
Curzon Mall 7
SL1 . . . . 34 A3
Cygnet Ho SL6 . . . 19 A4
Cypress Ho SL3 . . 36 C1

D

Dagmar Rd SL4 . . 50 B4
Dair House Sch
SL2 . . . . 13 A3
Dairy Ct SL6 . . . . . 40 B2
Dalby Gdns SL6 . . 18 A4
Dale Ct SL1 . . . . . . 33 A3
Dalton Gn 14 SL3. 36 A1
Damson Gr SL1 . . 33 A3
Dandridge Cl SL3 . 35 B1
Danes Ct SL6 . . . . 17 B2
Danes Gdns SL6 . . 3 A1
Darrell Cl SL3. . . . 36 A2
Dartmouth Ct 2
SL1 . . . . 34 A2
Darvill's La SL1 . . 33 B3
Darwin Rd SL3. . . 36 A4
Dashwood Cl SL3 . 35 A1
DATCHET 47 A1
DATCHET
COMMON 47 B1
Datchet Pl SL3. . . 46 C1
Datchet Rd
Old Windsor SL4 . . . 51 B2
Slough SL3. . . . . . . 34 A1
Windsor SL4 . . . . . . 45 B2
Datchet St Mary's CE
Prim Sch SL3 . . . . 46 C1
Datchet Sta SL3 . . 46 C1
Davidson Rd 8
SL3 . . . . 36 A1

Dawes East Rd
SL1 ....11 A1
Dawes Moor Cl
SL2 ....25 A2
Dawson Cl SL4....49 B4
Deacon Ct SL4....48 B4
Deal Ave SL1 ....22 A2
Dean Cl SL4 ......48 B3
Dean La SL6......2 A3
Deans Cl SL2 .....14 C3
Deansfield Cl SL6 ..7 B1
Dean View SL6......2 C1
Decies Way SL2...14 B3
DEDWORTH......43 C1
Dedworth Dr SL4 .44 A1
Dedworth Green Fst
Sch SL4 ....48 C4
Dedworth Manor
SL4 ....44 A1
Dedworth Mid Sch
SL4 ....43 C1
Dedworth Rd SL4 .48 B4
Deena Cl SL1 .....21 C1
Deep Field SL3 ...46 C2
Deerswood SL6...18 C4
Dell Cl SL2 ....4 B2
Dell The SL6.....26 A1
Delta Cl SL6......18 A1
Dene Ho SL4......50 A3
Denham Cl SL6 ...17 A1
Denholme Lodge
SL3 ....46 C2
Denmark St SL6 ..17 C3
Dennis Way SL1...21 B1
Denny Rd SL3.....36 A2
Derek Rd SL6.....19 A3
Derwent Dr
Burnham SL1......21 A3
Maidenhead SL6 ...17 B3
Desborough Cotts
SL6 ....19 C4
Desborough Cres
SL6 ....27 A4
Desborough Sch
SL6 ....27 C4
Deseronto Wharf Ind
Est SL3 ....35 C3
Devereux Rd SL4..50 B4
Deverills Way
SL3 ....37 A2
Devon Ave SL1...23 A2
Devonshire Cl
SL2 ....12 C2
Devonshire Gn
SL2 ....12 C2
Devonshire Lodge [10]
SL6 ....18 A1
Dhoon Rise SL6...18 A1
Diamond Rd SL1 ..34 C3
Diana Cl SL3......25 C2
Ditton Park Cvn Site
[2] SL3.........36 A1
Ditton Park Rd
SL3 ....47 C3
Ditton Rd SL3.....47 B2
Doddsfield Rd
SL2 ....12 B1
Dolphin Ct SL1...34 C3
Dolphin Rd SL1 ..34 C3
Donnington Gdns
SL6 ....18 A4
Dorchester Cl
SL6 ....16 C4
Dornels SL2......25 A2

DORNEY........31 A2
Dorney Court*
SL4 ....30 C2
DORNEY REACH..30 A2
Dorney Reach Rd
SL6 ....30 A2
Dorney Sch SL6...30 A2
Dorset Lodge [9]
SL6 ....18 A1
Dorset Rd SL4 ...45 A1
Douglas La TW19..53 C4
Douglas Rd SL2...23 B3
Dove House Cres
SL2 ....11 C1
Dover Rd SL1 .....22 A2
Dower Pk SL4 ....48 C2
Downing Path
SL2 ....21 C4
Down Pl SL4.....42 B3
Downs Rd SL3 ...35 B3
Drake Ave SL3 ...35 B1
Drew Mdw SL2.....4 B3
Drive The
Datchet SL3......46 C1
Slough SL3.......35 C3
Dropmore Rd SL1 11 A4
Drummond Ho [4]
SL4 ....50 B3
Duchess St SL1 ...31 C4
Dudley Ct SL1....34 B2
Duffield La SL2 ....5 B1
Duffield Pk SL2 ..14 B1
Dukes Pl SL1 .....24 A1
Duke St SL4 .....45 A2
Dunbar Cl SL2 ....24 A1
Dunboyne Pl SL4..51 B2
Duncannon Cres
SL4 ....48 B3
Duncansby Ho
SL1 ....34 B3
Duncroft SL4.....49 A3
Dundee Rd SL1 ..22 B3
Dunholme End
SL6 ....27 B2
Dunster Gdns SL1 22 B1
Dunwood Ct SL6 .27 A4
Dupre Cl SL1 ....31 C3
Durham Ave SL1 ..22 B2
Duvall Ct SL1 ....34 B2
Dyson Cl SL4 ....49 C3

E
Earlsfield SL6.....29 A1
Earls La SL1 ......32 A4
East Berkshire Coll
Slough SL3.......36 B3
Windsor SL4.....50 A4
Eastbourne Rd
SL1 ....22 B2
Eastbridge SL2 ...34 C4
EAST BURNHAM .12 B3
East Burnham Cotts
SL2 ....12 B3
East Burnham La
SL2 ....12 B3
East Cres SL4.....44 A1
Eastcroft SL2 ....22 C4
East Dr SL1.......13 C1
Eastfield Cl [4]
SL1 ....34 B2
Eastfield Rd SL1 .20 B3
East Rd SL6......17 C2
East Terr SL4.....45 C1
Ebsworth Cl SL6 ..9 A2
Eden Cl SL3 .....36 B1

Edinburgh Ave
SL1 ....22 C2
Edinburgh Gdns
SL4 ....50 B4
Edinburgh Ho
SL1 ....34 A3
Edinburgh Rd SL6..7 C1
Edith Rd SL6......16 B2
Edmunds Way
SL2 ....24 C2
Edwards Ct SL1 ..33 C3
Egerton Rd SL2 ..21 C4
Egremont Gdns
SL1 ....32 B4
EGYPT 4 A3
Egypt La
Farnham Common
SL2.............4 A3
Hedgerley SL2......4 A4
Egypt Wood Cotts
SL2............4 A4
Eight Acres SL1 ..20 B4
Elderfield Rd SL2 ..5 B1
Elizabeth Cl SL6 ...3 A2
Elizabeth Ct
[1] Slough SL1....34 B3
[5] Windsor SL4...50 A4
Elizabeth Way
SL2 ....14 A3
Ellesmere Cl SL3..46 B3
Elliman Ave SL2...24 A1
Ellington Ct SL6 ..19 A2
Ellington Gdns
SL6 ....19 A2
Ellington Pk SL6 .17 C4
Ellington Prim Sch
SL6 ....18 A4
Ellington Rd SL6 .19 A2
Ellis Ave SL1.....33 C3
Ellison Cl SL4.....4 A3
Ellison Ho [22] SL4 .45 B1
Elmar Gn SL2.....12 B1
Elm Cl SL2........4 B1
Elm Cotts SL6.....40 B3
Elm Croft SL3.....47 A1
Elm Gr SL6......17 C2
Elmhurst Ct SL3 .36 B3
Elmhurst Rd SL3 .36 B3
Elm Rd SL4......49 C3
Elmshott La SL1 .21 C1
Elmslie Ct [4] SL6..17 C2
Elmwood SL6......8 C3
Elmwood Rd SL2.24 C1
Eltham Ave SL1 ..31 C3
Elton Dr SL6......17 B3
Ely Ave SL1......23 A3
Embankment The
TW19...........52 C2
Ember Rd SL3 ...36 C3
Emerald Ct SL1 ..33 C3
Emilia Cl SL6 ....18 A4
Emlyn Bldgs SL4 .45 B2
Endfield Pl SL6 ...16 B1
Ennerdale Cres
SL1 ....21 A3
Erica Cl SL1 .....21 C1
Errington Dr SL4..44 B1
Eskdale Gdns SL6 28 C1
Essex Ave SL2 ...23 A3
ETON...........45 A3
Eton Cl SL3......46 B3
Eton Coll SL4.....45 A3
Eton Coll Mus*
SL4 ....45 A3
Eton Ct SL4.....45 A3
Eton End PNEU Sch
SL3 ....46 B3

Eton Porny CE Fst
Sch SL4 ....45 B3
Eton Rd SL3 .....46 B3
Eton Riverside
SL4 ....45 B2
Eton Sq SL4 .....45 B2
ETON WICK......43 C4
Eton Wick CE Fst Sch
SL4 ....44 B4
Eton Wick Rd SL4.44 C4
Eton Wlk [1] SL1 ..33 C2
Evenlode SL6.....18 B3
Everard Ave SL1 .33 C3
Evergreen Oak Ave
SL4 ....51 B3
Eyre Gn SL2 .....12 B1

F
Fairacre SL6......17 A1
Fairacres Ind Est
SL4 ....48 B4
Faircroft SL2 .....22 C4
Fairfield App
TW19...........53 A4
Fairfield Ave SL3..47 B2
Fairfield Cl SL3 ..47 B2
Fairfield La SL2...12 C2
Fairfield Rd
Burnham SL1......11 A1
Wraysbury TW19...53 A4
Fairford Rd SL6 ..18 A3
Fairlawn Pk SL4 ..48 C2
Fairlea SL6.......26 C2
Fairlie Rd SL1 ....22 B3
Fairlight Ave SL4..50 B4
Fair View Cotts
SL6 ....2 C2
Fairview Rd
Burnham SL6......20 B2
Slough SL2.......22 A4
Fairway SL6......27 C4
Fairway The
Burnham SL1......11 A2
Maidenhead SL6 ..26 C2
Falkland Ho SL6 .18 A3
Fallows The SL6..18 B4
Falmouth Rd SL1..22 B2
Fane Way SL6....27 B4
Faraday Cl SL2....22 C3
Faraday Rd SL2 ..22 C3
Farm Cl
Holyport SL6......41 A4
Maidenhead SL6 ..16 B2
Farm Cres SL2....25 A3
Farm Dr SL4.....52 B4
Farmers Cl SL6 ..26 B3
Farmers Way SL6 .26 B3
Farm Rd
Burnham SL6......20 B1
Maidenhead SL6 ..16 B2
Farm Yd SL4.....45 B2
Farnburn Ave SL1 22 C3
FARNHAM
COMMON........4 C1
Farnham Common
Inf Sch SL2.......4 A3
Farnham Common
Jun Sch SL2 ......4 A3
Farnham La SL2 ..11 C1
FARNHAM PARK .13 A3
Farnham Park La
SL2 ....13 A3
Farnham Rd SL1,
SL2 ....23 A2
FARNHAM
ROYAL..........13 A2

Farthingales The
SL6 ....18 C2
Farthing Green La
SL2 ....14 C3
Fawcett Rd SL4...44 C1
Fawley Cl SL6.....7 B1
Fellstead Ct SL6 ..17 A1
Ferndale Pk Cvn Pk
SL6 ....41 C3
Fern Dr SL6......20 C2
Fernley Ct SL6....17 B4
Ferrers Cl SL1 ...31 C4
Ferry End SL6.....29 A3
Ferry La
Bourne End SL8....3 C4
Cookham SL6......3 C2
Ferry Rd SL6......29 A3
Fetty Pl SL6 .....27 B3
Field Hurst SL3 ..36 A1
Fielding Gdns
SL3 ....35 A3
Fielding Rd SL6...16 C3
Fieldings The SL6 .40 B2
Fields The SL1 ...33 B3
Fieldview Ct SL1 ..23 A3
FIFIELD..........41 B1
Fifield Rd SL6....41 B2
Fifield Way Cotts
SL6 ....41 B1
Filey Spur SL1...32 C3
Filmer Rd SL4 ...48 B4
Finch Cl SL6.....27 B4
Fircroft Cl SL2 ....5 C1
Fircroft Ct SL2....5 C1
Firfield SL6.......40 C4
Firs Ave SL4.....49 A3
Firs La SL6......26 A3
First Cres SL1....23 A3
Firs The [1] SL6...17 C2
Fir Tree Ave SL2...24 A4
FISHERY.........18 C1
Fishery Rd SL6...29 A4
Fishguard Spur
SL1 ....34 C3
Fiveways SL4 ....48 C4
Flamborough Spur
SL1 ....32 B3
Fleetbrook Ho
SL3 ....47 B1
Fleetwood Rd
SL2 ....24 A1
Fleming Ct SL3 ..35 A2
Florence Ave SL6 .18 B3
Foliejohn Way
SL6 ....38 A4
Folkestone Ct
SL3 ....36 B1
Follett Cl SL4 ....52 B4
Fontwell Cl SL6...16 B3
Forest Gn SL6....40 B1
Forest Rd SL4....48 C4
Forest View Cotts
SL6 ....41 A1
Forge Dr SL2......8 B1
Forlease Cl SL6...18 B1
Forlease Dr SL6...18 B1
Forlease Rd SL6 .18 B1
Formby Cl SL3....37 A2
Forsythia Gdns
SL3 ....35 C2
Foster Ave SL4...48 C3
Fosters Path SL2..22 A4
Fotherby Ct SL6...18 B1
Fotheringay Gdns
SL1 ....22 B1
Foundation Pk
SL6 ....26 A3

Foundry Ct SL2 . . .34 A4
Fountain Gdns
SL4 . . . . .50 B3
Foxborough Cl
SL3 . . . . .36 B1
Foxborough Ct
SL6 . . . . .27 C3
Foxborough Prim
Sch SL3 . . . . .36 B1
Foxherne SL3 . . . . .35 A3
Foxhollow Dr SL2 . . 4 B2
Fox Rd SL3 . . . . . . .35 B1
Frances Ave SL6 . .19 A4
Frances Rd SL4 . . .50 B4
Francis Way SL1 . .21 B1
Franklin Ave SL2 . .22 C3
Franklyn Cres
SL4 . . . . .48 B3
Frank Sutton Way
SL1 . . . . .23 B1
Frantons The SL6 .16 B2
Frascati Way SL6. .18 A2
Fraunchies Ct
SL1 . . . . .23 C1
Freemans Cl SL2. . 5 C1
Frenchum Gdns
SL1 . . . . .21 C1
Frensham Wlk SL2 . 4 B2
Friary Island
TW19 . . . . .52 C3
Friary Rd TW19 . .52 C4
Friary The SL4 . . . .52 C4
Frithe The SL2 . . . .24 C2
Frogmore Cl SL1. . 32 B3
Frogmore Ct 11
SL6 . . . . .18 A2
Frogmore Dr SL4 .51 A4
Frogmore Flats
SL4 . . . . .51 A4
Frymley View SL4 .43 B2
Fullbrook Cl SL6 . .18 B3
Fullers Yd SL6 . . . . .8 C1
Furness SL4 . . . . . .48 A4
Furness Pl 8 SL4 .48 A4
Furness Row 9
SL4 . . . . .48 A4
Furness Sq 6
SL4 . . . . .48 A4
Furness Way SL4. .48 A4
Furness Wlk 7
SL4 . . . . .48 A4
Furnival Ave SL2 . .22 C3
Furrow Way SL6 . .26 B3
Furzen Cl SL2. . . .12 B1
FURZE PLATT 7 B1
Furze Platt Bus Ctr
Pk SL6. . . . . .7 B1
Furze Platt Halt
SL6 . . . . .17 C4
Furze Platt Inf Sch
SL6 . . . . .17 A4
Furze Platt Jun Sch
SL6 . . . . .17 A4
Furze Platt Rd
SL6 . . . . .16 C4
Furze Platt Senior
Sch SL6 . . . . 7 A1
Furze Rd SL6 . . . . .17 B4
Fuzzens Wlk SL4 . .48 C4

G

Gables Cl
Datchet SL3. . . . . . .46 B3
Maidenhead SL6 . .18 C3
Gage Cl SL6 . . . . . .27 C3
Gainsborough SL6 . 8 A4

Gainsborough Dr
SL6 . . . . .27 B2
Galahad Cl SL1 . . 32 B3
Galloway Chase
SL2 . . . . .24 B1
Gallys Rd SL4 . . . .43 B1
Galvin Rd SL1. . . .23 A1
Garden Cl SL6 . . . .26 B4
Garden Mews
SL1 . . . . .34 A4
Garden Mews The
SL6 . . . . .16 C2
Gardner Ho SL6. . .17 C4
Gardner Rd SL6. . . .7 B1
Garfield Pl 1 SL4 50 B4
Garnet Cl SL1. . . . .32 B3
Garrard Rd SL2 . . .22 A4
Garretts La SL6 . . . 8 A1
Garson La TW19. . .53 A3
Garthlands SL6 . . . .7 B1
Gascon's Gr SL2 . .22 B4
Gas La SL6 . . . . . .28 C2
Gatehouse Cl SL4 .49 C3
Gatewick Cl SL1 . .33 A4
Gatward Ave SL6. .26 B2
Gaveston Rd SL2. .12 A1
Gays La SL6 . . . . .40 C3
GEORGE GREEN. .25 C2
George Green Rd
SL3 . . . . .25 C2
George V Pl SL4. . .45 B2
Gerrards Cross Rd
SL2 . . . . .5 C2
Gervaise Cl SL1 . . .32 A4
Gibraltar La SL6 . . . 2 A4
Gibson Ct 15 SL3. .36 A1
Gilbert Way 6
SL3 . . . . .36 A1
Gilliat Rd SL1. . . . .23 C1
Gillott Ct SL6 . . . . .18 A3
Gilman Cres SL4 . .48 B3
Gilmore Cl SL3. . . .35 A3
Gilson Ct SL4 . . . .52 C3
Gladstone Ind Est
SL6 . . . . .17 C3
Gladstone Way
SL1 . . . . .32 B4
Glanmor Rd SL2 . .24 C1
Glebe Cl SL6. . . . . .30 A3
Glebe Rd
Maidenhead SL6 . .28 C4
Old Windsor SL4 . . .51 C1
Glenavon Gdns
SL3 . . . . .35 A2
Glenfields SL2 . . . .14 A3
Glenore SL6 . . . . . . 3 B3
Glen The SL3 . . . . .35 A1
Glentworth Pl
SL1 . . . . .33 A4
Gloucester Ave
SL1 . . . . .23 A3
Gloucester Pl SL4 50 B4
Gloucester Rd SL6 . 7 C1
Glynwood Ho 3
SL6 . . . . .18 B2
Godolphin Inf Sch
SL1 . . . . .23 A2
Godolphin Jun Sch
SL1 . . . . .23 A2
Godolphin Rd SL1 23 B1
Golden Ball La SL6 . 6 B2
Golden Oak Cl SL2 . 4 B1
Goldsworthy Way
SL1 . . . . .21 A2
Goodman Pk SL2. .35 A4
Goodwin Rd SL2 . .21 A1

Goodwin Villas
SL1 . . . . .32 A4
Goose Gn SL2. . . .12 C2
Gordon Rd
Maidenhead SL6 . . .17 B2
Windsor SL4 . . . . . .49 A4
Gore Rd SL1 . . . . .10 C1
Gore The SL1 . . . . .10 B1
Gorse Meade SL1 .32 C4
Gorse Rd SL6 . . . . . 2 C1
Goslar Way SL4 . .49 C4
Gosling Gn SL3 . . .35 C2
Gosling Rd SL3 . . .35 C2
Goswell Hill SL4 . .45 B1
Goswell Rd SL4 . . .45 B1
Gowings Gn SL1 . .31 C3
Grace Ct SL1 . . . . .33 A4
Grafton Cl
Maidenhead SL6 . . . 7 C1
Slough SL3. . . . . . . .25 C2
Graham Cl SL6. . . .27 A4
Graham Rd SL6 . . . 2 C1
Grampian Way
SL3 . . . . .36 B1
Grange Cl TW19. . .53 B4
Grange Gdns SL2 . . 4 C2
Grange La SL6 . . . . 3 A3
Grange Rd SL6. . . . 3 A2
Grange The SL4 . . .51 C1
Grangewood SL3 .25 A3
Grant Ave SL1 . . . .23 C2
Granville Ave SL2 .23 B3
Grasholm Way
SL3 . . . . .37 A2
Grasmere SL4 . . . .43 C2
Grasmere Ave
SL2 . . . . .24 B1
Grasmere Par
SL2 . . . . .24 C1
Grassy La SL6 . . . .17 C2
Gratton Dr SL4. . . .48 C2
Gray Ct 11 SL4 . . .49 B4
Gray's Mon* SL2 .14 A1
Grays Park Rd
SL2 . . . . .14 B1
Grays Pl SL2. . . . . .34 A4
Grays Rd SL1 . . . . .34 A4
Great Hill Cres
SL6 . . . . .17 A1
Greenacre SL4 . . .48 C4
Green Cl
Burnham SL6. . . . . .20 B2
Maidenhead SL6 . . .18 A4
Greendale Mews
SL2 . . . . .24 B1
Greenfern Ave
SL1 . . . . .21 A2
Greenfields SL6. . .28 B4
Green La
Burnham SL1. . . . . .11 B3
Datchet SL3. . . . . . .46 C1
Farnham Common
SL2. . . . . .4 A1
Fifield SL6. . . . . . . .41 A1
Maidenhead SL6 . . .18 B1
Windsor SL4 . . . . . .49 C4
Greenlands Ct 2
SL6 . . . . .16 C3
Green Lane Ct
SL1 . . . . .11 A1
Greenleaf Ct SL3. .46 B3
Green Leys SL6 . . .18 B1
Greenock Rd SL1 .22 B2
Greenside SL2 . . . .22 B3
Green The
Burnham SL1. . . . . .20 C4
Datchet SL3. . . . . . .46 C2

Green The continued
Slough SL1. . . . . . . .33 B2
Wraysbury TW19. . .53 B4
Greenway SL1 . . . .10 C2
Greenways Dr
SL6 . . . . .16 B3
Greenway The
SL1 . . . . .31 B4
Gregory Dr SL4 . . .52 B4
Grenfell Ave SL6. .18 A1
Grenfell Pl SL6. . . .18 A1
Grenfell Rd SL6. . .17 C1
Grenville Cl SL1. . .10 C2
Gresham Rd SL1 . .22 B2
Greystoke Rd SL2 .22 A3
Griffin Cl
Maidenhead SL6 . . .27 C4
Slough SL1. . . . . . . .33 A3
Gringer Hill SL6. . .17 C3
Grosvenor Ct SL1 .23 C2
Grosvenor Dr SL6 .19 A3
Grove Cl
Old Windsor SL4 . . .52 B3
2 Slough SL1. . . . .34 B2
Grove Ct SL6. . . . . .17 B2
Grove House SL4. .52 C3
Grove Rd
Burnham SL1. . . . . .11 C3
Maidenhead SL6 . . .18 A2
Windsor SL4 . . . . . .50 B4
Groves Way SL6. . . 2 C1
Grove The SL1 . . . .34 B3
Guards Club Rd
SL6 . . . . .19 A2
Guards Rd SL4 . . .48 A4
Guards View SL4 . .45 B1
Guards Wlk 1
SL4 . . . . .48 A4
Gulliver's SL4. . . . .45 B3
Gwendale SL6 . . . .17 A4
Gwent Cl SL6 . . . .26 C3
Gwynne Cl SL4. . . .43 C1
Gypsy La
Stoke Poges SL2 . . . 5 A3
Stoke Poges SL2 . . . 5 A4

H

Haddon Rd SL6 . . .27 A4
Hadlow Ct SL1 . . . .33 A4
Hag Hill La SL6 . . .20 B2
Hag Hill Rise SL6. .20 B2
Haig Dr SL1 . . . . . .32 C3
Haileybury Ct SL4 49 B3
Hailey Ct SL6 . . . . .28 A4
Hale SL4 . . . . .44 A1
Halfway Hos SL6 . . 7 C3
Halifax Cl SL6. . . . .16 B3
Halifax Rd SL6 . . . .16 C3
Halifax Way SL6. . .16 B3
Halkingcroft SL3. .35 A3
Hall Ct SL3 . . . . . . .46 C2
Halldore Hill SL6. . 2 C2
Hallmark Ho SL1. .11 A1
Hall Mdw SL1 . . . .11 A2
Hambleden Wlk
SL6 . . . . .7 C1
Hamfield Cotts
SL6 . . . . .2 C2
Hamilton Gdns
SL1 . . . . .10 C1
Hamilton Ho SL6 .16 B1
Hamilton Rd SL1 . .22 B2
Hamilton Way SL2 . 4 B2
Hammond End SL2 4 A3
Hampden Ct SL1 . .14 B1

Hampden Rd
Maidenhead SL6 . . .16 C3
Slough SL3. . . . . . . .36 A3
Hampshire Ave
SL1 . . . . .23 A3
Hampshire Lodge 8
SL6 . . . . .18 A1
Hanbury Cl SL1 . . .20 B3
Hanley Cl SL4. . . . .43 B1
Hanover Cl
Slough SL1. . . . . . . .34 B2
Windsor SL4 . . . . . .44 A1
Hanover Gate SL1 32 B4
Hanover Mead
SL6 . . . . .29 A2
Hanover Way SL4 .44 A1
Harborough Cl
SL1 . . . . .31 B4
Harcourt TW19. . . .53 B4
Harcourt Cl SL6. . .30 A2
Harcourt Rd
Dorney SL6. . . . . . .30 A2
Windsor SL4 . . . . . .44 A1
Hardwick Cl SL6 . .16 B3
Hardy Cl SL1. . . . . .32 B4
Harefield Rd SL6. .16 B2
Hare Shoots SL6. .27 C4
Harewood Pl SL1 .34 B2
Hargrave Rd SL6. .17 B3
Harkness Rd SL1. .20 C3
Harley Ct SL1 . . . .33 A3
Harmer Mews
SL6 . . . . .18 C2
Harrington Cl SL4 49 A2
Harris Gdns SL1 . .33 A3
Harrison Way SL1 .31 B4
Harrogate Ct SL3 .36 B1
Harrow Cl SL6 . . . .17 C4
Harrow La SL6 . . . .17 C4
Harrow Mkt SL3. .36 A3
Harrow Rd SL3. . . .36 A3
Hartland Cl SL1. . .33 B4
Hartley Cl SL3 . . . .15 A3
Hartley Copse
SL4 . . . . .52 A4
Harvest Hill Rd
SL6 . . . . .28 A2
Harvey Ho SL3 . . .25 C2
Harvey Rd SL3 . . . .36 C4
Harwich Rd SL1. . .22 B2
Harwood Gdns
SL4 . . . . .52 B3
Haslemere Rd
SL4 . . . . .44 B1
Hasting Cl SL6 . . . .29 A1
Hastings Mdw
SL2 . . . . .14 B3
Hatchgate Gdns
SL1 . . . . .21 B4
Hatch La SL4 . . . . .49 B4
Hatch Pl SL6. . . . . . 2 C2
Hatch The SL4 . . . .43 A2
Hatfield Cl SL6. . . .17 A1
Hatfield Rd SL1 . . .34 B3
Hatton Ave SL2 . . .23 B4
Hatton Ct SL4 . . . .50 A4
Havelock Bsns Pk
SL6 . . . . .17 A2
Havelock Cres
SL6 . . . . .16 C2
Havelock Rd SL6. .16 C2
Haven Of Rest
SL6 . . . . .18 C2
Hawker Ct SL3. . . .36 B3

Hawkes Cl SL3 . . . .36 C3
Hawkshill Rd SL2 .12 B1
Hawthorne Cres
SL1 . . . . .24 A2
Hawthorn Gdns
SL6 . . . . .27 C4
Hawthorn La SL2. .12 B4
Hawtrey Cl SL1 . . .34 C3
Hawtrey Rd SL4 . . .50 A4
Haydon Ct SL6 . . . .17 C1
Haymill Rd SL1,
SL2 . . . . .21 B4
Haynes Cl SL3 . . . .36 A1
Hayse Hill SL4 . . . .43 B1
Haywards Mead
SL4 . . . . .44 A4
Hazelhurst Rd
SL1 . . . . .11 B2
Hazell Cl SL6 . . . . .18 A3
Hazell Way SL2 . . . .5 B1
Hazelwood Ct SL6. .9 A1
Hazlemere Rd
SL2 . . . . .34 C4
Headington Cl
SL6 . . . . .16 B2
Headington Rd
SL6 . . . . .16 B2
Hearne Dr SL6 . . . .40 B4
Heathcote SL6. . . . .28 C1
Heathcote Ct **2**
SL4 . . . . .50 B3
Heatherside Gdns
SL2 . . . . .4 C1
Heathlands Dr
SL6 . . . . .16 B1
Hedingham Mews
SL6 . . . . .17 B2
Hedsor View Cotts
SL6 . . . . .3 A2
Helena Rd SL4 . . . .50 B4
Helen Cotts SL4. . .48 B4
Helston La SL4. . . .44 C1
Hemming Way
SL2 . . . . .12 C1
Hempson Ave
SL3 . . . . .35 A2
Hemsdale SL6 . . . .16 C4
Hemwood Rd SL4 .48 B3
Hencroft Mews **14**
SL1 . . . . .34 A3
Hencroft St N
SL1 . . . . .34 A3
Hencroft St S SL1 .34 A2
Hendons Way SL6 40 C4
Henley Lodge **12**
SL6 . . . . .18 A1
Henley Rd SL1 . . . .22 A2
Henry III Twr **4**
SL4 . . . . .45 B1
Henry Rd SL1 . . . . .33 B3
Hermitage Ct SL3 .35 A2
Hermitage La SL4 49 B3
Heron Dr SL3 . . . .36 C2
Herons Pl SL6 . . . . .9 A2
Herschel Gram Sch
SL1 . . . . .23 A2
Herschel St SL1. . .34 A3
Hetherington Cl
SL2 . . . . .12 A1
Hever Cl SL6. . . . . .17 A1
Heynes Gn SL6. . . .26 C2
Heywood Ave SL6 38 B4
Heywood Court Cl
SL6 . . . . .26 B1

Heywood Farm Barns
SL6 . . . . .38 C4
Heywood Gdns
SL6 . . . . .38 B4
Hibbert Rd SL6 . . .28 C3
Hibbert's Alley **20**
SL4 . . . . .45 B1
Highfield Ct SL2 . .12 C3
Highfield La SL6 . .26 B3
Highfield Rd
Maidenhead SL6 . . .16 C3
Windsor SL4 . . . . . .49 A3
Highfields Sch
SL6 . . . . .17 C2
Highgrove Pk SL6 17 C3
Highlands The SL2 . 4 B2
High Mdws SL6 . . . .9 A2
High Rd SL6 . . . . . . .2 C1
High St Mall **1**
SL6 . . . . .18 A2
High St
Bray SL6 . . . . .29 A3
Burnham SL1. . . . . .11 A1
Chalvey SL1. . . . . . .33 B2
Cookham SL6. . . . . . .3 C2
Datchet SL3. . . . . . .46 C1
Eton SL4 . . . . .45 B3
Maidenhead SL6 . .18 A2
Slough, Langley
SL3. . . . . .36 B2
Slough, Upton SL1. .34 A3
Taplow SL6 . . . . . .19 C4
Windsor SL4 . . . . .45 A1
Wraysbury TW19. . .53 C4
High Town Rd
SL6 . . . . .18 A2
HIGHWAY 16 C2
Highway Ave SL6. .16 B2
Highway Rd SL6 . .16 C1
Hilgrove Ho SL6 . .17 B4
Hillary Rd SL3 . . . .35 C3
Hillcrest Ave SL6. . .2 C1
Hillersdon SL2 . . . .24 C4
Hill Farm Rd SL6 . . .9 C1
Hill Ho SL6 . . . . . . .19 B4
Hillmead Ct SL6. . .20 A3
Hill Pl SL2 . . . . . . .12 C4
Hillside
Maidenhead SL6 . .27 B4
Slough SL1. . . . . . .33 C3
Hills La SL6. . . . . . . .2 B2
Hilltop Fst Sch
SL4 . . . . .48 C3
Hill View Rd
TW19. . . . . .53 A4
Hilperton Rd **3**
SL1 . . . . .33 C3
Hindhay La SL6 . . . .7 A2
Hinksey Cl SL3 . . . .36 C3
Hinton Rd SL1 . . . .21 C1
Hitcham Grange
SL6 . . . . .19 C4
Hitcham Ho SL1 . .20 B4
Hitcham La SL1,
SL6 . . . . .10 A1
Hitcham Rd SL1,
SL6 . . . . .20 B3
Hobbis Dr SL6 . . . .16 B1
Hockley La SL2 . . .14 C4
Hogarth Cl SL1 . . .21 C1
Hogfair La SL1. . . .21 A4
Hollybush Hill
SL2 . . . . .14 C4
Holly Cl SL2 . . . . . . .4 B3
Holly Cres SL4 . . . .48 B4
Holly Ct SL1 . . . . . .21 C1

Holly Dr
Maidenhead SL6 . . .18 A3
Windsor SL4 . . . . . .50 C1
Holmanleaze SL6 .18 B3
Holmedale SL2 . . .25 A1
Holmlea Rd SL3. . .47 B1
Holmlea Wlk SL3. .47 A1
Holmwood Cl SL6 26 C4
Holy Family RC Prim
Sch SL3 . . . . .36 A1
Holyhead Mews
SL1 . . . . .21 B2
HOLYPORT. 40 B2
Holyport CE Prim
Sch SL6 . . . . .40 C3
Holyport Manor Sch
SL6 . . . . .39 C1
Holyport Rd SL6 . .40 C4
Holyport St SL6. . .40 B3
Holy Trinity CE Prim
Sch SL3 . . . . .3 C2
Home Farm Way
SL3 . . . . .15 A3
Home Mdw SL2. . .13 A2
Homer Fst Sch
SL4 . . . . .43 B1
Homers Rd SL4 . . .43 B1
Homeside Cl SL6. . .7 C1
Homestead Rd
SL6 . . . . .27 B3
Homewood SL3. . .25 B2
Hornbeam Gdns **7**
SL1 . . . . .34 B2
Horseguards Dr
SL6 . . . . .18 C2
Horsemoor Cl
SL3 . . . . .36 B2
Horseshoe Cloisters
2 SL4 . . . . .45 B1
Horsham Reach
SL6 . . . . .9 A1
Horton Cl SL6. . . . .19 A4
Horton Grange
SL6 . . . . .19 A4
Horton Rd SL3 . . . .47 B1
Houston Ct **4**
SL4 . . . . .50 A4
Howard Ave SL2 . .23 C3
Howards Gate
SL2 . . . . .13 A1
Howarth Rd SL6 . .18 B1
Hoylake Cl SL1 . . .31 C3
Hubert Rd SL3 . . . .35 B2
Hub The **7** SL6 . . .18 A2
Hudson Pl **9** SL3 .36 A1
Hughenden Cl
SL6 . . . . .17 A1
Hughenden Rd
SL1 . . . . .23 B2
Hull Cl SL1 . . . . . . .33 A3
Humber Way SL3 .36 B2
Hungerford Ave
SL2 . . . . .23 C3
Hungerford Dr SL6 7 C2
Hunsford Lodge
SL4 . . . . .49 B3
Huntercombe Cl
SL6 . . . . .21 A2
Huntercombe Hospl
SL6 . . . . .21 A1
Huntercombe La N
SL6 . . . . .21 A2
Huntercombe La S
SL6 . . . . .21 A1
Huntercombe Spur
SL1 . . . . .21 A1
Hunter Ct SL1. . . . .21 A3

Hunters Mews
SL4 . . . . .45 A1
Hunters Way SL1. .31 C3
Huntington Pl
SL3 . . . . .36 C3
Hunt's La SL6 . . . . .9 C2
Huntswood La SL1,
SL6 . . . . .10 A3
Hurricane Way
SL3 . . . . .36 C1
Hurstfield Dr SL6 .20 C2
Hurst Rd SL1 . . . . .21 B3
Hurworth Ave
SL3 . . . . .35 A2
Huxley Cl SL2. . . . .24 C4
Hylle Cl SL4 . . . . . .43 C1

I

Ilchester Cl SL6. . .27 A4
Illingworth SL4 . . .48 C3
Imperial Ct SL4 . . .49 B3
Imperial Rd SL4. . .49 B3
India Rd SL1 . . . . . .34 C3
Ingleglen SL2. . . . . . .4 A2
Inkerman Rd SL4. .32 A1
Inniscrown Ho
SL3 . . . . .46 C2
Institute Rd SL6. . .20 A2
In The Ray SL6 . . . .18 A2
Iona Cres SL1 . . . . .21 C2
Ipswich Rd SL1 . . .22 B2
Irving Ho SL4 . . . . .48 C4
Islet Park Dr SL6. . .9 A2
Islet Park Ho SL6 . .9 A2
Islet Pk SL6. . . . . . . .9 A2
Islet Rd SL6. . . . . . . .9 A2
Ives Rd SL3 . . . . . . .36 B3
Ivy Cl SL6. . . . . . . .40 B2
Ivy Cres SL1 . . . . . .22 A1

J

Jacob Cl SL4 . . . . . .43 C1
Jakes Ho SL6 . . . . .18 B3
James Elliman Sch
SL2 . . . . .23 C1
James St SL4 . . . . .45 B1
Jardine Cotts SL2 . 5 C3
Jarratt Ho SL4 . . . .49 C3
Jefferson Cl SL3 . .36 B2
Jellicoe Cl SL1. . . .32 C3
Jennery La SL1 . . .11 A1
Jesus Hospital
SL6 . . . . .29 A2
John F Kennedy
Meml* TW20. . . . . .53 A1
Jonathan Ct SL6. .17 C2
Jourdelay's Pas
SL4 . . . . .45 B3
Journeys End SL2 23 C3
Jubilee Cotts SL3 .36 C1
Jubilee Way SL3 . .47 A2
Juniper Ct
Slough, Cippenham
SL1. . . . . .21 C1
Slough, Upton SL1. .34 B3
Juniper Dr SL6 . . . .18 C3
Jutland Ho SL4 . . .49 A4

K

Kaywood Cl SL3. . .35 A2
Keats La SL4. . . . . .45 A3
Keble Rd SL1 . . . . .17 A3
Keel Dr SL1. . . . . . .33 A3
Keeler Cl SL4 . . . . .48 C3

Keepers Farm Cl
SL4 . . . . .48 C4
Kelpatrick Rd SL1 21 B2
Kelsey Cl SL6 . . . . .27 B2
Kempe Cl SL3. . . . .37 A2
Kemsley Chase
SL2 . . . . .13 A3
Kendal Cl SL2. . . . .24 B1
Kendal Dr SL2 . . . .24 B1
Kendall Pl SL6 . . . .27 A3
Kendrick Rd SL3 . .34 C2
Kenilworth Cl
SL1 . . . . .34 A2
Kenneally SL4 . . . .48 A4
Kenneally Cl **11**
SL4 . . . . .48 A4
Kenneally Pl **12**
SL4 . . . . .48 A4
Kenneally Row **13**
SL4 . . . . .48 A4
Kenneally Wlk **10**
SL4 . . . . .48 A4
Kennedy Cl
Farnham Common
SL2. . . . . .4 B1
Maidenhead SL6 . .17 A1
Kennedy Ho SL1 . .31 B4
Kennel La SL6 . . . . .2 A2
Kennet Rd SL6 . . . .18 A3
Kennett Rd SL3 . . .36 C3
Kent Ave SL1 . . . . .23 A3
Kent Lodge **6**
SL6 . . . . .18 A1
Kentons La SL4 . . .49 A4
Kent Way SL6 . . . . .17 C4
Kenwood Cl SL6 . .16 B2
Keppel Spur SL4 . .52 B3
Keppel St SL4. . . . .50 B4
Kestrel Path SL2 . .21 C4
Keswick Ct SL2 . . .24 A1
Keys Pl SL6. . . . . . .18 A1
Khalsa Prim Sch
SL2 . . . . .24 B2
Kidderminster Rd
SL2 . . . . .12 B1
Kidwells Cl SL6 . . .18 A3
Kidwells Park Dr **13**
SL6 . . . . .18 A2
Killarney Dr SL6 . .17 C2
Kiln Pl SL6 . . . . .6 B2
Kimber Cl SL4 . . . .49 B3
Kimberley Cl SL3. .36 C2
Kimbers Dr SL1. . .11 B1
Kimber's La SL6 . .27 C2
Kimbolton **3** SL6 .18 C3
King Edward Ct **6**
SL4 . . . . .45 B1
King Edward St
SL1 . . . . .33 B3
King Edward VII Ave
SL4, SL3. . . . . .45 C3
King Edward VII
Hospl SL4. . . . . . . .50 A3
Kingfisher Ct SL2 .22 C4
Kinghorn La SL6 . . .7 B2
Kinghorn Pk SL6. . .7 B2
King John's Cl
TW19. . . . . .52 C4
Kingsbury Dr SL4 .52 A3
Kings Chase **16**
SL6 . . . . .18 A1
King's Court Fst Sch
SL4 . . . . .52 B3
Kingsfield SL4 . . . .43 B1
Kings Gr SL1. . . . . . .7 C1
Kings Grove Ind Est
SL6 . . . . .17 C1

Kingsley Path SL2 21 B4
Kingsmead Ho SL1 33 A4
Kingsoak Ct SL6 26 C2
Kings Rd SL4 50 B4
King's Rd SL1 33 C2
King's Road Ho 3 SL4 50 B4
King St SL6 18 A1
King Stable St SL4 45 B2
Kingsway
Farnham Common SL2 4 B1
Slough SL3 35 A2
Kingsway Mews SL2 4 B1
Kings Wlk 4 SL6 18 A2
Kingswood Ct SL6 28 A4
Kingswood Ho SL1 23 A3
Kinnaird Cl SL1 21 A2
Kipling Ct SL4 49 C4
Kirkwall Spur SL1 23 C3
Knightsbridge Ct 7 SL3 36 B2
Knights Cl SL4 43 B1
Knight's Pl 8 SL4 50 A4
Knolton Way SL2 25 A2
Knowle Croft SL6 27 C4
Knowsley Cl SL6 16 B4
Kola Ho SL2 24 C1

L

Laburnham Rd SL6 17 C1
Ladbrooke Rd SL1 33 B2
Ladyday Pl SL1 33 A4
Lady Elizabeth Ho 3 SL6 17 C2
Laggan Rd SL6 18 A4
Laggan Sq SL6 18 A4
Lake Ave SL1 23 B1
LAKE END 30 C3
Lake End Ct SL6 20 B2
Lake End Rd SL4, SL6 30 C4
Lakeside SL6 18 C4
Lakeside Dr SL2 14 A3
Lake View SL6 18 B4
Lambert Ave SL3 35 C2
Lambourne Ct SL6 19 A2
Lambourne Dr SL6 27 A2
Lambton Ho SL4 49 B3
Lamesley Ho SL6 17 C1
Lammas Ave SL4 50 B4
Lammas Ct SL4 50 A4
Lammas Rd SL1 21 B3
Lancaster Ave SL2 23 A4
Lancaster Rd SL6 16 C3
Lancastria Mews SL6 17 B2
Lancelot Cl SL1 32 B3
Langdale Cl SL6 18 B1
Langdown Way SL6 27 B4
LANGLEY 36 B3
Langley Broom SL3 36 A1
Langley Bsns Ctr SL3 36 B4
Langley Bsns Pk SL3 36 B4
Langley Gram Sch SL3 36 A2
Langley Manor Sch SL3 35 C4
Langley Rd SL3 35 C2
Langley Sta SL3 36 B4
Langleywood Sch SL3 35 C2
Langton Cl
Maidenhead SL6 17 B3
Slough SL1 31 B4
Langton's Mdw SL2 4 B1
Langworthy End SL6 40 C3
Langworthy La SL6 40 B3
Lansdowne Ave SL1 33 C4
Lansdowne Ct
Slough SL1 33 C4
Taplow SL6 19 A2
Lanterns Wlk SL6 18 C2
Larch Cl SL2 22 C3
Larchfield Prim Sch SL6 27 C3
Larchfield Rd SL6 27 C4
Larchmoor Pk SL2 5 C2
Larkfield SL6 40 C4
Larkings La SL2 14 C3
La Roche Cl SL3 35 A2
Lascelles Ho 4 SL1 34 B3
Lascelles Rd SL3 34 C2
Lassell Gdns SL6 18 C2
Laurel Ave SL3 35 C3
Laurels The 8 SL3 36 B2
Lautree Gdns SL6 2 C2
Lawkland SL2 13 A1
Lawn Cl SL3 47 A2
Lawn The SL3 47 A1
Lawrence Ct SL4 50 A4
Lawrence Way SL1 21 B3
Laxton Gn SL6 27 A2
Leaholme Gdns SL1 21 B3
Lea Inf Sch SL2 24 C1
Lea Jun Sch SL2 24 C1
Ledger's Rd SL1 33 B3
Leeds Rd SL1 23 C1
Lees Cl SL6 26 C4
Lees Gdns SL6 26 C4
Leeson Gdns SL4 31 C1
Legoland Windsor★ SL4 48 B1
Leigh Pk SL3 46 C2
Leigh Rd SL1 22 C1
Leigh Sq SL4 48 B4
Leighton Gdns SL6 18 C4
Leiston Spur SL1 23 C2
Leith Cl SL1 34 B4
LENT 20 C4
Lent Gn SL1 20 C4
Lent Green La SL1 20 C4
LENT RISE 20 B3
Lent Rise Comb Sch SL1 20 C3
Lent Rise Rd SL1 20 C4
Leopold Mall 6 SL1 34 A3
Lerwick Dr SL1 23 C3
Leslie Dunne Ho SL4 48 C4
Lesters Rd SL6 2 B1
Lewes Ct SL1 33 A3
Lewins Farm Ct SL1 22 A1
Lewins Way SL1 22 A1
Lexington Ave SL6 27 B4
Liddell SL4 48 A3
Liddell Pl SL4 48 A3
Liddell Sq 14 SL4 48 A4
Liddell Way SL4 48 A3
Lidstone Ct SL3 25 C2
Lightlands La SL6 8 A4
Lilac Ct SL2 12 A1
Lilley Way SL1 31 C4
Lillibrooke Cres SL6 26 B2
Lime Ave SL4 46 A2
Limes The SL4 43 A1
Lime Tree Ct SL4 52 C3
Lime Wlk SL6 16 B3
Linchfield Rd SL3 47 A1
Lincoln Ct 3 SL1 33 C2
Lincoln Hatch La SL1 21 A4
Lincoln Rd SL6 16 C3
Lincoln Way SL1 21 B1
Linden Ave SL6 17 B4
Linden Dr SL2 13 A3
Linden Ho SL3 36 C1
Lindores Ho SL6 40 C3
Lindores Rd SL6 40 C3
Lingholm Cl SL6 17 A1
Link Rd SL3 47 A1
Linkswood Rd SL1 11 A2
Link The SL2 24 C2
Lismore Pk SL2 24 A2
Litcham Spur SL1 23 B2
Little Acre SL4 49 B3
Littlebrook Ave SL2 21 C3
Little Buntings SL4 49 A3
Littledown Cotts SL1 34 A4
Littledown Rd SL1 34 A4
Littledown Sch SL1 24 A1
Littlefield Gn SL6 38 A1
LITTLEFIELD GREEN 38 A1
Littleport Spur SL1 23 C2
Little Sutton La SL3 37 A1
Little Woodlands SL4 49 A3
Liverpool Rd SL1 22 C2
Lochinvar Cl SL1 32 C3
Lock Ave SL6 9 A1
Lockbridge Ct SL6 19 A3
Locke Gdns SL3 35 A3
Lockets Cl SL4 43 B1
Lock La SL6 27 A3
Lock Mead SL6 9 A1
Lock Path SL4 43 B3
Locksley Ct 4 SL1 33 C2
Loddon Dr SL6 17 B3
Loddon Spur SL1 23 C2
Lodge Cl SL1 33 A3
Lodge The SL2 24 C3
Lodge Way SL4 48 C3
Lodgings of the Military Knights 3 SL4 45 B1
London Rd
Datchet SL3 47 A2
Slough SL3 35 B1
Longbourn SL4 49 B3
Long Cl SL2 12 C4
Long Close Prep Sch SL3 34 B2
Long Dr SL1 11 A1
Longfield SL2 4 C4
Long Furlong Dr SL2 21 C4
Long La
Cookham Rise SL6 7 B4
Holyport, Touchen-end SL6 39 C1
Longleat Gdns SL6 17 B1
Longmead SL4 43 C1
Longmead La SL1 11 B4
Long Readings La SL2 12 C1
Long Wlk The★ SL4 50 B3
Longwood Ave SL3 36 C1
Longworth Dr SL6 19 A4
Lonsdale Cl SL6 18 B4
Lonsdale Way SL6 41 A4
Look Ahead SL1 33 C3
Loosen Dr SL6 26 B2
Lord Raglan Ho SL4 50 A3
Loring Rd SL4 44 A1
Lorne Cl SL1 32 C2
Losfield Rd SL4 43 C1
Lovegrove Dr SL2 22 A4
Lovejoy La SL4 48 B4
Lovett Gdns SL6 9 A2
Lowbrook Dr SL6 26 B2
Lowbrook Prim Sch SL6 26 B2
Lower Boyndon Rd SL6 17 C1
Lower Britwell Rd SL2 21 B4
Lower Cippenham La SL1 22 A1
Lower Cookham Rd SL6 9 A1
Lower Lees Rd SL2 12 C1
Lower Rd SL6 2 C2
Lower Ventnor Cotts SL6 2 A3
Lower Ward SL4 45 B2
Lowestoft Dr SL1 21 B2
Ludlow Ho SL6 17 C1
Ludlow Rd SL6 17 C1
Luff Cl SL4 48 C3
Lundy Ct SL1 21 C1
Lutman La SL6 8 A1
Lydford Ave SL2 23 B3
Lydsey Cl SL2 12 B1
Lyell Pl E SL4 48 A3
Lyell Pl W SL4 48 A3
Lyell Rd SL4 48 A3
Lyell Wlk E SL4 48 A3
Lyell Wlk W SL4 48 A3
Lynch Hill La SL1 11 C1
Lynch Hill Prim Sch SL2 12 A1
Lynden Cl SL6 40 C3
Lyndhurst Ave SL6 2 C1
Lyndwood Dr SL4 52 A4
Lyndwood Par SL4 52 A4
Lyneham Gdns SL6 16 C4
Lyngfield Pk SL6 41 B3
Lynton Gn SL6 17 C2
Lynwood Ave SL3 35 B2
Lysander Mead SL6 19 A3

M

Mackenzie Mall 3 SL1 34 A3
Mackenzie St 2 SL1 34 A3
Magna Carta La TW19 53 B2
Magnolia Gdns SL3 35 A2
Magpie Way SL2 22 A4
MAIDENHEAD 18 A1
MAIDENHEAD COURT 9 A3
Maidenhead Court Pk SL6 8 C2
Maidenhead Rd
Cookham Rise SL6 3 A1
Windsor SL4 43 C2
Maidenhead Sta SL6 18 A1
Maidenhead Trad Pk SL6 28 C1
Main Dr SL0 37 C3
Major's Farm Rd SL3 47 B2
Malders La SL6 7 A2
Mallard Cl SL1 10 C2
Mallard Dr SL1 22 A1
Mallow Pk SL6 17 A4
Malpas Rd SL2 24 C1
Malt House Cl SL4 52 B3
Malton Ave SL1 22 C1
Malvern Rd SL6 17 B4
Manfield Cl SL2 12 B1
Manor Ct
Slough, Cippenham SL1 32 A4
5 Slough, Upton Park SL1 34 A2
Manor Farm Cl SL4 49 A3
Manor Farm Cotts SL4 51 B1
Manor Farm Ho SL4 49 A3
Manor Gr SL6 41 B1
Manor House La SL3 46 C1
Manor La SL6 27 C3
MANOR PARK 23 B4
Manor Rd
Maidenhead SL6 27 C3
Windsor SL4 48 C4
Manor Way SL6 40 B3
Mansel Cl SL2 24 C3
Mansell Cl SL4 48 C4
Maple Cl SL6 27 A4
Maple Cres SL2 24 C1
Maple Ct SL4 50 A3

Mapledurham Wlk SL6 7 C2
Maplin Pk SL3 36 C4
Marbeck Cl SL4 43 B1
Marches The SL4 33 B1
Marcia Ct SL1 32 A4
Marescroft Rd SL2 21 C4
Marina Way SL1 21 B1
Marish Ct SL3 36 B3
Marish Prim Sch SL3 36 B3
Marish Wharf Ind Est SL3 35 C3
Market La SL3 37 A3
Market St
 Maidenhead SL6 18 A2
 [8] Windsor SL4 45 B1
Marlborough Cl SL6 16 B1
Marlborough Ct SL1 21 C2
Marlborough Ho [5] SL6 18 A1
Marlborough Rd
 Maidenhead SL6 16 B1
 Slough SL3 35 B1
Marlow Lodge [13] SL6 18 A1
Marlow Rd SL6 18 A2
Marshfield SL3 47 A1
Marshgate Trad Est SL6 20 B2
Marsh La SL6 19 C1
Martin Cl SL4 43 B1
Martin Rd
 Maidenhead SL6 18 A3
 Slough SL1 33 C2
Martin's Plain SL2 14 A2
Marunden Gn SL2 12 A1
Mary Morgan Ct SL2 23 B3
Maryside SL3 35 C3
Mascoll Path SL2 12 A1
Mason's Ct SL1 21 C1
Masons Rd SL1 21 C1
Maudsley Ho SL6 18 C2
Maxwell Ct SL1 21 A4
Maybury Cl SL1 21 B2
Mayfield Dr SL4 49 B3
Mayflower Way SL2 4 B3
Maynard Ct SL4 44 B1
Maypole Rd SL6 20 B3
Mead Ave SL3 36 C4
Mead Cl SL3 36 C4
Meadfield Ave SL3 36 B3
Meadfield Rd SL3 36 C3
Mead Haze SL6 9 A1
Meadow Cl SL4 51 C1
Meadow La SL4 45 A2
Meadow Rd SL3 35 C2
Meadow View La SL6 39 C3
Meadow Way
 Dorney SL6 30 A3
 Fifield SL6 41 B1
 Old Windsor SL4 52 B4
Meads The
 Stoke Poges SL2 14 B1
 [4] Windsor SL4 49 B4
Mead Way SL1 21 B3
Mead Wlk SL3 36 C4
Medallion Pl SL6 18 C2
Mede Cl TW19 53 A2
Melbourne Ave SL1 23 A2
Mellor Wlk [17] SL4 45 B1
Melton Ct SL6 18 A1
Mendip Cl SL3 36 B1
Mercian Way SL1 31 B4
Mercia Rd SL6 27 A3
Mere Rd SL1 34 A2
Merlin Ct [3] SL6 16 C3
Merton Cl SL6 27 A2
Merton Ct [10] SL1 34 B2
Merton Rd SL1 34 B2
Merwin Way SL4 48 B3
Meryton Ho SL4 49 B3
Michael Cl SL6 27 A4
Midcroft SL2 22 C4
Middle Gn SL3 25 C1
MIDDLE GREEN 35 C4
Middlegreen Rd SL3 35 B4
Middlegreen Trad Est SL3 35 B3
Middle Wlk SL1 10 C1
Mildenhall Rd SL1 23 C2
Milford Ct SL1 34 B3
Millennium Mews SL1 33 C4
Miller's La SL4 52 A4
Mill La
 Taplow SL6 19 A3
 Windsor SL4 44 B2
Mills Spur SL4 52 B3
Mill St SL2 34 A4
Millstream La SL1 31 C4
Mill West SL2 34 A4
Milner Rd SL1 20 B3
Milton Rd SL2 23 B4
Milverton Cl SL6 26 C2
Mina Ave SL3 35 B3
Minniecroft Rd SL1 10 C1
Minster Way SL3 36 A4
Minton Rise SL6 20 C2
Mirador Cres SL2 24 C1
Misbourne Ct SL3 36 B2
Missenden Gdns SL1 20 C2
Mitchell Cl SL1 32 B3
Moat Dr SL2 25 A3
Moffy Hill SL6 7 C1
Molyns Mews SL1 31 C4
Moneyrow Gn SL6 40 B2
MONEYROW GREEN 40 B2
Monkey Island Ct SL6 41 C3
Monkey Island La SL6 29 C1
Monksfield Way SL2 12 B1
Monks Rd SL4 48 B4
Montague Rd SL1 24 A1
Montagu Rd SL3 46 C1
Montbatten Ct SL3 35 C2
Montem La SL1 33 B3
Montem Prim Sch SL1 32 C3
Montgomery Pl SL2 25 A2
Montpellier Ct SL4 50 A4
Montrose Ave
 Datchet SL3 47 A2
 Slough SL1 22 C2
Montrose Dr SL6 16 B1
Montrose Way SL3 47 B2
Monycrower Dr SL6 17 C2
Moorbridge Rd SL6 18 B2
Moore Cl SL1 32 C3
Moor End SL6 41 A4
Moores La SL4 32 A1
Moorfield Terr SL6 18 B3
Moor Furlong SL1 31 C4
Moorings The
 Old Windsor SL4 52 C3
 Windsor SL4 44 B2
Moor La SL6 18 A4
Moorlands Dr SL6 16 A3
Moorside Cl SL6 18 A4
Moorstown Ct [7] SL1 33 C3
Moray Dr SL2 24 B2
Moreau Wlk SL3 25 C2
Moreton Way SL1 31 B4
Morley Cl SL3 36 A4
Morrice Cl [3] SL3 36 B2
Morris Ct SL4 43 C1
Mortimer Rd SL3 35 B2
Mosaic Apartments The SL1 33 C3
Mossy Vale SL6 17 B4
Moundsfield Way SL1 31 C3
Mountbatten Cl [6] SL1 34 B2
Mountbatten Sq [7] SL4 45 A1
Mount Cl SL2 4 B3
Mulberry Ave SL4 51 A4
Mulberry Dr SL3 47 C4
Mulberry Wlk SL6 17 A3
Mundesley Spur SL1 23 C2
Murrin Rd SL6 17 A3
MYRKE 34 A1
Myrke The SL3 34 A1
Myrtle Cres SL2 24 A1

N

Napier Rd SL6 16 C1
Nashdom SL1 10 A4
Nash Rd SL3 36 B2
Needham Cl SL4 43 C1
Nelson Cl SL3 35 B1
Nelson Rd SL4 49 A3
Neo Apartments [2] SL1 34 B3
Neptune Way SL1 31 C3
Neve Ho SL6 18 A3
Neville Cl SL2 5 B1
Neville Ct SL1 11 A1
Newberry Cres SL4 48 B4
Newbery Way SL1 33 B3
Newbury Dr SL6 18 C1
Newchurch Rd SL2 22 A3
Newhaven Spur SL2 22 C4
Newlands Dr SL6 16 B2
Newlands Girls' Sch SL6 16 B2
Newlands Ho SL6 16 B1
New Market [12] SL6 18 A2
Newport Rd SL2 21 C4
New Rd
 Cookham Rise SL6 2 C2
 Datchet SL3 47 B1
 Holyport SL6 40 C3
 Slough SL3 36 B3
New Sq SL1 34 A3
Newton Cl SL3 36 A4
Newton Ct SL4 52 A4
Newton La SL4 52 B4
Newtonside SL4 52 A4
Newton Side Orch SL4 52 A4
Nicholas Gdns SL1 31 C4
Nicholas Winton Ct SL6 18 B3
Nicholls SL4 48 A3
Nicholls Wlk SL4 48 A3
Nicholsons Ctr [5] SL6 18 A2
Nicholsons La SL6 18 A2
Nightingale Ct [9] SL1 34 B2
Nightingale La SL6 7 B2
Nightingale Pk SL2 12 A4
Nightingale Pl SL6 3 A2
Nightingale Wlk SL4 50 A3
Nine Acres SL1 32 A4
Nixey Cl SL1 34 B3
Noble Ct SL2 34 A4
Norden Cl SL6 27 A3
Norden Mdws SL6 27 A4
Norden Rd SL6 27 A4
Norelands Dr SL1 11 A2
Norfolk Ave SL1 23 A3
Norfolk Park Cotts SL6 18 A3
Norfolk Rd SL6 18 A3
Normans The SL2 24 C2
Norreys Dr SL6 27 B3
Northampton Ave SL1 23 A2
Northborough Rd SL2 22 C4
North Burnham Cl SL1 10 C2
North Cl SL4 44 A1
North Cotts SL2 13 A1
Northcroft SL2 22 C4
Northdean [5] SL6 18 A4
Northern Rd SL2 23 B4
Northfield Rd
 Eton SL4 32 A1
 Maidenhead SL6 18 A4
North Gn
 [3] Maidenhead SL6 18 A4
 Slough SL1 23 C1
Northmead Rd SL2 22 A3
North Pk SL0 37 B3
North Rd SL6 17 C2
North Star La SL6 17 A1
North Terr SL4 45 C2
NORTH TOWN 8 A1
North Town Cl [1] SL6 18 A4
North Town Mead [4] SL6 18 A4
North Town Moor SL6 18 A4
North Town Rd SL6 18 A4
Northumbria Rd SL6 26 C3
Norway Dr SL2 24 C3
Norwich Ho SL6 17 C3
Nursery La SL3 35 B4
Nursery Pl SL4 52 B4
Nursery Rd SL6 20 C2
Nursery Way TW19 53 A4

O

Oaken Gr SL6 17 A4
Oakfield Ave SL1 32 C4
Oakfield Fst Sch SL4 49 C4
Oakhurst SL6 8 C3
Oak La SL4 44 B1
Oakley Cres SL1 23 C1
Oakley Green Rd SL4 42 C2
Oakridge Pl SL2 4 B3
Oak Stubbs La SL6 30 A3
Oak Tree Dr SL3 36 C1
Oakvew Gdns SL3 36 A2
Oakwood Ct SL1 23 C2
Oast House Cl TW19 53 B3
Oatlands Dr SL1 23 B2
Oban Ct SL1 33 B3
Ockwells Rd SL6 27 A1
Odencroft Rd SL2 12 B1
Odney La SL6 3 C2
Oldacres SL6 18 C2
Old Court Cl SL6 26 C2
Oldershaw Mews SL6 16 C3
Old Ferry Dr TW19 53 A4
Oldfield Prim Sch SL6 18 C1
Oldfield Rd SL6 18 C2
Oldfield Rd Ind Est SL6 18 C2
Old Fives Ct SL1 10 C1
Old Forge Cl SL6 28 B2
Old House Ct SL3 25 B2
Old Kiln Ind Est SL6 6 B2
Old Marsh La SL6 30 A3
Old Mill La SL6 29 B3
Old Orchard SL6 27 C4
Old Post Office La [10] SL6 18 A2
Old School Ct TW19 53 B3
Oldway La SL1 31 B4
OLD WINDSOR 52 A3
Oliver Ct SL1 21 C1
Olivia Dr SL3 36 A1
One Pin La
 Farnham Common SL2 4 B3
 Farnham Common SL2 4 C4
Opal Ct SL3 25 A4
Opecks Cl SL2 24 C4
Opendale Rd SL1 20 C3

Oppidan SL6 . . . . . . **21** A2
Orchard Ave
Slough SL1 . . . . **21** B3
Windsor SL4 . . . . . . **44** B1
Orchard Bungalow Mobile Home Pk
SL2 . . . . **12** A4
Orchard Cl SL6 . . . . **28** B2
Orchard Gate SL2 . . **4** B2
Orchard Gdns SL6 . . **3** C2
Orchard Gr SL6 . . . **17** A2
Orchard Lodge
SL1 . . . . **31** C4
Orchard Mill SL8 . . . **3** C4
Orchard Rd SL4 . . . **52** B4
ORCHARDVILLE . . **20** C4
Orchardville SL1 . . **20** C4
Orchard Way SL3 . **35** C4
Orkney Ct SL6 . . . . . **9** C4
Orwell Cl SL4 . . . . . **50** B3
Osborne Ct SL4 . . . **50** A4
Osborne Lodge [9]
SL4 . . . . **50** A4
Osborne Mews
SL4 . . . . **50** A4
Osborne Rd SL4 . . . **50** B3
Osborne St SL1 . . . **34** A3
Osney Rd SL6 . . . . . . **7** C1
Ostler Gate SL6 . . . **17** A4
Our Lady of Peace RC Inf Sch SL1 . . . **21** A3
Our Lady of Peace RC Jun Sch SL1 . . **21** A3
Ouseley Lodge
SL4 . . . . **52** C3
Ouseley Rd TW19 . . **53** A3
Owen Cl [5] SL3 . . . **36** A1
Oxford Ave
Burnham SL1 . . . . . . **10** C2
Slough SL1 . . . . **22** A3
Oxford Rd SL4 . . . . **45** A1
Oxford Rd E SL4 . . . **45** A1

P

Paddock Cl SL6 . . . **26** B1
Paddock Cotts
SL6 . . . . **26** B1
Paddock The
Datchet SL3 . . . . **46** C1
Maidenhead SL6 . . . . **7** A1
Padstow Cl SL3 . . . **35** C2
Pages Wharf SL6 . . **19** A3
Paget Dr SL6 . . . . . **26** B3
Paget Rd SL3 . . . . . **36** A2
Pagoda The SL6 . . . **18** C4
Palace Cl SL1 . . . . . **32** A4
Paley St SL6 . . . . . . **38** C1
Palmers Cl SL6 . . . **26** B2
Palmerston Ave
SL3 . . . . **34** C2
Pamela Row SL6 . . **40** B3
Pantile Row SL3 . . **36** B2
Parade The
Farnham Common SL2 . . . . **4** B1
Windsor SL4 . . . . . . **43** B1
Parish La SL2 . . . . . . **4** B4
Park Cl SL4 . . . . **50** B4
Park Cnr SL4 . . . . . **48** C3
Parkgate SL1 . . . . . **21** A4
Park Ho SL6 . . . . . . **17** C1
Park La SL3 . . . . **34** C2
Parkland Ave SL3 . **35** B1
Park Lawn SL2 . . . . **13** A1
Park Par SL2 . . . . . **13** A2
Park Rd SL2 . . . . . . **13** C2
Parkside SL6 . . . . . **17** B4
Parkside Lodge [11]
SL3 . . . . **34** B2
Parkside Wlk SL1 . **34** B2
Park St
Maidenhead SL6 . . . **18** A2
Slough SL1 . . . . **34** A3
Windsor SL4 . . . . . . **45** B1
Parkview SL6 . . . . . **18** A2
Parkview Chase
SL1 . . . . **21** C2
Parlaunt Park Prim Sch SL3 . . . . **36** C3
Parlaunt Rd SL3 . . **36** C2
Parliament La SL1,
SL6 . . . . **10** A4
Parry Gn N SL3 . . . **36** A2
Parry Gn S SL3 . . . . **36** B2
Parsonage La
Farnham Common SL2 . . . . **13** B3
Windsor SL4 . . . . . . **44** B1
Parsons Rd SL3 . . . **36** A1
Parson's Wood La
SL2 . . . . **13** B4
Partridge Mead
SL6 . . . . **8** A1
Patricia Cl SL1 . . . . **21** C1
Pavilions The SL4 . **44** C1
Paxton Ave SL1 . . . **33** A2
Payton Hos SL6 . . . . **2** C1
Peace La SL6 . . . . . . **3** A1
Pearce Cl SL6 . . . . . **18** A4
Pearce Dr SL6 . . . . . **3** A2
Pearce Rd SL6 . . . . **18** A4
Pearl Gdns SL1 . . . **32** C4
Peartree Cl SL1 . . . **32** A4
Peascod Pl [16]
SL4 . . . . **45** B1
Peascod St SL4 . . . **45** B1
Peel Cl SL4 . . . . **49** C3
Peel Ct SL1 . . . . **22** C3
Pelham Ct SL6 . . . . **17** C2
Pelling Hill SL4 . . . **52** B2
Pemberley Lodge
SL4 . . . . **49** B3
Pemberton Rd
SL2 . . . . **21** C4
Pendeen Ct SL1 . . . **32** B4
Penling Cl SL6 . . . . . **2** C1
Penn Ho SL1 . . . . . . **11** A1
Pennine Rd SL2 . . . **22** B3
Penn Mdw SL2 . . . . **14** B3
Penn Rd
Datchet SL3 . . . . **47** B1
Slough SL2 . . . . **23** B4
Penn Wood Prim Sch
SL2 . . . . **23** B4
Pennylets Gn SL2 . **14** B4
Penshurst Rd SL6 **27** B4
Pentland Rd SL2 . . **22** B3
Penwood Ct SL6 . . **16** C2
Penyston Rd SL6 . . **17** A2
Penzance Spur
SL2 . . . . **22** C4
Pepler Way SL1 . . . **10** C1
Percy Pl SL3 . . . . . . **46** C1
Perrycroft SL4 . . . . **49** A3
Perryfields Way
SL1 . . . . **20** C4
Perry Ho SL1 . . . . . **20** C4
Perryman Way
SL2 . . . . **12** A1
Perth Ave SL1 . . . . . **22** C2
Perth Trad Est
SL1 . . . . **22** C3
Peterhead Mews
SL3 . . . . **36** B1
Petersfield Ave
SL2 . . . . **34** B4
Peters La SL6 . . . . . **40** C3
Petty Cross SL1 . . . **21** C2
Petworth Ct SL4 . . **44** B1
Pevensey Rd SL2 . . **22** B3
Pheasants Croft
SL6 . . . . **26** B3
Philberds Lodge
SL6 . . . . **40** C4
Philbye Mews
SL1 . . . . **32** A3
Phipps Cl SL6 . . . . . **26** B1
Phipps Rd SL1 . . . . **21** C3
Phoenix Ct SL6 . . . **27** B3
Pickfords Gdns
SL1 . . . . **33** C4
Pickwick Terr
SL2 . . . . **24** C1
Pierson Rd SL4 . . . **43** B1
Pine Cl SL6 . . . . **16** C2
Piner Cotts SL4 . . . **48** C3
Pink La SL1 . . . . **10** C2
Pinkneys Dr SL6 . . **16** A3
Pinkneys Farm
SL6 . . . . **16** C4
PINKNEYS GREEN **16** B4
Pinkneys Rd SL6 . . **16** B3
Pipers Cl SL1 . . . . . **11** A1
Pipers Ct SL1 . . . . . **11** A1
Pitts Rd SL1 . . . . . . **33** A4
Plackett Way SL1 . **31** B4
Plaines Cl SL1 . . . . **32** A4
Plough La SL2 . . . . **14** C3
Ploughlees La
SL1 . . . . **23** C1
Pluto Cl SL1 . . . . . . **31** C3
Plymouth Rd SL1 . . **21** C3
Pocketts Yd SL6 . . . . **3** C2
Pococks La SL4 . . . **45** C4
Points The SL6 . . . . **26** C2
Pollard Cl SL4 . . . . **51** C1
Pool La SL1 . . . . **23** C1
Poolmans Rd SL4 . **48** B3
Popes La SL6 . . . . . . **2** A2
Poplar Ho SL3 . . . . **36** A1
Poplars Gr SL6 . . . . . **8** C1
Portland Bsns Ctr
SL3 . . . . **46** C1
Portland Cl SL2 . . . **21** B4
Portlock Rd SL6 . . **17** A2
Portsmouth Ct
SL1 . . . . **23** C1
Post Office Cotts
SL2 . . . . **14** B4
Post Office La
SL3 . . . . **25** B2
Poulcott TW19 . . . . **53** B4
Poundfield La SL6 . **3** A2
Pound The SL1 . . . . **21** B4
Powis Cl SL6 . . . . . . **26** C3
Powney Rd SL6 . . . . **17** A2
Poyle La SL1 . . . . . . **10** C2
Precincts The
SL1 . . . . **21** A4
Preston Rd SL2 . . . **25** A1
Prestwood SL2 . . . **24** C2
Priest Hill SL4,
TW20 . . . . **52** C1
Prince Albert's Wlk
SL3, SL4 . . . . **46** C1
Prince Andrew Cl
SL6 . . . . **18** C4
Prince Andrew Rd
SL6 . . . . **18** C4
Prince Consort Cotts
SL4 . . . . **50** B4
Princes Cl SL4 . . . . **44** A4
Princess Ave SL4 . . **49** C3
Princess Christians Hospl SL4 . . . . **45** A1
Princess Margaret Hospl The SL4 . . . . **50** B4
Princess St [19]
SL6 . . . . **18** A1
Princes St SL1 . . . . **34** C3
Priors Cl
Maidenhead SL6 . . . **28** C1
[5] Slough SL1 . . . . . **34** B2
Priors Rd SL4 . . . . . **48** B3
Priors Way SL6 . . . **28** C1
Priors Way Ind Est
SL6 . . . . **28** C1
Priory Hts SL1 . . . . **21** C2
Priory Rd SL1 . . . . . **21** A3
Priory Sch SL1 . . . . **21** B3
Priory Way SL3 . . . **46** C2
Progress Bsns Ctr
SL1 . . . . **21** B2
Prospect Ct SL2 . . . . **4** B1
Prospect Pl [3]
SL4 . . . . **50** B3
Providence Pl [14]
SL6 . . . . **18** A2
Prudential Bldgs [1]
SL1 . . . . **34** A3
Pulse The [2] SL6 . . **18** B2
PUNT HILL **17** A1
Pursers Ct SL2 . . . . **23** C1
Pursell Cl SL6 . . . . **26** B2
Purton Ct SL2 . . . . . **13** A4
Purton La SL2 . . . . **13** A4

Q

Quadrant The SL6 **18** B1
Quadrivium Point
SL1 . . . . **33** A4
Quantock Cl SL3 . . **36** B1
Quaves Rd SL3 . . . . **35** A2
Queen Anne Royal Free CE Fst Sch The SL4 . . . . **50** B3
Queen Anne's Ct [9]
SL4 . . . . **45** A1
Queen Anne's Rd
SL4 . . . . **50** A2
Queen Charlotte St
[10] SL4 . . . . **45** B1
Queen Elizabeth's Wlk SL4 . . . . **51** A4
Queens Acre SL4 . . **50** B2
Queens Acre Ho [6]
SL4 . . . . **50** B3
Queen's Cl SL4 . . . **51** B1
Queens Ct SL1 . . . . **24** A1
Queens Gate Cotts
SL4 . . . . **50** B2
Queen's La [8]
SL6 . . . . **18** A2
Queensmead SL3 . **46** C1
Queensmere Sh Ctr
SL1 . . . . **34** A3
Queens Rd
Eton SL4 . . . . **44** A4
Slough SL1 . . . . **24** A1
Windsor SL4 . . . . . . **50** A4
Queen's Rd SL3 . . . **46** C2
Queen St SL6 . . . . . **18** A2
Queen's Terr [5]
SL4 . . . . **50** B3
Queensway SL6 . . . . **7** C1
Queens Wlk Mall [3]
SL6 . . . . **18** A2
Queen Victoria's Wlk
SL4 . . . . **46** A1
Quinbrookes SL2 . . **25** A2

R

Radcot Ave SL3 . . . **36** C3
Radcot Cl SL6 . . . . . . **7** C2
Radnor Way SL3 . . **35** C1
Ragstone Rd SL1 . . **33** C2
Railway Terr SL2 . . **34** A4
Rainsborough Chase
SL6 . . . . **26** C2
Raleigh Cl SL1 . . . . **32** B4
Ralston Ct [25] 25 . . . **45** B1
Rambler Cl SL6 . . . **20** C2
Rambler La SL3 . . . **35** A2
Ramsey Ct SL2 . . . . **21** B4
Randall Cl SL3 . . . . **36** A1
Randall Ct SL4 . . . . **52** A4
Randolph Rd SL3 . . **35** C2
Ravens Field SL3 . . **35** B3
Ravensworth Rd
SL2 . . . . **12** B1
Rawcliffe Ho SL6 . . **18** B1
Ray Dr SL6 . . . . **18** C2
Rayfield SL6 . . . . . . **18** C3
Ray Lea Cl SL6 . . . . **18** C3
Ray Lea Rd SL6 . . . **18** C3
Ray Lodge SL6 . . . . **18** C2
Ray Lodge Mews
SL6 . . . . **18** C2
Ray Mdw SL6 . . . . . **18** B4
Ray Mead Ct SL6 . . **19** A4
Ray Mead Rd SL6 . **19** A3
Ray Mill Rd E SL6 . **18** C4
Ray Mill Rd W
SL6 . . . . **18** B3
Raymond Rd
Maidenhead SL6 . . . **17** B2
Slough SL3 . . . . **36** B3
Ray Park Ave SL6 . **18** C3
Ray Park La SL6 . . . **18** C2
Ray Park Rd SL6 . . **18** C3
Rays Ave SL4 . . . . . **44** A2
Ray St SL6 . . . . **18** C2
Reade Ct SL2 . . . . . . **4** B1
Recognition Ho [9]
SL4 . . . . **49** B4
Rectory Cl
Farnham Royal SL2 . . . . **13** A1
Windsor SL4 . . . . . . **44** B1
Rectory Rd SL6 . . . **19** C4
Rectory Terr SL2 . . **13** A2
Red Brick Cotts [13]
SL4 . . . . **45** B1
Red Cottage Mews
SL3 . . . . **35** A2
Red Ct SL1 . . . . **33** C4
Reddington Dr
SL3 . . . . **35** C1
Redford Rd SL4 . . . **43** B1
Red Lion Cotts
SL2 . . . . **24** C4
Redriff Cl SL6 . . . . . **17** B1
Red Roofs SL6 . . . . **19** A2
Redwood SL1 . . . . . **10** C2

Redwood Gdns
SL1 . . . . .23 B1
Redwoods The
SL4 . . . . .50 B3
Reeve Rd SL6 . . . . .40 C3
Reform Rd SL6 . . . .18 C2
Regal Ct SL6 . . . . . .28 C1
Regent Ct
9 Maidenhead
SL6 . . . . .18 A2
Slough SL1 . . . . . . .23 C2
Windsor SL4 . . . . . .45 B1
Regents Pl SL6 . . .17 B2
Regional Ho SL1 . .34 B3
Reid Ave SL6 . . . . .27 C4
Repton Cl SL6 . . . .27 A2
Retreat The SL6 . . .41 B2
Revesby Cl SL6 . . .27 B2
Ribstone Rd SL6 . .26 C2
Ricardo Rd SL4 . . .52 B4
Richard Dodd Pl **16**
SL1 . . . . .34 A3
Richards Way SL1 . 32 B4
Richings Pl SL0 . . .37 C3
Richmond Cres
SL1 . . . . .34 B4
Rickman's La SL2 . . 5 A1
Ridgebank SL1 . . .22 A1
Ridge Ct SL4 . . . . .50 A3
Riding Court Rd
SL3 . . . . .47 B2
Riding Ct SL3 . . . .47 A3
Ridings The SL6 . . .16 B2
Rigby Lodge SL1 . .23 C2
Ripley Cl SL3 . . . . .35 C1
Risborough Rd
SL6 . . . . .17 C3
Riseley Rd SL6 . . . .17 B2
Riverbank The
SL4 . . . . .44 C2
River Ct SL6 . . . . . .19 A2
River Gdns SL6 . . .29 B3
Riverine SL6 . . . . . .19 A3
River Rd SL6 . . . . . .19 A1
Riversdale SL3 . . . . 3 C4
Riversdale Cotts
SL8 . . . . 3 C4
Riversdale Ct SL8 . . 3 C4
Riverside TW19 . . .52 C3
Riverside Wlk SL4 . 45 B2
River St SL4 . . . . . .45 B2
Riverway SL4 . . . . .45 A2
Rixman Cl SL6 . . . .27 B4
Rixon Cl SL3 . . . . . .25 C2
Robin Hood Cl
SL1 . . . . .32 A4
Robin Par SL2 . . . . . 4 B2
Robinson Ct SL6 . .27 C3
Robin Willis Way
SL4 . . . . .52 A4
Rochfords Gdns
SL2 . . . . .35 A4
Rochford Way
SL6 . . . . .20 B2
Rockall Ct SL3 . . . .36 C3
Roddell Cl SL1 . . . .24 A1
Roebuck Gn SL1 . . .31 C4
Rogers La SL2 . . . .14 A3
Rokesby Rd SL2 . . .12 A1
Rolls La SL6 . . . . . .39 C3
Roman Lea SL6 . . . . 3 A2
Roman Pl SL6 . . . . .17 A1
Romney Lock Rd
SL4 . . . . .45 B2

Romsey Cl SL3 . . . .36 A3
Romsey Dr SL2 . . . . 4 C4
Ronaldsay Spur
SL1 . . . . .23 C3
Rosebank Cl SL6 . . . 2 C2
Rose Cotts SL6 . . . .27 A2
Rose Hill SL1 . . . . .10 B4
Rosehill Ct SL1 . . .34 B2
Roseleigh Cl SL6 . .16 B2
Roses La SL4 . . . . . .48 B4
Rose Wlk SL2 . . . . .22 C3
Rosewood Way
SL2 . . . . 4 B2
Rosken Gr SL2 . . . .12 C2
Rossiter Cl SL3 . . .35 C1
Ross Rd SL6 . . . . . .27 C3
Rowanhurst Dr SL2 . 4 B2
Rowan Way SL2 . . .22 C3
Rowland Cl SL4 . . .48 B3
Rowley La SL3 . . . .15 B3
Roxborough Way
SL6 . . . . .26 A3
Roxwell Cl SL1 . . . .31 C4
Royal Cotts SL6 . . . . 2 A2
Royal Free Cl **18**
SL4 . . . . .45 B1
Royal Mews SL4 . .45 B1
Royston Way SL1 . .21 B3
Ruby Cl SL1 . . . . . .32 B3
Ruddlesway SL4 . .43 B1
Ruscombe Gdns
SL3 . . . . .46 B2
Rushes The SL6 . . .19 A1
Rushington Ave
SL6 . . . . .28 A4
Russell Ct SL6 . . . .18 A2
Russell St SL4 . . . .50 B4
Russet Rd SL6 . . . .27 A2
Rutherford Cl SL4 . 44 A1
Rutland Ave SL1 . .23 A3
Rutland Gate SL6 . .17 A1
Rutland Pl SL6 . . . .17 A1
Rutland Rd SL6 . . .17 B1
Rycroft SL4 . . . . . . .49 A3
Rydings SL4 . . . . . .49 A3
Rye Cl SL6 . . . . . . .26 B3
Rye Ct **1** SL1 . . . .34 B2
Rylstone Cl SL6 . . .27 A2
Ryvers End SL3 . . .36 A3
Ryvers Prim Sch
SL3 . . . . .35 B2
Ryvers Rd SL3 . . . .36 A3

S

Sadlers Mews
SL6 . . . . .18 C2
Saffron Cl SL3 . . . .46 C1
Sage Ct SL4 . . . . . .52 A3
St Adrian's Cl SL6 26 C3
St Albans Cl **12**
SL4 . . . . .45 B1
St Alban's St SL4 . .45 B1
St Andrew's Ave
SL4 . . . . .49 A4
St Andrew's Cl
Old Windsor SL4 . . .52 A4
Wraysbury TW19 . . .53 B4
St Andrews Cotts **1**
SL4 . . . . .49 B4
St Andrew's Cres
SL4 . . . . .49 A4
St Andrews Ct **2**
SL1 . . . . .33 C2
St Andrew's Way
SL1 . . . . .21 B1

St Anthony's RC Prim
Sch SL2 . . . . .23 A4
St Bernard's Prep
Sch SL1 . . . . .34 C3
St Bernard's RC
Gram Sch SL3 . . . .35 A3
St Bernards Rd
SL3 . . . . .35 A2
St Catherines Ct **8**
SL4 . . . . .49 B4
St Chad's Rd SL6 . .26 C3
Saint-Cloud Way
SL6 . . . . .18 B2
St Columba's Cl
SL6 . . . . .26 C3
St David's Cl SL6 . .26 B3
St Edmund Campion
RC Prim Sch
SL6 . . . . .16 C1
St Edward's RC Fst
Sch SL4 . . . . .44 B1
St Edward's Royal
Free Ecumenical
Mid Sch SL4 . . . . .44 B1
St Elmo Cl SL2 . . . .23 B4
St Elmo Cres SL2 . .23 B4
St Ethelbert's RC
Prim Sch SL2 . . . . .24 B2
St George's Cl
SL4 . . . . .43 C1
St George's Cres
SL1 . . . . .21 B1
St Georges Lodge
SL6 . . . . 3 C2
St George's Sch
SL4 . . . . .45 B2
St Ives Rd SL6 . . . .18 B2
St James Pl SL1 . . .21 A2
St James Wlk SL0 . 37 C4
St John's Beaumont
Sch SL4 . . . . .52 B1
St Johns Dr SL4 . . .49 B4
St Johns Rd
Slough SL2 . . . . . . .24 B1
Windsor SL4 . . . . . .49 B4
St Joseph's RC High
Sch SL2 . . . . .24 B2
St Laurence Way
SL1 . . . . .34 B2
St Leonard's Ave
SL4 . . . . .50 A4
St Leonards Hill
SL4 . . . . .48 C3
St Leonard's Rd
SL4 . . . . .50 A3
St Luke's CE Prim
Sch SL6 . . . . .18 A3
St Luke's Rd
Maidenhead SL6 . . .18 A3
Old Windsor SL4 . . .52 A4
St Margaret's Rd
SL6 . . . . .16 B2
St Mark's Cres
SL6 . . . . .16 C2
St Mark's Hospl
SL6 . . . . .17 A2
St Mark's Pl SL4 . .50 A4
St Mark's Rd
Maidenhead SL6 . . .17 B2
Windsor SL4 . . . . . .50 A4
St Mary's CE Prim
Sch SL1 . . . . .34 B2
St Mary's Cl SL6 . .18 B2
St Mary's Farnham
Royal CE Prim Sch
SL2 . . . . .13 A1

St Mary's RC Prim
Sch SL6 . . . . .8 A1
St Mary's Rd SL3 . .35 C3
St Mary's Wlk **16**
SL6 . . . . .18 A2
St Michael's Ct
SL2 . . . . .21 B4
St Nicholas' CE Comb
Sch SL6 . . . . .19 C4
St Patrick's Cl
SL6 . . . . .26 C3
St Pauls Ave SL2 . .34 B4
St Paul's Ct **20**
SL6 . . . . .18 A1
St Peter's CE Comb
Sch SL1 . . . . .10 C1
St Peter's Cl
Burnham SL1 . . . . . .20 C4
Old Windsor SL4 . . .51 B1
St Peter's Lodge
SL6 . . . . .27 C4
St Peter's Rd SL6 . . 7 B1
St Pirans Sch SL6 17 C4
Salisbury Ave SL2 23 A3
Salisbury Ct SL6 . .27 C4
Salisbury Mews
SL2 . . . . .23 A4
Salters Cl SL6 . . . . .18 B2
Salters Rd SL6 . . . .18 B2
SALT HILL 33 B4
Salt Hill Ave SL1 . .33 A4
Salt Hill Dr SL1 . . .33 A4
Salt Hill Mans
SL1 . . . . .33 A4
Salt Hill Way SL1 . .33 B4
Sampsons Gn SL2 12 A1
Sandisplatt Rd
SL6 . . . . .16 B1
Sandlers End SL2 .22 C4
Sandown Rd SL2 . .22 A3
Sandpipers Pl SL6 . 2 C1
Sandringham Ct
SL1 . . . . .21 B2
Sandringham Rd
SL6 . . . . 7 C1
Sands Farm Dr
SL1 . . . . .21 A4
Sandy Mead SL6 . .41 A4
Satis Ho SL3 . . . . . .47 A2
Savoy Ct SL6 . . . . . .18 A4
Sawyers Cl SL6 . . .26 B1
Sawyer's Cl SL4 . . .43 C2
Sawyers Cres SL6 26 B1
Saxon Cl SL3 . . . . . .36 A4
Saxon Gdns SL6 . . .19 B4
Saxon Lodge SL1 . .32 B4
Saxon Way SL4 . . .52 B4
Scafell Rd SL2 . . . .22 A3
Scarborough Way
SL1 . . . . .32 C3
Scholars Wlk SL3 . 36 B4
School La
Cookham SL6 . . . . . . 3 C2
Maidenhead SL6 . . .17 C4
Slough SL2 . . . . . . .24 A1
Stoke Poges SL2 . . .14 C4
Scotlands Dr SL2 . . 4 A1
Scott Cl SL2 . . . . . . 4 B2
Seacourt Rd SL3 . .36 C2
Second Cres SL1 . .23 A3
Seer Green Ho
SL1 . . . . .11 A1
Sefton Cl SL2 . . . . .14 A3
Sefton Paddock
SL2 . . . . .14 B4
Sefton Park Cotts
SL2 . . . . .14 B3

Sefton Park Sch
SL2 . . . . .14 C4
Selim Ct **5** SL1 . . .34 B3
Selwyn Cl SL4 . . . .48 C4
Selwyn Pl SL1 . . . .22 A1
Sermed Ct SL2 . . . .35 A4
Servite Ho SL6 . . . .18 C3
Seymour Cl SL6 . . .26 C2
Seymour Ho SL3 . .35 C3
Seymour Rd SL1 . .33 B3
Shackleton Rd
SL1 . . . . .24 A1
Shaftesbury Ct
Maidenhead SL6 . . .27 C4
6 Slough SL1 . . . .33 C3
Shaggy Calf La
SL2 . . . . .24 B1
Shakespeare Lodge
SL1 . . . . .32 A4
Shamaa Ho **15**
SL1 . . . . .34 A3
Sharman Row **11**
SL3 . . . . .36 A1
Sharney Ave SL3 . .36 C3
Shaw Ct SL4 . . . . . .51 B1
SHAW FARM 50 C2
Shaw Gdns **13**
SL3 . . . . .36 A1
Shaw The SL6 . . . . . 2 C1
Sheehy Way SL2 . .24 C1
Sheepcote Rd
Eton SL4 . . . . .44 B4
Windsor SL4 . . . . . .48 C4
Sheephouse Rd
SL6 . . . . 8 C1
Sheet St SL4 . . . . . .45 B1
Sheffield Rd SL1 . .23 A2
Shelley Cl **16** SL3 . .36 A1
Shelton Ct SL3 . . . .35 A2
Shenston Ct **23**
SL4 . . . . .45 B1
Shenstone Dr SL1 21 B4
Shepherds Ct SL4 48 C4
Sherborne Ct SL6 .17 C1
Sherbourne Dr
Maidenhead SL6 . . .27 A2
Windsor SL4 . . . . . .49 A2
Sherbourne Wlk
SL2 . . . . 4 B3
Shergold Way SL6 . 3 A1
Sheridan Ct
SL6 . . . . .18 C3
Slough SL1 . . . . . . .21 C1
Sheringham Ct **5**
SL6 . . . . .17 C2
Sherman Rd SL1 . .23 C3
Sherwood Cl SL3 . .35 C2
Sherwood Ct SL3 . .36 A1
Sherwood Dr SL6 . .16 B1
Shifford Cres SL6 . . 7 C2
Shirley Ave SL4 . . .44 A1
Shirley Rd SL6 . . . .27 A4
Shoppenhangers Rd
SL6 . . . . .27 A2
Shoppenhanger's Rd
SL6 . . . . .27 C3
Shoreham Rise
SL2 . . . . .21 B4
Shortfern SL2 . . . . .25 A2
Sidney Rd SL4 . . . .48 A3
Silchester Ho SL6 . 18 C3
Silchester Manor Sch
SL6 . . . . .19 B2
Silco Dr SL6 . . . . . .17 C1
Silver Cl SL6 . . . . . .26 B4

Silverstone Mews
SL6 . . . . .27 A3
Silvertrees Dr
SL6 . . . . .26 B4
Simmons Cl 🖸
SL3 . . . . .36 B2
Simpson Cl SL6 . . .18 C3
Simpsons Way
SL1 . . . . .33 C4
Sinclair Rd SL4 . . .50 A3
Sir Robert Mews
SL3 . . . . .36 B1
Sir Sydney Camm Ho
SL4 . . . . .44 C1
Skerries Ct 🖸
SL3 . . . . .36 B2
Skydmore Path
SL2 . . . . .12 A1
SLOUGH 33 B4
Slough Bsns Ctr
SL1 . . . . .33 C4
Slough & Eton CE
Coll SL1 . . . . .33 B2
Slough Gram Sch
SL3 . . . . .34 C2
Slough Interchange
Ind Est SL2 . . . . . .34 B4
Slough Mus* SL1 .34 B3
Slough Rd
Datchet SL3 . . . . . .46 C3
Eton SL4 . . . . .33 C1
Slough Sta SL1 . . .34 A4
Slough Trad Est
SL1 . . . . .22 C2
Smithfield Cl SL6 .26 A2
Smithfield Rd SL6 26 B2
Smiths La SL4 . . . .43 C1
Snape Spur SL1. . .23 C2
Snowball Hill
Maidenhead SL6 . . .38 B4
White Waltham
SL6. . . . . .38 C3
Snowden Cl SL4 . .48 B2
Somerford Cl SL6 .18 C3
Somerlea SL6. . . . . .9 A2
Somersby Cres
SL6 . . . . .27 C2
Somerset Lodge 🖪
SL6 . . . . .18 A1
Somersham 🖪
SL6 . . . . .18 C3
Somerville Rd
SL4 . . . . .45 A4
Sophie Gdns SL3 . .35 B3
Sospel Ct SL2. . . . .13 A2
South Cl SL1. . . . . .21 B1
Southcroft SL2 . . .22 C4
South Field Cl
SL4 . . . . .31 A2
Southfield Gdns
SL1 . . . . .20 C3
Southgate Ho
SL6 . . . . .18 A2
South Gn SL1 . . . . .23 C1
Southlea Rd SL3 . .51 C4
South Meadow La
SL4 . . . . .45 A3
South Rd SL6 . . . . .17 C1
South Terr SL4 . . . .45 C1
South View SL6 . . . .2 C2
Southwold Spur
SL3 . . . . .37 A4
Southwood Gdns
SL6 . . . . .7 C4
Southwood Rd SL6 7 C4
Sovereign Beeches
SL2 . . . . .4 A1

Spackmans Way
SL1 . . . . .33 B2
Spencer Rd SL3. . .36 A3
Spencers Cl SL6 . .17 B3
Spencers La SL6 . . .2 C2
Spencers Rd SL6. .17 B3
Sperling Rd SL6. . .18 A4
Spinners Wlk SL4 .45 A1
Spinney SL1 . . . . . .32 C4
SPITAL 49 C2
Spitfire Cl SL3 . . . .36 B2
Springate Field
SL3 . . . . .35 C3
Spring Cl SL6. . . . . .8 A1
Springfield SL1 . . .34 B2
Springfield Cl
SL4 . . . . .49 C4
Springfield Ct
SL6 . . . . .18 C2
Springfield Pk
SL6 . . . . .41 A4
Springfield Rd
SL4 . . . . .49 C4
Spring Hill SL6. . . .27 C2
Spring La
Cookham Dean
SL6. . . . . .7 A4
Farnham Common
SL2. . . . . .13 A4
Slough SL1. . . . . . . .32 A4
Spruce Ct 🗓 SL1. .34 A2
Spur The SL1 . . . . .21 B3
Stafferton Way
SL6 . . . . .18 B1
Stafford Ave SL2 . .23 A4
Stafford Cl SL6 . . .20 C2
Staines Rd TW19 . .53 C2
Stamford Rd SL1. .17 A1
Stanhope Rd SL1. .21 B2
Stanley Cotts SL2 .34 A4
Stanley Gn E SL3. .36 A2
Stanley Gn W SL3 .36 A2
Stanley Ho SL4 . . .51 B1
Stanley Spencer Art
Gall* SL6. . . . . .3 C2
Stanton Way SL3. .35 C1
Startins La SL6 . . . .2 A3
Starwood Ct SL3 . .35 A2
Station App 🗓
SL6 . . . . .18 A1
Station Hill SL6 . . .36 B4
Station Ho SL3. . . .46 C1
Station Par SL6 . . . .3 A1
Station Rd
Cookham Rise SL6. . .3 A2
Slough, Langley
SL3. . . . . .36 B4
Slough SL1. . . . . . . .21 C2
Taplow SL6 . . . . . . .20 A2
Staunton Rd SL2 . .23 B3
Stephenson Ct 🗓
SL1 . . . . .34 A3
Stephenson Dr
SL4 . . . . .44 C2
Stewart Ave SL1 . .24 A3
Stewart Cl SL6 . . . .41 B1
Stewarts Dr SL2 . . .4 A3
Stile Rd SL3 . . . . . .35 B2
Stirling Cl SL4 . . . .48 B4
Stirling Gr SL6. . . .12 A3
Stirling Pl 🗓 SL6 .16 C3
Stirling Rd SL1. . . .22 C3
Stockdales Rd
SL4 . . . . .32 A1
Stockwells SL6 . . .19 B4
Stoke Court Dr
SL2 . . . . .14 A3

Stoke Gdns SL1 . . .34 A4
Stoke Gn SL2 . . . . .24 B4
STOKE GREEN . . .24 C4
Stoke Park Ave
SL2 . . . . .13 A1
STOKE POGES . . .14 A2
Stoke Poges La SL1,
SL2 . . . . .23 C2
Stoke Poges Sch The
SL2 . . . . .14 A4
Stoke Rd SL2 . . . . .24 A2
Stokesay SL2 . . . . .24 A1
Stoke View SL1 . . .34 A4
Stoke Wood SL2 . . .5 B3
Stompits Rd SL6 . .41 A3
Stomp Rd SL1 . . . .21 A3
Stonebridge Field
SL4 . . . . .44 C4
Stonefield Pk SL6 17 A2
Stone House La
SL6 . . . . .2 A4
Stoney La SL2 . . . .12 B3
Stoney Meade
SL1 . . . . .32 C4
Stornaway Rd
SL3 . . . . .37 A2
Stour Cl SL1 . . . . . .32 C2
Stovell Rd SL4 . . . .44 C2
Stowe Rd SL1. . . . .21 C1
Straight Rd SL4 . . .52 B4
Strande La SL6 . . . .8 A4
Strande Pk SL6 . . . .8 A4
Strande View Wlk
SL6 . . . . .8 A4
Stranraer Gdns
SL1 . . . . .33 C4
Stratfield Ct SL6 . .18 C3
Stratfield Rd SL1. .34 B3
Stratford Cl SL2. . .21 B4
Stratford Gdns
SL6 . . . . .27 A3
Streamside SL1. . .32 A4
Stroma Cl SL1 . . . .21 B1
Stroud Cl SL4. . . . .48 B3
Stroud Farm Rd
SL6 . . . . .40 C3
Stuart Cl SL4 . . . . .49 A4
Stuart Way SL4 . . .49 A4
STUD GREEN 40 A2
Sturt Gn SL6. . . . . .39 C3
Suffolk Cl SL1 . . . .21 C2
Suffolk Ct 🔁 SL6. .18 A3
Suffolk Rd SL6. . . .27 B3
Sumburgh Way
SL1 . . . . .23 C3
Summerlea SL1. . .32 C4
Summerleaze Rd
SL6 . . . . .18 B4
Summers Rd SL1. .11 A1
Sunbury Ct SL4 . . .45 B3
Sunbury Rd SL4. . .45 B3
Sun Cl SL4. . . . . . . .45 B3
Sunderland Rd
SL6 . . . . .16 C3
Sun La SL6 . . . . . . .18 A2
Sunnymede Cotts
SL6 . . . . .18 C4
Sun Pas 🔞 SL4 . . .45 B1
Surly Hall Wlk
SL4 . . . . .44 A1
Surrey Ave SL2. . . .23 A4
Sussex Cl SL1. . . . .34 C3
Sussex Ho SL2 . . . .4 B1
Sussex Keep SL1. .34 C3
Sussex Lodge 🔽
SL6 . . . . .18 A1
Sussex Pl SL1, SL3 34 C2

Sutherland Grange
SL4 . . . . .43 B2
SUTTON 37 A1
Sutton Ave SL3 . . .35 A3
Sutton Cl
Cookham SL6. . . . . .3 C2
Maidenhead SL6 . . .27 A4
Sutton La SL3. . . . .37 A1
Sutton Rd SL6 . . . . .3 C1
Swabey Rd SL3 . . .36 B2
Swanbrook Ct 🖸
SL6 . . . . .18 B2
Swan Terr SL4 . . . .44 C2
Switchback Cl SL6 . 7 B1
Switchback Rd N
SL6 . . . . .7 C2
Switchback Rd S
SL6 . . . . .7 B1
Switchback The
SL6 . . . . .7 B1
Sycamore Cl SL6. .27 A2
Sycamore Ct SL4. .50 A3
Sycamore Wlk
SL3 . . . . .25 C2
Sydenham Gdns
SL1 . . . . .33 A3
Sydney Gr SL1 . . . .23 A2
Syke Cluan SL0 . . .37 C4
Sykes Rd SL1 . . . . .22 C2
Sylvester Rd SL6. . .7 C1

T

Talbot Ave SL3. . . .36 A4
Talbot Ct SL4 . . . . .49 C3
Talbot Pl SL3 . . . . .47 A1
Talbots Dr SL6 . . . .16 C1
Tamarisk Way
SL1 . . . . .32 B4
Tamar Way SL3 . . .36 C2
Tangier Ct SL4 . . . .45 B3
Tangier La SL4 . . . .45 B3
Tapestries Hall
SL4 . . . . .51 B1
Tapestries The
SL4 . . . . .51 B1
TAPLOW 19 C4
Taplow Common Rd
SL1 . . . . .10 B2
Taplow Quay SL6 .19 A2
Taplow Rd SL6 . . . .20 B2
Taplow Sta SL6 . . .20 A2
Tatchbrook Cl
SL6 . . . . .18 B3
Tavistock Cl SL6 . .16 B3
Taylors Ct SL6 . . . .16 C3
Teesdale Rd SL2 . .22 A3
Teikyo Sch (UK)
SL3 . . . . .15 B4
Telford Dr SL1 . . . .32 B3
Templegate SL4 . .50 A4
Temple Rd SL4. . . .50 B4
Temple Way SL2 . . .4 B2
Templewood Gate
SL2 . . . . .4 B2
Templewood La
SL2 . . . . .4 C3
Tennyson Way
SL2 . . . . .21 C4
Terrace The SL6. . .29 A2
Terrent Ct SL4 . . . .49 B4
Terry's La SL6 . . . . .3 A3
Testwood Rd SL4. .40 C3
Thamebridge Ct 🖸
SL6 . . . . .18 C3
Thames Ave SL4 . .45 B2
Thames Bank SL6 19 A2

Sil–Tru 65

Thames Cres SL6 . .8 C1
Thames Mead
SL4 . . . . .43 C1
Thames Rd SL3 . . .36 C3
Thames Side SL4 .45 B2
Thames St SL4. . . .45 B2
Thames Valley
Nuffield Hospl The
SL3 . . . . .15 A3
Thames Valley Univ
SL1 . . . . .33 C4
Thatchers Dr SL6 .26 B4
Thicket Gr SL6. . . .16 A2
Third Cres SL1. . . .23 A3
Thirkleby Cl SL1 . .33 A4
Thirlmere Ave
SL1 . . . . .21 A3
Thomas Ct SL6. . . .26 B1
Thompkins La
SL2 . . . . .12 B4
Thompson Cl SL3 .36 B2
Thorndike SL2 . . . .22 C3
Thorn Dr SL3 . . . . .25 C2
Thorn Rd SL1 . . . . .39 B4
Thurlby Way SL6. .27 B2
Thurley Cotts SL3 14 C2
Thurston Rd SL1 . .23 C2
Tilbury Wlk SL3. . .36 C3
Tilstone Ave SL4 . .31 C1
Tilstone Cl SL4. . . .43 C4
Timbers Wlk SL6. .26 C4
Timberwood SL2. . .4 C4
Tinkers La SL1 . . . .48 B4
Tintagel Ho SL1. . .33 A4
Tintern Ct SL1 . . . .33 A2
Tiree Ho SL2. . . . . .22 C3
Tithe Barn Dr SL6 41 C4
Tithe Cl SL4 . . . . . .41 A4
Tithe Ct SL3 . . . . . .36 B2
TITTLE ROW 26 B4
Tobermory Cl SL3 35 C1
Tockley Rd SL1 . . .10 C1
Tollgate SL6 . . . . . .16 B1
Tomlin Rd SL2 . . . .32 C4
Topaz Cl SL1. . . . . .32 C4
Torquay Spur SL2 .12 C1
Tower Ho 🗓 SL1 . .33 C3
Town Sq 🗓 SL1 . . .34 A3
Tozer Wlk SL4 . . . .48 B3
Tracey Ave 🗓
SL3 . . . . .36 A1
Transcend 🖸 SL4 .50 A4
Travic Rd SL2. . . . .12 A1
Travis Ct SL2 . . . . .12 C1
Treesmill Dr SL6 . .27 A2
Trelawney Ave
SL3 . . . . .36 A3
Trelawney Ind Ct
SL3 . . . . .35 C2
Trenchard Rd SL6 40 C3
Trent Villas Est
SL3 . . . . .46 A4
Tressell The SL6. . .17 B1
Trevelyan Ct SL4 . .49 C4
Trevelyan Mid Sch
SL4 . . . . .50 A2
Trevose Ho SL2 . . .22 C4
Trinity Ho SL6 . . . . .3 A1
Trinity Pl SL4 . . . . .50 A4
Trinity St Stephens
CE Fst Sch SL4. . . .44 C1
Troutbeck Cl SL2. .24 B1
Trumper Way SL1 .32 A4
Truro Cl SL6 . . . . . .16 B2

66 Tub–Win

Tubwell Rd SL2 . . .14 C3
Tudor Ct SL6. . . . . . .9 A1
Tudor Gdns SL1. . .21 A3
Tudor La SL4 . . . . .52 C3
Tudor Way SL4. . . .43 C1
Tuns La SL1. . . . . .33 A3
Turks Head Ct
SL4 . . . . .45 B2
Turner Rd SL3 . . . .35 A3
Turnoak Pk SL4 . .48 C2
Turpins Gn SL6 . . .26 B4
Turton Way SL1 . . .33 B2
Tuscany Ct **2**
SL6 . . . . .17 C2
Twinches La SL1 . .32 C4
Two Mile Dr SL1 . .31 C3
Twynham Rd SL6. .16 C2
Tyle Pl SL4 . . . . . . .51 B1
Tyler Wlk **4** SL3 . .36 A1
Tyndale Mews
SL1 . . . . .32 C3
Tyrell Gdns SL4 . . .49 A3

U

Ullswater Cl SL1 . .21 A3
Umberville Way
SL2 . . . . .12 A1
Underhill Cl SL6 . .17 C1
Upcroft SL4 . . . . . .49 C3
Upper Bray Rd
SL6 . . . . .29 A2
Upper Lees Rd
SL2 . . . . .12 C1
Upper Ventnor Cotts
SL6 . . . . .2 A3
UPTON 34 B2
Upton Cl SL1 . . . . .34 A2
Upton Court Rd
SL3 . . . . .34 C1
Upton Hospl SL1 . .34 A2
Upton House Sch
SL4 . . . . .50 A4
UPTON LEA 24 B1
Upton Lea Par
SL2 . . . . .24 C1
UPTON PARK 34 A2
Upton Pk SL1 . . . .34 A2
Upton Rd SL1, SL3 .34 B2
Urbis Apartments
SL4 . . . . .48 C4
Uxbridge Rd SL1, SL2,
SL3 . . . . .25 A1

V

Vale Gr SL1 . . . . . . .33 C2
Vale Rd SL4. . . . . . .44 A1
Valley End SL3 . . . .25 A4
Vansittart Est SL4 .45 A1
Vansittart Rd SL4 .44 C1
Vantage Rd SL1 . . .32 C4
Vanwall Bsns Pk
SL6 . . . . .27 A4
Vanwall Rd SL6 . . .27 A3
Vaughan Copse
SL4 . . . . .33 B1
Vaughan Gdns
SL4 . . . . .32 A1
Vaughan Way SL2 .22 A4
Venus Cl SL2. . . . . .22 A4
Verdon Ct SL2 . . . .12 C1
Vermont Rd SL2 . .22 A4
Verney Rd SL3 . . . .36 B2

Vicarage Cl SL6. . . .3 C2
Vicarage Dr SL6 . .29 A3
Vicarage Flats
SL4 . . . . .45 B3
Vicarage Gdns
SL6 . . . . .38 A3
Vicarage La TW19 .53 C2
Vicarage Rd SL6 . .18 A3
Vicarage Wlk SL6 .29 A3
Victor Cl SL6. . . . . .16 C3
Victoria Cotts SL6. . .2 A3
Victoria Ct SL1. . . .33 C4
Victoria Ho SL4 . . .51 B1
Victoria Rd
Eton SL4 . . . . .44 A4
Slough SL2. . . . . . .34 C4
Victoria St
10 Slough SL1. . . . .34 A3
Windsor SL4 . . . . .45 B1
Victor Rd SL4 . . . . .50 A3
Village Rd SL4 . . . .30 C2
Village Sh Ctr The **5**
SL1 . . . . .34 A3
Villiers Ct SL4 . . . .44 C2
Villiers Rd SL2 . . . .23 B3
Vine Ct SL2 . . . . . . .5 C1
Vine Rd SL2 . . . . . . .5 B1
Viscount Ct SL4. . .45 A1
Vivien Cl SL6 . . . . . .3 A1

W

Wade Dr SL1. . . . . .32 B4
Wagner Cl SL6. . . .26 A2
Wakefield Cres
SL2 . . . . .5 B1
Wakelins End SL6. . .2 C2
Waldeck Ho SL6 . .18 B2
Waldeck Rd SL6 . .18 B2
Walker Cres SL3 . .36 A1
Walker Ct SL6. . . . .17 B2
Walker Rd SL6 . . . .28 B3
Walk The SL4 . . . . .44 B4
Wallace Wlk SL4 . .46 A4
Wallis Ct SL1 . . . . .34 B3
Walnut Lo SL1 . . . .33 B2
Walpole Rd
Old Windsor SL4 . . .52 B3
Slough SL1. . . . . . .22 B2
Waltham Cl SL6. . .26 A1
Waltham Rd SL6 . .38 A4
Walton La SL2 . . . .12 A2
Ward Gdns SL1 . . .21 C1
Ward Royal **5**
SL4 . . . . .45 A1
Ward Royal Par **2**
SL4 . . . . .45 A1
Warner Cl SL1 . . . .31 C4
Warners Hill SL6. . .2 A3
Warren Cl SL3 . . . .35 C2
Warren Ct SL2 . . . .4 B2
Warrington Ave
SL1 . . . . .23 A2
Warrington Spur
SL4 . . . . .52 B3
Warwick Ave SL2. .23 A4
Warwick Cl SL6. . .26 C3
Warwick Ct **2**
SL4 . . . . .50 A4
Washington Dr
Slough SL1. . . . . . .21 B1
Windsor SL4 . . . . .48 C3
Waterbeach Cl
SL1 . . . . .23 B2
Waterbeach Rd
SL1 . . . . .23 B2
Waterman Ct SL1 .31 C4

WATER OAKLEY . .42 A3
Water Oakley Cotts
SL4 . . . . .42 A3
Water Oakley Farm
Cotts SL4 . . . . . . .42 A3
Waterside Dr SL3 .36 A4
Waterside Lodge
SL6 . . . . .19 A3
Waters Reach
SL6 . . . . .18 B4
Wavell Gdns SL2 . .12 A1
Wavell Rd SL6 . . . .16 C1
Waverley Rd SL1 . .23 A3
Waylands TW19 . . .53 B4
Wayside Mews
SL6 . . . . .18 A3
Webb Cl SL3 . . . . . .35 B1
Webster Cl SL6 . . .26 B4
Weekes Dr SL1. . . .32 C3
Welbeck Rd SL6 . .27 B4
Welby Cl SL6 . . . . .26 B3
Welden SL2. . . . . . .25 A2
Wellbank SL6 . . . . .19 C4
Wellcroft Rd SL1 . .32 C4
Wellesley Ho SL4 .44 C1
Wellesley Path
SL1 . . . . .34 B3
Wellesley Rd SL1. .34 B3
Wellhouse Rd SL6. .7 C1
Wellington Cl **4**
SL6 . . . . .16 C3
Wellington Rd
SL6 . . . . .17 B2
Wellington St SL1 34 B3
Wells Cl SL4 . . . . . .44 B2
Wendover Rd SL1 .20 C3
Wentworth Ave
SL2 . . . . .12 B1
Wentworth Cres
SL6 . . . . .17 A1
Wentworth Ind Ct **1**
SL2 . . . . .12 B1
Wessex Ct **24** SL4 .45 B1
Wessex Prim Sch
SL6 . . . . .26 C3
Wessex Way SL6 . .26 C3
Wessons Hill SL6. . .2 A2
Westborough Ct
SL6 . . . . .17 A1
Westborough Rd
SL6 . . . . .17 A1
Westbrook SL6 . . .41 C4
Westcoign Ho
SL6 . . . . .18 C3
West Cres SL4 . . . .44 A1
Westcroft SL2 . . . .22 C4
West Ct SL6. . . . . . .29 A3
West Dean SL6. . . .18 A3
West End Ct SL2 . .14 A3
West End La SL2 . .13 C3
Western House Prim
Sch SL1 . . . . .32 A3
Westfield Rd
Maidenhead SL6 . . .16 C2
Slough SL2. . . . . . .22 C4
Westgate Cres
SL1 . . . . .22 A1
Westgate Ret Pk
SL1 . . . . .22 B1
Westgate Sch The
SL1 . . . . .32 B4
Westlands Ave
SL1 . . . . .21 A2
Westlands Cl SL1 .21 A2
Westmead SL4. . . .49 C3
West Mead SL6 . . . .8 A1

Westmorland Rd
SL6 . . . . .17 B1
Weston Rd SL1. . . .22 A3
West Point SL1 . . .31 B4
West Rd SL6 . . . . . .17 C2
West St SL6. . . . . . .18 A2
Westwood Gn SL6. .3 A1
Wethered Rd SL1 .20 C3
Wexford Ct SL6 . . .18 C2
Wexham Court Prim
Sch SL2 . . . . .25 A2
Wexham Park Hospl
SL2 . . . . .25 A4
Wexham Park La
SL3 . . . . .25 A4
Wexham Rd SL1,
SL2 . . . . .24 C1
Wexham Sch SL2. .25 A3
Wexham St SL3 . . .14 C2
WEXHAM
STREET. 15 A3
Wexham Woods
SL3 . . . . .25 A3
Wharf Rd TW19 . . .53 A3
Wheatbutts The
SL4 . . . . .32 A1
Wheatfield Cl SL6 26 B3
Wheatlands Rd
SL3 . . . . .35 A2
Wheatsheaf Par
SL4 . . . . .51 B1
Wheatstone Cl
SL3 . . . . .34 B2
Whitby Rd SL1. . . .23 A1
Whitchurch Cl SL6 .7 C2
Whiteacres Dr
SL6 . . . . .41 A4
Whitebrook Pk
SL6 . . . . .9 A3
White Cl SL1. . . . . .33 B4
Whiteford Rd SL2 .23 C3
Whitehall SL6 . . . .18 C4
White Hart Rd
2 Maidenhead
SL6. . . . . .18 A2
Slough SL1. . . . . . .33 B2
Whitehaven SL1 . .24 A1
White Horse Rd
SL4 . . . . .48 B4
Whitehouse Way
SL3 . . . . .35 B2
Whiteley SL4 . . . . .43 C2
White Lilies Island
SL4 . . . . .44 C2
White Paddock
SL6 . . . . .26 B1
White Rock SL6. . .18 C4
Whites La SL3 . . . .46 C3
Whittaker Rd SL2 .21 C4
Whittenham Cl
SL2 . . . . .34 B4
Whittle Parkway
SL1 . . . . .21 B2
Whurley Way SL6 . .7 C1
Whyteladyes La
SL6 . . . . .2 C1
Wickets The SL6 . .17 A2
Widbrook Rd SL6 . .8 C2
Wiggington Ho
SL4 . . . . .45 B2
Wilberforce Mews **15**
SL6 . . . . .18 A2
Wildgreen N **1**
SL3 . . . . .36 B2
Wildgreen S **2**
SL3 . . . . .36 B2
Wilford Rd SL3. . . .36 A2

Willant Cl SL6 . . . .26 A1
William Ellis Cl
SL4 . . . . .52 A4
William Hartley Yd
SL3 . . . . .24 C4
William St
Slough SL1. . . . . . .34 A4
Windsor SL4 . . . . .45 B1
Willoners SL2. . . . .22 B2
Willoughby Rd
SL3 . . . . .36 B3
Willowbrook SL4. .33 B1
Willow Cl SL6. . . . .17 B4
Willow Dr SL6 . . . .28 C1
Willow Par SL3 . . .36 B3
Willow Pk SL2 . . . .14 B4
Willow Pl SL4. . . . .45 A3
Willows Riverside Pk
The SL4 . . . . .43 A2
Willows The SL4 . .43 B2
Willow Wood Cl
SL1 . . . . .10 C2
Wilmot Rd SL1. . . .10 C1
Wilton Cres SL4. . .48 B3
Wiltshire Ave SL2 .23 A4
Wiltshire Lodge **2**
SL6 . . . . .18 A1
Winbury Ct SL6 . . .17 C2
Winbury Sch SL6. .28 C3
Winchester Dr
SL6 . . . . .26 C2
Winch Terr SL4. . . .48 B4
Windermere Way
SL1 . . . . .21 A2
Windmill Cl SL4. . .49 C4
Windmill Rd
Cookham Rise SL6. . .2 C1
Slough SL1. . . . . . .33 B4
Windrush Ave
SL3 . . . . .36 C3
Windrush Way
SL6 . . . . .18 A3
WINDSOR 45 C2
Windsor Boys' Sch
The SL4 . . . . .44 C1
Windsor Bsns Ctr
The SL4 . . . . .45 A2
Windsor Castle★
SL4 . . . . .45 C2
Windsor Cl SL1 . . .21 A4
Windsor & Eton
Central Sta SL4 . .45 B1
Windsor & Eton
Riverside Sta
SL4 . . . . .45 B2
Windsor Girls' Sch
SL4 . . . . .49 B3
Windsor Hall SL4 .51 A3
Windsor La SL1 . . .21 A4
Windsor Rd
Datchet SL3. . . . . .46 B2
Englefield Green SL4,
TW19, TW20 . . . . .53 B1
Fulmer SL2 . . . . . . .5 C3
Maidenhead SL6. . .41 C4
Oakley Green SL4 . .42 B2
Slough SL1. . . . . . .23 C3
Wraysbury TW19. . .53 B4
Windsor Royal Sta **5**
SL4 . . . . .45 B2
Winkfield Rd SL4. .48 C1
Winsford Par **4**
SL1 . . . . .34 A2
Winston Ct SL6 . . .16 C3
Winter Hill SL6 . . . .2 A4
Winter Hill Rd SL6 .6 B3

Wintoun Path
SL2 . . . .**21** C4
Winvale SL1 . . . . . .**33** C2
Winwood
Slough SL2. . . . .**25** A2
Windsor SL4 . . . . . .**44** A1
Withey Cl SL4. . . . .**43** C1
Withycroft SL3. . . .**25** C2
Wolf La SL4. . . . . . .**48** C3
Wood Cl SL4. . . . . .**50** A2
Woodcote SL6 . . . .**17** B1
Wood End Cl SL2. . .**4** C4
Woodfield Dr SL6 .**16** B1
Woodford Way
SL2 . . . .**12** B1
Woodhurst Rd
SL6 . . . .**18** C4
Woodhurst South
SL6 . . . .**19** A4
Wood La SL1. . . . . .**32** B3

Woodland Ave
Slough SL1. . . . . . .**23** B1
Windsor SL4 . . . . . .**49** A2
Woodland Glade
SL2 . . . .**4** C4
Woodland Grange
SL0 . . . .**37** C3
Woodlands Bsns Pk
SL6 . . . .**26** B1
Woodlands Cotts
SL2 . . . .**4** B2
Woodlands Farm
SL6 . . . .**2** A1
**WOODLANDS
PARK** **26** A1
Woodlands Park Ave
SL6 . . . .**26** B1
Woodlands Park
Prim Sch SL6 . . . .**38** B4

Woodlands Park Rd
SL6 . . . .**26** B1
Woodmoor End
SL6 . . . .**3** C2
Woodstock Ave
SL3 . . . .**35** B1
Woodstock Cl
SL6 . . . .**18** A4
Wootton Way SL6 .**17** A1
Worcester Cl SL6 .**27** B2
Worcester Gdns
SL1 . . . .**33** B3
Wordsworth Rd
SL2 . . . .**21** B4
Worple The TW19 .**53** C4
Worster Rd SL6 . . . .**2** C1
WRAYSBURY. **53** B4
Wraysbury Prim Sch
TW19. . . . .**53** B4
Wren Ct SL3 . . . . . .**36** B3

Wright SL4 . . . .**48** A3
Wright Sq SL4 . . . .**48** A3
Wright Way SL4. . .**48** A3
Wyatt Rd SL4 . . . . .**48** B3
Wylands Rd SL3. . .**36** B2
Wymers Cl SL1. . . .**10** C2
Wymers Wood Rd
SL1 . . . .**10** B2
Wyndham Cres
SL1 . . . .**10** C2

Y

Yarmouth Rd SL1 .**23** A1
Ye Meads SL6. . . . .**30** A4
Ye Meads Cotts
SL6 . . . .**30** A4
Yeovil Ent Ctr
SL1 . . . .**22** A3
Yeovil Rd SL1 . . . . .**21** C3

Yew Tree Cl SL6 . . .**17** C3
Yew Tree Rd SL1 . .**34** B2
York Ave
Slough SL1. . . . .**23** B2
Windsor SL4 . . . . . .**49** C4
York Rd
Maidenhead SL6 . . .**18** B2
Windsor SL4 . . . . . .**49** C4

Z

Zetland Ct SL6 . . . .**18** C3

List of numbered locations

In some busy areas of the maps it is not always possible to show the name of every place.

Where not all names will fit, some smaller places are shown by a number. If you wish to find out the name associated with a number, use this listing.

The places in this list are also listed normally in the Index.

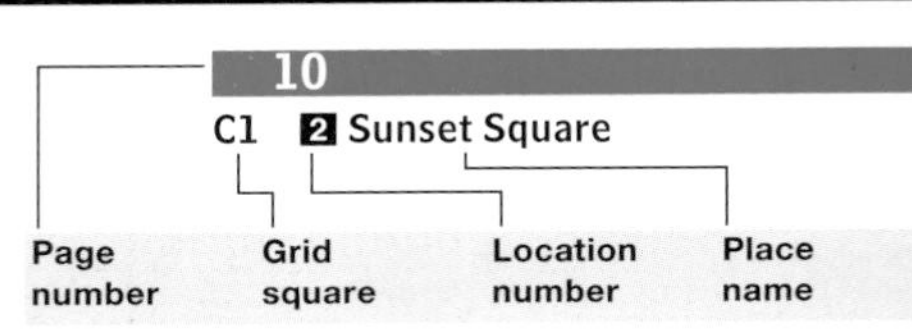

| Page number | Grid square | Location number | Place name |

10
C1 **2** Sunset Square

12

B1 **1** Wentworth Ind Ct

16

C3 **1** Stirling Pl
2 Greenlands Ct
3 Merlin Ct
4 Wellington Cl

17

C2 **1** Firs The
2 Tuscany Ct
3 Lady Elizabeth Ho
4 Elmslie Ct
5 Sheringham Ct

18

A1 **1** Berkshire Lodge
2 Wiltshire Lodge
3 Somerset Lodge
4 Buckingham Ho
5 Marlborough Ho
6 Kent Lodge
7 Sussex Lodge
8 Hampshire Lodge
9 Dorset Lodge
10 Devonshire Lodge
11 Cornwall Lodge
12 Henley Lodge
13 Marlow Lodge
14 Courtlands
15 Cookham Lodge
16 Kings Chase
17 Station App
18 Cullern's Pass
19 Princess St
20 St Paul's Ct
A2 **1** High St Mall
2 White Hart Rd
3 Queens Wlk Mall
4 Kings Wlk
5 Nicholsons Ctr
6 Broadway Mall
7 Brock Lane Mall
8 Queen's La
9 Regent Ct

10 Old Post Office La
11 Frogmore Ct
12 New Market
13 Kidwells Park Dr
14 Providence Pl
15 Wilberforce Mews
16 St Mary's Wlk
A3 **1** Cordwallis Est
2 Suffolk Ct
A4 **1** North Town Cl
2 Alyson Ct
3 North Gn
4 North Town Mead
5 Northdean
B2 **1** Colonnade
2 Pulse The
3 Glynwood Ho
4 Chapel Arches
5 Bridge Ct
6 Swanbrook Ct
7 Hub The
C3 **1** Barbicus Ct
2 Somersham
3 Kimbolton
4 Sheridan Ct
5 Thamebridge Ct

33

C2 **1** Eton Wlk
2 St Andrews Ct
3 Lincoln Ct
4 Locksley Ct
C3 **1** Burlington Ct
2 Burlington Rd
3 Hilperton Rd
4 Tower Ho
5 Ashbourne Ho
6 Shaftesbury Ct
7 Moorstown Ct

34

A2 **1** Spruce Ct
2 Dartmouth Ct
3 Albert Cl
4 Winsford Par
5 Manor Ct
A3 **1** Prudential Bldgs
2 Mackenzie St
3 Mackenzie Mall

4 Buckingham Gdns
5 Village Sh Ctr The
6 Leopold Mall
7 Curzon Mall
8 Chandos Mall
9 Town Sq
10 Victoria St
11 Bisham Ct
12 Bembridge Ct
13 Stephenson Ct
14 Hencroft Mews
15 Shamaa Ho
16 Richard Dodd Pl
B2 **1** Rye Ct
2 Grove Cl
3 Chatham Ct
4 Eastfield Cl
5 Priors Cl
6 Mountbatten Cl
7 Hornbeam Gdns
8 Church View
9 Nightingale Ct
10 Merton Ct
11 Parkside Lodge
B3 **1** Elizabeth Ct
2 Neo Apartments
3 Clifton Lodge
4 Lascelles Ho
5 Selim Ct
6 Alpha St N

36

A1 **1** Calder Ct
2 Ditton Park Cvn Site
3 Bessemer Ct
4 Tyler Wlk
5 Owen Cl
6 Gilbert Way
7 Beckett Chase
8 Davidson Rd
9 Hudson Pl
10 Chaplin Mews
11 Sharman Row
12 Tracey Ave
13 Shaw Gdns
14 Dalton Gn
15 Gibson Ct
16 Shelley Cl
B2 **1** Wildgreen N
2 Wildgreen S

3 Morrice Cl
4 Anvil Ct
5 Skerries Ct
6 Simmons Cl
7 Knightsbridge Ct
8 Laurels The

45

A1 **1** Cambridge Ho
2 Ward Royal Par
3 Christian Sq
4 Crescent Villas
5 Ward Royal
6 Bowes-Lyon Cl
7 Mountbatten Sq
8 Charles Ho
9 Queen Anne's Ct
B1 **1** Castleview Ho
2 Horseshoe Cloisters
3 Lodgings of the Military Knights
4 Henry III Twr
5 Windsor Royal Sta
6 King Edward Ct
7 Amberley Pl
8 Market St
9 Church St
10 Queen Charlotte St
11 Church La
12 St Albans Cl
13 Red Brick Cotts
14 Burford Ho
15 Copperfield Ho
16 Peascod Pl
17 Mellor Wlk
18 Royal Free Ct
19 Sun Pas
20 Hibbert's Alley
21 Chariott's Pl
22 Ellison Ho
23 Shenston Ct
24 Wessex Ct
25 Ralston Ct

48

A4 **1** Guards Wlk
2 Charlton Pl
3 Charlton Wlk

4 Charlton Sq
5 Charlton Row
6 Furness Sq
7 Furness Wlk
8 Furness Pl
9 Furness Row
10 Kenneally Wlk
11 Kenneally Cl
12 Kenneally Pl
13 Kenneally Row
14 Liddell Sq

49

B4 **1** St Andrews Cotts
2 Albion Pl
3 St Catherines Ct
4 Meads The
5 Concorde Ct
6 Canterbury Mews
7 Cedar Ct
8 Bridgeman Ct
9 Recognition Ho
10 Cloisters The
11 Gray Ct
12 Convent Ct

50

A4 **1** Camperdown Ho
2 Warwick Ct
3 Chelmsford Ct
4 Houston Ct
5 Elizabeth Ct
6 Transcend
7 Crossways Ct
8 Knight's Pl
9 Osborne Lodge
10 Aberdeen Lodge
B3 **1** Cornel Ho
2 Heathcote Ct
3 Prospect Pl
4 Drummond Ho
5 Queen's Terr
6 Queens Acre Ho
B4 **1** Garfield Pl
2 Alexandra Ct
3 King's Road Ho
4 Coachman's Lodge